Entry *of* Claims
for
Georgia Landholders
- 1733-1755 -

Compiled by:

Mrs Pat Bryant
Deputy Surveyor General
Georgia Surveyor General Department
Office of the Secretary of State

Southern Historical Press, Inc.
Greenville, South Carolina

This volume was reproduced
from a personal copy located in
the Publishers private library

All rights reserved. No part of this publication may be reproduced,
stored in a retrieval system, transmitted in any form, posted
on the web in any form or by any means without the
prior written permission of the publisher.

Please direct all correspondence and book orders to:
SOUTHERN HISTORICAL PRESS, Inc.
1071 Park West Blvd.
Greenville, SC 29611

Published 1975 by:
 Mrs. Pat Bryant
ISBN #978-1-63914-664-2
Printed in the United States of America

Dedicated to

The Honorable Ben W. Fortson, Jr.,

Secretary of State of Georgia

and

Who in all things, in all ways, encourages
the dissemination of things historical
in his beloved State of Georgia, and
no less in his beloved America.

and to

The Honorable Ann Adamson

Assistant Secretary of State

Who with utmost ability, patience and graciousness
executes the myriad duties of her office.

CONTENTS

Preface viii

Introduction x

Proclamations of Governor Reynolds xiv

Example of original page in manuscript . . xvii

Entry of Claims 1

Index to names and places 209

PREFACE

This manuscript gives some much needed historical information on those settlers who received land in Georgia under the Trustees for Establishing the Colony of Georgia in America, from the landing at Yamacraw Bluff in 1733 to the first Royal Governor in 1754.

One finds concise data here concerning the location of properties of these early Georgians, and in many instances this material shows how and when the property was acquired. The <u>Entry of Claims</u> is particularly important because there is very little original manuscript material in Georgia before 1755.

There remains another document which precedes the <u>Entry of Claims</u>. It is in the Georgia Surveyor General Department and gives the names of those settlers who arrived with Oglethorpe and received the first lots in Savannah. There are some 80 names in this record and there are plans to compile and publish it as soon as possible. No doubt some names are shown in both documents, but it is felt that it should be done. With that completed, the Surveyor General Department of the Office of the Secretary of State will have published the land owners from December 21, 1733 to June 6, 1775, or from the settling of the colony up to the Revolution. In the future, it is hoped that those grants from 1775 to 1800 can be done.

Altogether there are some 1,474,699 grants of land and surveys under the jurisdiction of this department of the Office of Secretary of State, and it is doubtful that all of them will ever be published. There is not enough time, nor staff, nor money.

To the historians who have been so encouraging, goes our grateful appreciation. And to those great people of Georgia who have cheered us on, we wish to say that we never could have done it without your stimulation and interest.

Mrs. Lilla Hawes, Director of the Georgia Historical Society, gave us a map of Savannah which she had compiled and offered to let us use it in this document. Because of the extra costs of folding and insertation we could not use it. However, that important map is in the Historical Society in Savannah and a copy is here. To Lilla, goes our warm thanks for her welcome help and our regrets that it could not be used.

Edwin Bridges, that excellent scholar and now Administrative Assistant to Miss Carroll Hart, Director of the Georgia Archives, read the manuscript and critized it until I finally wouldn't let him read it again, but he still has my affectionate gratitude.

To my own staff, Miss Janice Blake and Mr. Marion Hemperley, who caught my many errors and who did my share of the work while I was doing this, ... well, they know how I feel about them.

And if it were not for the best boss in the world, Ben Fortson, Secretary of State and Surveyor General, who scratched up the money - somehow ! - this work would never have been done at all. All of us should thank Mr. Ben for his great love of Georgia and his willingness to publish some of Georgia's history.

Mrs. Pat Bryant
December 29, 1975

INTRODUCTION

Of the thirteen original colonies, only Georgia began as a trusteeship. The youngest and most southern of the colonies was governed by "The Trustees for Establishing the Colony of Georgia in America." Under that government no records of land conveyances to the settlers were kept in Georgia, although lists of these were sent to the Accountant of Plantations in London.

Because of the lack of land records during the earliest period of Georgia's history, it was decided to publish the "Entry of Claims, 1755" which was so graciously loaned to the Surveyor General Department by Miss Ruth Corry, Head of Central Research, of the Department of Archives and History. This volume documents all land holdings of those persons in Georgia during the period of the trustees up to 1755.

King George II issued the charter to the trustees for the new colony in June 1732. The area in Georgia as described in that document was "all those lands, countries, and territories ... which lies from the most northern stream of a river ... called the Savannah ... unto ... the most southern stream ... called the Altamaha and westward from the heads of the said rivers ... in direct lines to the South Seas." Three main objectives were set forth in the charter for the benefit of England and the protection of her colonies already established in North America.

First, Georgia was established as a philanthropic venture to relieve the great unemployment condition in England. Second, the colony was to provide raw materials for the manufactories in the old country, and third, and most important in the minds of the Royal Government, this small settlement was to establish a military buffer zone between South Carolina and the foreign encroach-ments from the southward.

Twenty-one trustees were named in the charter and 15 of that body were to act as "The Council." The Council attended to the business of overseeing the new colony and reported to the larger body regularly. One of the most prominent of the trustees was James Edward Oglethorpe who came to Georgia with the first colonists in 1733.

Immediately, Oglethorpe laid out the town called Savannah and shortly thereafter treated with the various heads of the Creek towns for a small area within the larger confines of the charter lands. Each free white male was allotted 50 acres of land which consisted of a town lot 60 feet by 90 feet, five acres for a garden lot, and the balance of 45+ acres for a farm lot. No more than 500 acres were to be allotted to any one person. Fee simple titles to the land were not given by the trustees. As a corporation they held all titles to the chartered lands.

That the trustees were indeed a corporation is borne out numerous times in the charter where they were designated as such. In one instance that document states, " ... we (King George II) would be graciously pleased to Erect and Settle a corporation ...." In another statement the charter speaks of " ... our will and pleasure is that the first president of the said corporation shall be ... John Lord Viscount Percival ...." As a corporation, the trustees allotted all lands in tail male which restricted any but male heirs from inheritance, and forbade disposition of any individual property by deed, mortgage, or will.

Discontent over tenure of land mounted. By June 1739, resentment had increased so much that the system was relaxed sufficiently to allow daughters to inherit in the absence of male heirs, and widows could reside in the "mansion" and share a portion of the land left by their deceased husbands, for their life time. By 1750, the dissatisfaction of the settlers over land strictures was so pronounced that all restraints were removed.

The trustees were to keep the charter for 21 years, but on June 20, 1752, one year early, they relinquished it to George II, and the seal was defaced. Georgia was now a Royal Province.

Not until August 6, 1754 did the Crown commission John Reynolds of England as Captain-General and Governor-in-Chief in and over the Province of Georgia. One of the governor's first acts was to deal with the problem of land titles. Titles were to be transferred from the Corporate body of the trustees to the governmental body of the English Crown. On January 1, 1755, Reynolds issued a proclamation " ... to give publick notice that all such persons as hold or possess any lands within his Majesty's Colony of Georgia, by virtue of grants from the late Trustees ... shall be finally released from all conditions of such grants .... " Fresh grants were to be issued in his Majesty's name under the public seal of the new colony and persons should appear by themselves, or their attorneys could appear for them.

The 7th day of April, 1755, was the final day for claims to be entered and every claimant to land was to " ... lay before me (Reynolds) for my inspection a particular account in writing of all the lands they claim to hold, either in their own name or in the name of any other person, with a particular description of the situation and extent of such lands, and the right and claim they have to, and the tenure by which they claim to hold the same ...."

Apparently, many entries were not filed by the 7th of April and the Council and Assembly "respectfully" requested that an extension be made. The second proclamation of May 26, 1755, extended the time for the entering of claims to June 30th of that year. In it, Reynolds further noted that all persons to whom he had issued warrants for surveys of land, should, forwith, " ... apply to the Surveyor General to have their land laid out ...." The governor also reminded the people that quit rents must be paid on their property. A quit rent was a traditional token of loyalty paid by a freeholder to his sovereign or lord for commutation of services. It was usually a very small amount which amounted to a few shillings, one or two peppercorns or even a single rose. Grants of land in his Majesty's name were subject to the payment of two shillings sterling for every hundred acres, and five acres a year were to be cleared out of every 100 acres.

Over a 1000 claimants registered their claims to property, giving a description of their holdings and how and when they acquired them. Some, like John Peter Briton, who held property in Savannah, stated that he had received his land from the trustees in 1738. Others, like Ann Graham, whose property was located in Josephs

Town, said that she had received it originally from "General" Oglethorpe. George Peters who held a lot in Savannah, described his land as having been granted by the trustees to his father in the year 1733.

    Some descriptions of property actually give a chain of title for a parcel of land. A few later claims appear herein and were acquired through Governor Reynolds. But, more particularly, this manuscript covers a period which is not as well known as the Royal Provincial era of 1755-1775.

Georgia

By his Excellency John Reynolds, Esqr.,
Captain-General, Governor and Commander
in Chief in and over his Majesty's said
Province

A Proclamation

Whereas I am commanded by his Majesty to give publick notice that all such persons as hold or possess any lands within his Majesty's Colony of Georgia, by virtue of grants from the late Trustees or from persons acting under their authority or by virtue of Allottments made by the President and Council of Assistants, not exceeding Five Hundred acres to any one person, shall be finally released from all conditions of such grants and allottments, and the arrears of quit-rents due thereon totally remitted, on condition that they do within a certain time specified by me, appear by themselves or sufficient attorneys before me in Council, and take out fresh grants in his Majesty's name under the publick seal of the said Colony, for the lands they claim to be in possession of under such grants and allottments, subject to the payment of Two Shillings Sterling for every hundred acres so granted, to commence within two years from the date of the grant, and that the said grantees shall likewise be obliged to clear and cultivate at the rate of five acres per year for every hundred acres contained in their grants, in failure of which such grants shall be void, provided nevertheless and it is his Majesty's express will and pleasure that nothing herein contained shall extend or be construed to extend to, establish or confirm a right in any person or persons to lands which they claim to hold by virtue of grants or by allottments, which grants or allottments have been forfeited by a noncompliance with the terms and conditions thereof, or which they claim to hold under allottments of more than Five Hundred acres to any one person.

I have therefore thought fit to issue this my Proclamation charging and requiring all persons whatsoever that on or before the 7th day of April next, they do lay before me for my inspection, a particular account in writing of all the lands they claim to hold, either in their own name or in the name of any other person, with a particular description of the situation and extent of such lands, and the right and claim they have to, and the tenure by which they claim to hold the same, in order, if it shall be thought proper, to their obtaining fresh grants for the same in his Majesty's name.

Hereof none are to fail, as they will answer to the contrary.

     Given under my hand and the seal of his
     Majesty's said Colony, at Savannah, the
     1st day of January 1755, and in the 28th
     year of his Majesty's reign.

By his Excellency's command   J. Reynolds
James Habersham, Secty
     God Save the King

       ***

Georgia

     A Proclamation

Whereas by a Proclamation published the 1st day of January last particular advantages are offered to all persons holding lands in this Province, under grants from the late Trustees, or under allottments from the President and Court of Assistants either before or since the surrender of the charter, and they are directed to lay before me for my inspection, their respective claims, on or before the 7th day of April last, which time, upon an humble request made to me by an address from the Council and Assembly, I extended to the 30th day of June next.

This is therefore, in his Majesty's name, to charge and command all persons concerned to pay due obedience thereto and bring in their titles and claims accordingly, on or before the last day of June next in order that they may appear before in Council on or before the 28th day of July next following, and take out fresh grants in his Majesty's name under the publick seal of the province, for the lands they claim under such grants or allottments or under any other title whatsoever, as they will answer the contrary, for their names with an account of the quantity of land that has been granted or allotted to them will be immediately transmitted to be laid before his Majesty, pursuant to his instructions on that head.

And in like manner, all persons who have obtained warrants for land from me, are required forthwith to apply to the Surveyor General to have their lands laid out, and that the payment of his Majesty's quit-rents may not be evaded, they within Ten days after the return of their warrants to take to take out regular grants for the lands so laid out; and it is his Majesty's express will and pleasure that the said warrants shall be returned within Six months at furthest after the date thereof, in failure of which they are void and of no effect.

                    Given under my hand and seal of his Majesty's said Colony, at Savannah, the 26th Day of May in the year of our Lord 1755 and in the 28th year of his Majesty's reign.

By his Excellency's command
James Habersham   Secty   J. Reynolds

                    God Save the King

                          ***

Claimants Names	No. acres	Situation of Lands	Original Grantees
Wm Buchanan	500	Claims [500] on the Main opposite to the Island Doboy in the Neighbourhood of Darian allotted him by the late President and Asistants the 21st December 1747	Wm Buchanan
Edward Barnard for Robert Germany	200	Claims two hundred acres of Land situated at a Place known by the Name of Micheals Creek about Ten Miles above Augusta bounded on all Sides by Vacant Land and granted by the late President and Asistants	Robert Germany
Do for John Germany	200	Claims [sic] two hundred acres of Land situated on Savannah River about four Miles above the Mouth of Broad River at a Place known by the Name of Cladon Mount Bounded North by Savannah River and on all other Sides by vacant Land, granted by the late President and Asistants	John Germany
		Claims two hundred Acres	

Claimant's Name: John Alther
Acres: 117

Situation of lands: On an island about 8 miles east south east of Savannah bounding east by lands of Gasper Hoffstetter and on other sides by creeks and marshes and was laid out by order of the late President and Assistants about 7 years ago.
Original grantee: John Alther

Claimant's Name: Elizabeth Anderson, widow, in behalf of herself and John Anderson, her son
Acres: 50

Situation of lands: A lot in Savannah number 10 in the Third Tything Lower New Ward alias Reynolds Ward with a Garden and Farm Lot.
Original grantee: James Anderson

Claimant's Name: Elizabeth Anderson, widow, in behalf of herself and John Anderson, her son
Acres: 500

Situation of lands: Lying south of a placed called Thunderbolt granted her said husband by the late President and Assistants.
Original grantee: James Anderson

Claimant's Name: Francis Arthur
Acres: 344

Situation of lands: Situated on a creek on the south side of Midway River and bounded northerly on Middleton Evans southerly on Edmund Tannatt easterly on said creek and westerly by vacant land being part of 500 acres granted him per warrant from the late President and Assistants 13th August 1753.
Original grantee: Francis Arthur

Claimant's Name: Francis Arthur
Acres: 100

Situation of lands: Situated on a creek on the north side of the aforesaid river and bounded northerly upon land of John Bennett southerly upon vacant land westerly upon

said creek and easterly upon vacant purchased from John Coffee and granted to him by warrant from the Board of President and Assistants dated 3rd May 1753.
Original grantee: John Coffee

Claimant's Name: Benjamin Brownjohn by Charles Watson
Acres: 50

Situation of lands: A town lot number 10 in Savannah in Hucks Tything Percival Ward with a Garden and Farm Lot thereto as brother and heir of William Brownjohn deceased.
Original grantee: None shown

Claimant's Name: William Bell by Charles Watson
Acres: 50

Situation of lands: A town lot number 9 in the first Tything lower ward alias Reynolds Ward with a Garden Lot and Farm Lot thereunto belonging as only heir and only son of Andrew Bell, deceased.
Original grantee: None shown

Claimant's Name: Leonard Bodell by Charles Watson
Acres: 1/8

Situation of lands: A town lot in Savannah number 2 in the fourth Tything lower New Ward alias Reynolds Ward containing 1/8 acre formerly Holmes and purchased by the said Bodell.
Original grantee: None shown

Claimant's Name: Leonard Bodell by Charles Watson
Acres: 50

Situation of lands: At Newington granted him by the late President and Assistants 1750.
Original grantee: Leonard Bodell

Claimant's Name: Reverend John Martin Bolzius by N. W. Jones
Acres: 500

Situation of lands: On a branch the northwest side of Savannah River called River Ness by warrant from late President and Assistants.
Original grantee: John Martin Bolzius

Claimant's Name: Reverend Harman Lemke by N. W. Jones
Acres: 500

Situation of lands: On the point of River Ness on Savannah River by warrant of President and Assistants.
Original grantee: Harman Lemke

Claimant's Name: Nicholas Cronberger by N. W. Jones
Acres: 200

Situation of lands: On the island in Savannah River opposite Purisburgh by warrant of late President and Assistants.
Original grantee: Cronberger

Claimant's Name: David Cutler Braddock by Charles Watson
Acres: 500

Situation of lands: On little Ogeehee (sic) River fronting on the said river east on lands of Richard Cooper north on lands late of James Papot west and on other lands of said Braddock south granted him about nine years since by the late President and Assistants.
Original grantee: David Cutler Braddock

Claimant's Name: David Cutler Braddock by Charles Watson
Acres: 400

Situation of lands: On the same river fronting said river east bounded by the tract above mentioned north by lands of Richard Cooper southand on lands of Peter Slyterman west purchased about seven years since of William Spood of South Carolina.
Original grantee: William Spood

Claimant's Name: John Peter Briton
Acres: 50

Situation of lands: A lot in Savannah number 6 Slopers Tything Percival Ward with a Garden and Farm Lot in the whole fifty acres granted him by the late Trustees in 1738.
Original grantee: John Peter Briton

Claimant's Name: James Baillou by Charles Watson
Acres: 50

Situation of lands: A town lot in Savannah number 1 Belitha Tything Heathcote Ward with a Garden and Farm Lot granted by the late Trustees in 1740 formerly Humphrey Brights.
Original grantee: Humphrey Bright

Claimant's Name: James Baillou by Charles Watson
Acres: 50

Situation of lands: A Town Lot number 2 in Savannah in the same Tything and Ward granted by the late Trustees in 1734 with Garden and Farm Lot.
Original grantee: James Baillou

Claimant's Name: James Baillou by Charles Watson
Acres: 200

Situation of lands: In or near Newington Village granted him by the late Presidents and Assistants in 1753.
Original grantee: James Baillou

Claimant's Name: James Baillou by Charles Watson on behalf of his son Isaac Baillou
Acres: 5 1/8

Situation of lands: Lot in Savannah number 5 Sloper Tything Percival Ward with a Garden Lot by deed of gift from Abraham Bignon in 1752.
Original grantee: Abraham Bignon

Claimant's Name: Peter Baillou by Charles Watson
Acres: 50 acres

Situation of lands: Town lot in Savannah number 3 in Wilmington Tything Darby Ward with Garden and Farm Lot in exchange with John Gready about the year 1741.
Original grantee: John Gready

Claimant's Name: Peter Baillou by Charles Watson
Acres: 50

Situation of lands: Town lot in Savannah number 4 Carpenters Tything Deckers Ward with Garden and Farm Lot purchased of Richard Warren in 1750.
Original grantee: None shown

Claimant's Name: Peter Baillou by Charles Watson
Acres: 50

Situation of lands: Lot in Abercorn purchased of George Langley.
Original grantee: Not shown

Claimant's Name: Peter Baillou by Charles Watson
Acres: 300

Situation of lands: On Midway River purchased of John Ballew (sic).
Original grantee: John Baillou

Claimant's Name: Peter Baillou by Charles Watson
Acres: 300

Situation of lands: On same river purchased of Jonathon Colkins.
Original grantee: John Colkins

Claimant's Name: Peter Baillou by Charles Watson
Acres: 200

Situation of lands: On the north side of said river called Plumb Park formerly Hancocks purchased by the said Baillou of John Milledge.
Original grantee: John Hencock (sic).

Claimant's Name: Peter Baillou by Charles Watson
Acres: 50

Situation of lands: At Midway aforesaid purchased of John Sloan.
Original grantee: John Sloan

Claimant's Name: Peter Baillou by Charles Watson
Acres: 50

Situation of lands: At Midway purchased of William Gore.
Original grantee: William Gore

Claimant's Name: Peter Baillou by Charles Watson for
                  Caleb Davis
Acres: 50

Situation of lands: Also said Baillou claims for Caleb Davis a lot in Savannah number 3 first Tything lower new ward alias Reynolds Ward with Garden and Farm lot granted by the late Trustees the town lot now under lease to the said Baillou.
Original grantee: None shown

Claimant's Name: Peter Baillou by Charles Watson
Acres: 300

Situation of lands: On an island known by the name of Whitmarsh granted by the late President and Assistants.
Original grantee: Peter Baillou

Claimant's Name: Richard Bennison by Charles Watson
Acres: 400

Situation of lands: At a place called Walnut Point about fifteen miles below Augusta bounded south east by Spirit Creek granted by the late President and Assistants.
Original grantee: Richard Bennison

Claimant's Name: Robert Bolton
Acres: 50

Situation of lands: Town lot number 3 in the 3rd Tything upper new ward with Farm Lot number 8 Garden Lot number 147 east of the town granted by the President and Assistants in 1749.
Original grantee: Robert Bolton

Claimant's Name: Robert Bolton
Acres: 89 6/8

Situation of lands: Two Farm Lots in the center of same granted by the President and Assistants in 1752.
Original grantee: Robert Bolton

Claimant's Name: Robert Bolton
Acres: 50

Situation of lands: Lot number 12 in New Village Skidoway by purchase from Thomas Hill.
Original grantee: Thomas Hill

Claimant's Name: Edward Barnard by right of his wife Henrietta Jane Barnard heir to James Fraser deceased
Acres: 500

Situation of lands: Bounded north west by Patt Brown southeast by Daniel Nunes northeast by Savannah River southwest by vacant land one town lot belonging to the same number 13 in Town of Augusta.
Original grantee: None shown

Claimant's Name: Edward Barnard by right of his wife Henrietta Jane Barnard heir to James Fraser deceased
Acres: 500

Situation of lands: About four miles below Augusta bounded northwest by Natt Bassett southeast by Thomas Bassett north east by Savannah River southwest by vacant land.
Original grantee: None shown

Claimant's Name: Edward Barnard
Acres: 50

Situation of lands: In the Township of Augusta bound north west by Patt Clark southeast by John Tinley (Finley?) north east by Benjamin Goldwire southwest by Ambrose Barr purchase of James Campbell.
Original grantee: None shown

Claimant's Name: William Butler
Acres: 500

Situation of lands: Between the Great Ogeechee and Midway Rivers on the south side of Sterlings Swamp granted by the late President and Assistants 14th September 1752.
Original grantee: William Butler

Claimant's Name: William Butler
Acres: Lot

Situation of lands: Lot in Hardwick number 23
Original grantee: None shown

Claimant's Name: Henry Bourquin by Charles Watson
Acres: 100

Situation of lands: On the western branch of Little Ogechee River adjoining lands of Philip Delegal and lands late of James Tebeau purchased of Peter Guirard.
Original grantee: Peter Guirard

Claimant's Name: Henry Bourquin by Charles Watson
Acres: 500

Situation of lands: Lying on the east side of the North branch of Little Ogeechee River bounded by lands of John Farmur and lands of Henry Parker purchased of Charles Watson known by the name of Rockingham allowed on 3rd May 1757.
Original grantee: Charles Watson

Claimant's Name: John Barnard by Charles Watson
Acres: 500

Situation of lands: On Wilmington Island granted by the late President and Assistants.
Original grantee: John Barnard

Claimant's Name: John Barnard in behalf of Timothy Barnard his son
Acres: 500

Situation of lands: On the same island by deed of gift from Captain Richard Kent to whom the same was granted by the late President and Assistants.
Original grantee: Richard Kent

Claimant's Name: John Barnard on behalf of Caleb Davis
Acres: 50

Situation of lands: Town lot in Savannah number 3 in the first Tything of the lower new ward alias Reynolds Ward with a Garden and Farm Lot granted said Davis by the late Trustees.
Original grantee: Allowed to William Bradley 20th March 1761 entered

Claimant's Name: John Barnard on behalf of Caleb Davis
Acres: 50

Situation of lands: Town lot number 10 in the first Tything of the lower new ward alias Reynolds Ward with a Garden and Farm Lot formerly Douglass
Original grantee: None shown

Claimant's Name: John Barnard on behalf of Caleb Davis
Acres: 50

Situation of lands: Town Lot number 1 Digby Tything Decker Ward with a Garden and Farm Lot formerly Jenkins.
Original grantee: None shown

Claimant's Name: John Barnard on behalf of Caleb Davis
Acres: 50

Situation of lands: Town Lot number 5 in Towers Tything
Deckers Ward with a Garden and Farm Lot formerly Thomas
Millichamps.
Original grantee: None shown

Claimant's Name: John Barnard on behalf of William Bradley
Acres: 50

Situation of lands: Town lot number 9 in Holland Tything
Percival Ward with a Garden and Farm Lot under the will
of--------Adlionby deceased.
Original grantee: None shown

Claimant's Name: William Butler in behalf of James Butler
                 Junior in trust
Acres: 500

Situation of lands: On the head of Collens's Creek near
Midway River on the north side of said river adjoining
to Peter Machu(torn - yn's ?) land granted by the late
President and Assistants 14th September 1752.
Original grantee: James Butler Junior

Claimant's Name: William Butler
Acres: 300

Situation of lands: On the south side of Great Ogechee
formerly ran out for Richard Burtley purchased from
Lewis Mutteair.
Original grantee: Richard Burtley

Claimant's Name: William Butler for Thomas Butler
Acres: 500

Situation of lands: On the north side of the Great Ogechee
fronting the said river by warrant from the late President
and Assistants 14th September 1752.
Original grantee: Thomas Butler

Claimant's Name: William Butler for John Parker
Acres: 500

Situation of lands: Near Midway River adjoining Peter McHugh's land by warrant from the late President and Assistants 14th September 1752.
Original grantee: John Parker

Claimant's Name: Thomas Bailey
Acres: 50

Situation of lands: Town lot number 8 in Laroche Tything Farm Lot number 4 Garden Lot number 78 south west of the town granted by the Late Trustees.
Original grantee: Thomas Bailey

Claimant's Name: Thomas Bailey
Acres: 50

Situation of lands: Town lot number 1 in Moor's Tything Farm Lot number 10 a Garden Lot number 63 west of the town by purchase from Richard Mellichamp.
Original grantee: Richard Millichamp (sic).

Claimant's Name: Thomas Bailey
Acres: 89 6/8

Situation of lands: Two Farm Lots in the center of Moor's Tything by allottment from the President and Assistants.
Original grantee: Thomas Bailey

Claimant's Name: Thomas Bailey
Acres: 5

Situation of lands: Garden Lot number 79 south west of the town by purchase of William Barbo.
Original grantee: William Barbo

Claimant's Name: Thomas Bailey
Acres: 100

Situation of lands: Lot at Tybee number 8 granted by the Honorable Trustees and claimed for the relict of John Cadman.
Original grantee: John Cadman

Claimant's Name: Henry Bourquin by Charles Watson allowed 3d May 1757
Acres: 500

Situation of lands: Lying on the western branch of Little Ogeechee River bounded by lands of Benedict Bourquin and lands late of James Tebeau granted by the late President and Assistants 1749 now called by the name of Bourdeaux.
Original grantee: Henry Bourquin.

Claimant's Name: John Barnard by Charles Watson on behalf of William Bradley
Acres: 100

Situation of lands: On any navigable river in Georgia by grant to the said Aglionby from the late Trustees entered in the office of the auditor of the Plantations (the lands have not yet been run out).
Original grantee: 20th March 17 1761 No such land to be found. Rejected.

Claimant's Name: John Barnard by Charles Watson on behalf of William Bradley
Acres: 500

Situation of lands: On the Little Ogechee River granted by the Late Trustees.
Original grantee: 20th March 1761. Allowed entered

Claimant's Name: John Barnard by Charles Watson on behalf of James Bradley
Acres: 50

Situation of lands: Lot in Savannah number 6 Digby Tything Decker Ward with a Garen and Farm Lot granted by the Late Trustees.
Original grantee: 20th March 1761. Allowed entered

Claimant's Name: John Barnard by Charles Watson on behalf
                   William Bradley, Junior
Acres: 50

Situation of lands: Lot in Savannah number 6 in the third
Tything of the lower new Ward alias Reynolds Ward with
Garden and Farm Lot granted by the late Trustees.
Original grantee: 20th March 1761 Entered

Claimant's Name: Mary Bowling spinster by Charles Watson
Acres: 5 1/8

Situation of lands: Lot in Savannah number 5 in Tyrconnel
Tything Darby Ward with a Garden Lot as daughter and heir
of Timothy Bowling her father deceased.
Original grantee: None shown

Claimant's Name: Mary Bowling by Charles Watson
Acres: 50

Situation of lands: Lot in Savannah number 2 in Wilmington
Tything Darby Ward with Garden and Farm Lot by gift from
Walter Fox deceased.
Original grantee: None shown

Claimant's Name: Benedict Bourquin by Charles Watson
Acres: 500

Situation of lands: On the western branch of Little Ogechee
River adjoining lands of Philip Delegal and Henry Bourquin
granted by the President and Assistants.
Original grantee: Benedict Bourquin

Claimant's Name: Michel Boreman by Charles Watson
Acres: 50

Situation of lands: Lying in Goshen purchased by him of
Philip Ports about 5 years ago.
Original grantee: Philip Portz (sic).

Claimant's Name: Michel Boreman by Charles Watson

Acres: 50

Situation of lands: Lying in Goshen and granted him by the late Trustees seven years ago.
Original grantee: Michel Boreman

Claimant's Name: Michel Boreman by Charles Watson
Acres: 50

Situation of lands: Lying at Black Creek about two miles from Goshen purchased by him of Leonard Plessing one year since.
Original grantee: None shown

Claimant's Name: Elisha Butler
Acres: 500

Situation of lands: Granted by the President and Assistants on the south side of the Great Ogeechee joining south easterly on David Black and north easterly on the said river.
Original grantee: Elisha Butler

Claimant's Name: Elisha Butler in behalf of William Butler his son
Acres: 500

Situation of lands: Granted by the President and Assistants on the south side of the above river called the Poplar Swamp bounded on all sides by vacant land.
Original grantee: William Butler

Claimant's Name: Joseph Butler, Senior
Acres: 300, 300, and 500

Situation of lands: 300 acres bought of David Black, 300 acres bought of Lewis Mutteair and 500 acres granted by the Council
Original grantee: Joseph Butler

Claimant's Name: Joseph Butler in behalf of Joseph Butler his son

Acres: 500

Situation of lands: Lands granted by the Council.
Original grantee: Joseph Butler, Junior

Claimant's Name: Joseph Butler in behalf of Shem Butler
Acres: 500

Situation of lands: Land granted by the Council.
Original grantee: Shem Butler

Claimant's Name: William Baker
Acres 500

Situation of lands: On a middle branch of North Newport by allotment of the late President and Assistants in July 11th 1752.
Original grantee: William Baker

Claimant's Name: Samuel Burnley
Acres: 500

Situation of lands: On the north side of North Newport by allotment of the late President and Assistants on July 11th 1752.
Original grantee: Samuel Burnley

Claimant's Name: None shown
Acres: 400

Situation of lands: On a southern branch of North Newport Swamp by allotment of the President and Assistants on August 8th 1752.
Original grantee: Elizabeth Baker, deceased

Claimant's Name: Samuel Bacon
Acres: 500

Situation of lands: On the south side of the south branch of Midway by allotment of the late President and Assistants July 11th 1752.
Original grantee: Samuel Bacon

Claimant's Name: Benjamin Baker
Acres: 500

Situation of lands: On the south side of the south branch
 of Midway by allotment of the late President and Assistants
Original grantee: Benjamin Baker

Claimant's Name: Richard Baker:
Acres: 500

Situation of lands: On a southern branch of North Newport
Swamp by allotment of the late President and Assistants.
Original grantee: Richard Baker

Claimant's Name: Sigmund Beltz
Acres: 62

Situation of lands: Bounding east on William DeBrahm's
south on Joseph Bryan and on all other sides by vacant
land by warrant from the President and Assistants on
April 6th 1754.
Original grantee: Sigmund Beltz

Claimant's Name: Sigmund Beltz
Acres: 50

Situation of lands: At Vernonburgh number 8 by purchase
of Jacob Stroubler
Original grantee: Jacob Stroubler

Claimant's Name: John Bennett by Thomas Ellis
Acres: 100

Situation of lands: On the north branch of Midway River
by the late President and Assistants
Original grantee: John Bennett

Claimant's Name: David T'Bear
Acres: 50

Situation of lands: In the Township of Vernonburgh by the
Late President and Assistants, number 7.
Original grantee: David T' Bear

Claimant's Name:　Joseph Barker
Acres:　　　　　　50

Situation of lands:　On the south side of Great Ogechee near Hardwick granted by the President and Assistants.
Original grantee:　Joseph Barker

Claimant's Name:　Joseph Barker
Acres:　　　　　　50

Situation of lands:　On the south branch of Coonoche (sic) granted by the President and Assistants.
Original grantee:　Joseph Barker

Claimant's Name:　William Beckett for Thomas Beckett by Charles Watson
Acres:　　　　　　50

Situation of lands:　On the Island Skidoway granted him by the late President and Assistants.
Original grantee:　Thomas Beckett

Claimant's Name:　William Beckett for Thomas Beckett by Charles Watson
Acres:　　　　　　50

Situation of lands:　On the Island Skidoway purchased of Alex. Ross formerly belonging to Hugh Lane:
Original grantee:　Hugh Lane

Claimant's Name:　William Beckett
Acres:　　　　　　100

Situation of lands:　At Half Moon Bluff on Skidoway Island granted by the President and Assistants.
Original grantee:　William Beckett

Claimant's Name:　Adrian Van Beverhoudt
Acres:　　　　　　500

Situation of lands: Upon Burmuda Island by allotment by the late President and Assistants.
Original grantee: Adrian Van Beverhoudt

Claimant's Name: Adrian Van Beverhoudt for John Van Beverhoudt
Acres: 500

Situation of lands: Upon Burmuda Island by allotment of the late President and Assistants.
Original grantee: John Van Beverhoudt

Claimant's Name: Francis Harris for John Bailey of Barbados
Acres: 500

Situation of lands: On the south side of the south branch of Little Ogechee River by warrant from the late President and Assistants to Joseph Phillips.
Original grantee: Joseph Phillips

Claimant's Name: Francis Harris for John Bailey of Barbados
Acres: None shown

Situation of lands: A Wharfe above the Upper Landing at Savannah.
Original grantee: Joseph Phillips

Claimant's Name: Keneth (sic) Baillie by Charles Watson
Acres: 500

Situation of lands: On Long Island near the head of Midway River granted by the late President and Assistants.
Original grantee: Keneth Baillie

Claimant's Name: ~~Keneth Baillie by Charles Watson~~
Acres: ~~250~~

Situation of lands: ~~On the same Island purchased of Abraham Frisby.~~
Original grantee: ~~Abraham Frisby~~
NOTE: ALL OF THE ABOVE IS CROSSED OUT. P. B.

18.

Claimant's Name: Keneth Baillie by Charles Watson
Acres: 500

Situation of lands: Near the same purchased of Probart Howarth.
Original grantee: Probart Howarth

Claimant's Name: Keneth Baillie by Charles Watson for Keneth Baillie his son
Acres: 50

Situation of lands: Near the above given him as a disbanded soldier.
Original grantee: Keneth Baillie, Jr.

Claimant's Name: Keneth Baillie by Charles Watson for Keneth Baillie his son
Acres: 50

Situation of lands: By gift from John Hargrove a disbanded soldier.
Original grantee: John Hargrove

Claimant's Name: John Casper Bate
Acres: 50

Situation of lands: At Goshen number 10 by warrant from the President and Assistants.
Original grantee: John Casper Bate

Claimant's Name: John Rae for Isaac Barksdale
Acres: 500

Situation of lands: Lying on the Uchee Island and part on the Main opposite the said island granted by the late President and Assistants.
Original grantee: Isaac Barksdale

Claimant's Name: John Rae for Rae and Barksdale
Acres: 500

Situation of lands: In Augusta purchased of Kenedy O'Brien having a plat and grant from the late Trustees.
Original grantee: None shown

Claimant's Name: John Rae
Acres: 50

Situation of lands: Lot in Savannah with a Garden and Farm Lot.
Original grantee: None shown

Claimant's Name: John Rae
Acres: 50

Situation of lands: Brier Creek with the priviledge (sic) of a ferry granted by General Oglethorpe.
Original grantee: None shown

Claimant's Name: John Rae
Acres: 400

Situation of lands: Lying on Savannah River granted by the late President and Assistants.
Original grantee: John Rae

Claimant's Name: David Douglass for James Bobby
Acres: 100

Situation of lands: On the north west side of the (scratched out and illegible) Great Ciokee (sic) on Savannah River granted by the late President and Assistants.
Original grantee: James Bobby

Claimant's Name: Patrick Brown, Daniel Clark and Lachlan McGillivray
Acres: 500

Situation of lands: In the Township of Augusta run out for Thomas Smith by order of James Oglethorpe Esqr. purchased jointly by them from said Smith.
Original grantee: None shown

Claimant's Name: William Clifton
Acres: 50

Situation of lands: Lot in Savannah number 8 in Broughton Street in Frederick Tything Darby Ward with five and forty five acre lots the former being the Garden Lot number 51 south east of Savannah the latter the Farm Lot number 8 letter D lying near the Trustees Farm purchased by him of Joseph Stanley.
Original grantee: None shown

Claimant's Name: William Clifton for John Graham
Acres: 50

Situation of lands: The town lot number 8 in Hucks Tything Percival Ward with the Garden Lot number 29 south west from the town and the Farm Lot number 3 thereto belonging.
Original grantee: None shown

Claimant's Name: James Campbell for Robert Gilbert
                   (struck out as shown here)
Acres: 50

Situation of lands: Town Lot number 10 in Carpenter's Tything a Farm Lot number 1 in Carpemter's Tything Garden Lot number 9 west of the town by purchase the 14th September 1754.
Original grantee: Robert Gilbert

Claimant's Name: James Campbell for William Mears the Heir
Acres: 50

Situation of lands: Town lot number 8 in Digby Tything Farm Lot number 6 in Digby Tything Garden Lot number 21 east of the town granted by the late Trustees to William Mears.
Original grantee: William Mears

Claimant's Name: James Campbell for the relict of
                   Samuel Pensyre
Acres: 100

Situation of lands: Tract on Tybee Island number 13 granted by the late Trustees to Samuel Pensyre.
Original grantee: Samuel Pensyre

Claimant's Name: Anthony Camuse
Acres: 50

Situation of lands: Lot in Savannah number 4 Tyrconnel Tything Darby Ward with a Garden and Farm Lot granted him by the late Trustees.
Original grantee: None shown

Claimant's Name: Anthony Camuse
Acres: 500

Situation of lands: Lying on Wilmington Island granted by the late President and Assistants in 1746.
Original grantee: Anthony Camuse

Claimant's Name: Jane Cary in behalf of her son John Cary an infant grandson and heir of Jeremiah Papot by Charles Watson
Acres: 50

Situation of lands: Lot in Savannah number 8 Sloper Tything Percival Ward with Garden and Farm Lots granted by the Trustees to Jeremiah Papot deceased.
Original grantee: None shown

Claimant's Name: Martin Campbell and Francis Macartin
Acres: 50

Situation of lands: Lot in the township of Augusta granted by James Oglethorpe Esqr to George Cornell and purchased by us from his son.
Original grantee: None shown

Claimant's Name: Martin Campbell and Francis Macartin
Acres: 499

Situation of lands: In the said township and town granted by James Oglethorpe Esqr. to Thomas Goodale purchased by us from the said Thomas.
Original grantee: None shown

Claimant's Name: Roderick McKintosh by George Cuthbert
Acres: 500

Situation of lands: Dickensons Neck Sapola River by allotment from the President and Assistants September 1753.
Original grantee: Roderick McKintosh

Claimant's Name: Roderick McKintosh by George Cuthbert
Acres: 50

Situation of lands: Joining the above by purchase of James Stuart Taylor who had it by allotment from the President and Assistants.
Original grantee: James Stuart Taylor (Taylor may mean "tailor.")

Claimant's Name: Ann Graham by George Cuthbert
Acres: 50

Situation of lands: Lot in Savannah by will of Patrick Graham who had same by grant of the Trustees in 1736.
Original grantee: Patrick Graham

Claimant's Name: Ann Graham by George Cuthbert
Acres: 50

Situation of lands: Lot in Savannah by will of Patrick Graham who purchased same of Marmaduke Cannon son of   Cannon who had it by grant from the Trustees in 1733.
Original grantee: Cannon

Claimant's Name: Ann Graham by George Cuthbert
Acres: 50

Situation of lands: Lot in Frederica by grant of General Oglethorpe in 1738.
Original grantee: None shown

Claimant's Name: Ann Graham by George Cuthbert
Acres: 500

Situation of lands: Ann Graham claims by her attorney George Cuthbert five hundred acres of land on Savannah River known by the name of Joseph's Town about ten miles to the north west of the Town of Savannah granted her by the name of Ann Cuthbert by General Oglethorpe.
Original grantee: None shown

Claimant's Name: Ann Graham by George Cuthbert
Acres: None shown

Situation of lands: Also a town lot in the Town of Hardwicke known by the number 44 granted by the late President and Assistants ~~to her late husband Patrick Graham~~.
Original grantee: Patrick Graham

Claimant's Name: Edward Carlton
Acres: 50

Situation of lands: Town lot number 7 in Heathcote Tything with Farm Lot number 3 in Heathcote Tything Garden Lot number 44 east of the town by purchase.
Original grantee: None shown

Claimant's Name: Edward Carlton
Acres: 300

Situation of lands: On the south side of Little Ogechee by allotment of the late President and Assistants.
Original grantee: Edward Carlton

Claimant's Name: John Cubbedge
Acres: 200

Situation of lands: On the north side of Midway River granted him by the President and Assistants about the year 1753.
Original grantee: John Cubbedge

Claimant's Name: John Cubbedge
Acres: 300

Situation of lands: On the west side of Cubbedge's Creek near Midway River purchased of Mr. John Edwards which was granted him by the President and Assistants about 1748/9.
Original grantee: John Edwards

Claimant's Name: John Cubbedge
Acres: 50

Situation of lands: On the north side of Midway River purchased of Mr. John Beacham granted him by the President and Assistants about the year 1751.
Original grantee: John Beacham

Claimant's Name: Christian Campher
Acres: 50

Situation of lands: Lot in the Town of Savannah number 4 in the third Tything of the Upper New Ward with the lands annexed.
Original grantee: Christian Campher

Claimant's Name: Christian Campher
Acres: 50

Situation of lands: Lot in the Town of Vernonburgh with the lands appertaining to it.
Original grantee: None shown

Claimant's Name: Thomas Carter
Acres: 300

Situation of lands: On the south side of Newport River by warrant of the President and Assistants.
Original grantee: Thomas Carter

Claimant's Name: Frances Coffey
Acres: 45

Situation of lands: Lot 143 in Savannah and a 45 acre (sic) thereto belonging by right of widowed executrix etc. of the late said Gibbons surgeon.
Original grantee: None shown

Claimant's Name: John Coffey
Acres: 100

Situation of lands: On Midway
Original grantee: None shown

Claimant's Name: Richard Cooper
Acres: 500

Situation of lands: On the south side of little Ogechee fronting the river and bounding on one side by lands granted to Joseph Summers and on the other side by lands granted to William Spood granted by the President and Assistants.
Original grantee: Richard Cooper

Claimant's Name: Richard Cooper
Acres: 50

Situation of lands: On Coonochee (sic) about 8 miles above the ford bounding on vacant lands.
Original grantee: Richard Cooper

Claimant's Name: Richard Cooper
Acres: 500

Situation of lands: On the south side of Little Ogechee fronting on the river bounding on one side to lands of David Cutler Braddock and on the other side by lands granted to William Wilson above-land-granted-to-John Rogerson.(sic)
Original grantee: John Rogerson

Claimant's Name: Thomas Collins
Acres: 100

Situation of lands: On the north side of Midway River granted him by the President and Assistants about the year 1741.
Original grantee: Thomas Collins

Claimant's Name: James Corneck
Acres: 50

Situation of lands: Lot in Savannah number 188 with the 5 and 45 acre lots.
Original grantee: None shown

Claimant's Name: Patrick Clark
Acres: 50

Situation of lands: Lot in the Township of Augusta bounded north west by Thomas Ross south west by William Clark south east by Gilbert Fyfe and north east by Savannah River granted by General Oglethorpe to Benjamin Crosswell and sold by him to Joseph Oaks and by him sold to Patrick Clark.
Original grantee: None shown

Claimant's Name: Patrick Clark
Acres: 50

Situation of lands: Lot number 28 in the Township of Augusta bounded north west by Richard Lee south east by Ambrose Barr south west by Thomas Webb north east by the Town Common granted to Nicholas Murphy a soldier and by him sold to John Tinly and purchased by Patrick Clark.
Original grantee: Nicholas Murphy

Claimant's Name: Patrick Clark
Acres: 50

Situation of lands: Lot number 29 (ditto) bounded (ditto) granted to Peter Gates and by him sold (ditto) and purchased by (ditto). NOTE: These are "dittos" as shown in the original.
Original grantee: Peter Gates

Claimant's Name: Patrick Clark
Acres: 300

Situation of lands: About 9 miles above Augusta bounded north west by Mathew Allen south east by Thomas Mooney south west by vacant land and north east by Savannah River granted by the President and Assistants in 1748.
Original grantee: Patrick Clark

Claimant's Name: Patrick Clark
Acres: 200

Situation of lands: On Broad River about 70 miles north west of Augusta bounded on all sides by vacant land by the President and Assistants the 29th September 1753.
Original grantee: Patrick Clark

Claimant's Name: John Crieter by Charles Watson
Acres: 50

Situation of lands: In the Township of Ebenezer lying east on a creek called Mill Creek south on John Gable and west on vacant lands by the late President and Assistants.
Original grantee: John Crieter

Claimant's Name: David Cunningham by Charles Watson
Acres: 50

Situation of lands: Lot in Savannah number 7 in the Second Tything Lower New Ward alias Reynolds Ward with Garden and Farm Lots granted him by the late President and Assistants.
Original grantee: David Cunningham

Claimant's Name: David Cunningham in behalf of his wife and James Brooks her son by Charles Watson
Acres: 50

Situation of lands: Lot in Savannah number 4 in the Second Tything Lower New Ward alias Reynolds Ward heretofore granted by the late Trustees to Francis Brooks her former husband deceased.
Original grantee: Francis Brooks

Claimant's Name: David Cunningham in behalf of his wife and James Brooks her son by Charles Watson.
Acres: 500

Situation of lands: On an island called Whitmarsh given her deceased husband by the late Trustees.
Original grantee: None shown

Claimants' Name: David Cunningham in behalf of his wife and John Brooks her son by Charles Watson
Acres: 50

Situation of lands: On the island of Skidoway granted his said wife while sole by the name of Ann Mouse.
Original grantee: None shown

Claimant's Name: William Clement
Acres: 5

Situation of lands: Town lot number 6 in the fourth Tything in Reynolds Ward with a Garden Lot granted by the President and Assistants in 1743.
Original grantee: William Clements

Claimant's Name: William Carr
Acres: 500

Situation of lands: On the north side of the north branch of Newport River granted by the late President and Assistants.
Original grantee: William Carr

Claimant's Name: William Clements
Acres: 300

Situation of lands: About three miles above Augusta adjoining north east of lands granted to John Kennedy granted by the President and Assistants.
Original grantee: William Clements

Claimant's Name: Frances Coffey
Acres: 50

Situation of lands: Town lot late Thomas Ormston number 5 in the Third Tything Upper New Ward.
Original grantee: None shown

Claimant's Name: John Cubbedge in behalf of George Cubbedge
Acres: 500

Situation of lands: North side of Midway River fronting on Midway Narrows granted by the late President and Assistants.
Original grantee: George Cubbedge

Claimant's Name: Peter Cupper (sic)
Acres: 50

Situation of lands: Lot at Goshen number 16 granted to Nicholas Ludholt.
Original grantee: None shown

Claimant's Name: Christian Dasher
Acres: 100

Situation of lands: Two fifty acre lots in the district of Joseph's Town adjoining together.
Original grantee: None shown

Claimant's Name: Raymond Demere
Acres: 50

Situation of lands: On St. Simon's Island near Frederica on the south side of the High Road to the German Village about a mile from the town bounded by Dr. Hawkins land and Dr. Holzendorf's granted by General Oglethorpe.
Original grantee: None shown

Claimant's Name: James Dean
Acres: 50

Situation of lands: In the Town of Augusta butting and bounding on the north by land of David Douglass and John Tinley granted by the President and Assistants.
Original grantee: None shown

Claimant's Name: James Dean
Acres: None shown

Situation of lands: Lot in Town of Savannah joining to Mrs. Dean given by the Trustees.
Original grantee: None shown

Claimant's Name: David Douglass
Acres: 50

Situation of lands: Lot in Augusta number 2 bought of John Burtley granted him by James Oglethorpe, Esqr.
Original grantee: None shown

Claimant's Name: David Douglas
Acres: None shown

Situation of lands: Adjoining to the former bought of John Tinly being part of his lot number 1.
Original grantee: None shown

Claimant's Name: David Douglass
Acres: 50

Situation of lands: Lot in Augusta number 14 bought of Benjamin Goldwire granted to him.
Original grantee: None shown

Claimant's Name: David Douglass
Acres: 50

Situation of lands: Lot in Augusta number 37 bought of Richard Begling a soldier granted to him.
Original grantee: None shown

Claimant's Name: David Douglass
Acres: 50

Situation of lands: Lot in Augusta number 3 bought by my son John of Samuel Williams granted by James Oglethorpe, Esqr.
Original grantee: None shown

Claimant's Name: David Douglass
Acres: 200

Situation of lands: On a place called Mill Creek above Augusta bought of Thomas Ross granted by the President and Assistants.
Original grantee: Thomas Ross

Claimants' Name: David Douglass
Acres: 500

Situation of lands: On Newport River granted by the President and Council.
Original grantee: David Douglass

Claimant's Name: Ann Demetre as the heir in tail by deed pole
Acres: 50

Situation of lands: Town lot in Savannah number 7 in Frederick Tything Derby Ward Garden Lot number 65 east Farm lot number 1 granted to Joseph Coles by the late Trustees.
Original grantee: Joseph Coles

Claimant's Name: Ann Demetre
Acres: 50

Situation of lands: Town lot in Savannah number 8 in Heathcote Tything Deckers Ward Garden Lot number 68 west Farm Lot number 7 by will of Thomas Salter who had it from the late Trustees.
Original grantee: Thomas Salter

Claimant's Name: Ann Demetre
Acres: 50

Situation of lands: Town lot in Savannah number 6 in Laroche Tything Heathcote Ward Garden Lot number 2 west Farm Lot number 6 as relict of William Harris who had it from the late Trustees.
Original grantee: William Harris

Claimant's Name: Ann Demetre
Acres: 50

Situation of lands: Town lot in Savannah number 3 in Tyrconnel Tything Derby Ward Garden Lot number 57 south east Farm Lot number 5 as heiress to Thomas Pratt.
Original grantee: Thomas Pratt

Claimant's Name: Ann Demetre
Acres: 50

Situation of lands: Town lot in Frederica number 27 in Tracy Ward with the land belonging formerly William Hughes Hayes who leaving the Colony was regranted to Laurence Raynour who leaving the colony General Oglethorpe purchased it of him December 3, 1742 and gave it to said Ann Demetre.
Original grantee: None shown

Claimant's Name: Ann Demetre
Acres: None shown

Situation of lands: House and garden in Frederica adjoining Samuel Goffs by purchase of Robert and Elizabeth Bateman June 3, 1749.
Original grantee: None shown

Claimant's Name: Ann Demetre
Acres: 50

Situation of lands: On Dickenson's Neck adjoining to Daniel Demetre by purchase of John Rutledge 15th June 1750.
Original grantee: John Rutledge

Claimant's Name: Ann Demetre as guardian to William Thomas Harris
Acres: 500

Situation of lands: About 3 miles below Savannah commonly called Salter's Island by grant Dec. 17th 1741 and given by will to William Thomas Harris by Thomas Salter Deceased.
Original grantee: Thomas Salter

Claimant's Name: Ann Demetre as guardian to William Thomas Harris
Acres: 350

Situation of lands: East on a creek of Sapola River and north of John Rutledges land by the President and Assistants 11th Dec. 1752.
Original grantee: William Thomas Harris

Claimant's Name: Daniel Demetre
Acres: 500

Situation of lands: On Newport River northerly southerly on Rutledge's land westerly on vacant land and easterly on marshes from the President and Assistants May 5th 1750.
Original grantee: Daniel Demetre

Claimant's Name: Daniel Demetre
Acres: 500

Situation of lands: On Smith's Island by purchase of John Smith 30th May 1754.
Original grantee: John Smith

Claimant's Name: James DeVeaux
Acres: 500

Situation of lands: On the west side of the north branch of Little Ogechee called Lebanon from the President and Assistants 25th Feb. 1752.
Original grantee: James DeVeaux

Claimant's Name: James DeVeaux Junr. by James DeVeaux Senr.
Acres: 500

Situation of lands: On Argyle Island from the President and Assistants 9 Dec. 1752.
Original grantee: James DeVeaux Junr.

Claimant's Name: James DeVeaux
Acres: 500

Situation of lands: On Skidoway Island known by the name of Springfield granted to Richard Palmer deceased by the President and Assistants 22d Augt. 1749 by purchase of said Palmer.
Original grantee: Richard Palmer

Claimant's Name: James DeVeaux
Acres: 50

Situation of lands: Town lot number 9 in Slopers Tything with Garden and Farm Lots number 46 and number 10 granted to Peter Baillou and since exchanged with John Gready who sold it to James DeVeaux.
Original grantee: None shown

Claimant's Name: James DeVeaux
Acres: 447/8

Situation of lands: Farm Lot containing 44 7/8 in Holland Tything Percival Ward number 5 purchased from William Barbo.
Original grantee: William Barbo

Claimant's Name: John DeVeaux
Acres: 500

Situation of lands: On the north branch of Little Ogechee River adjoining land there of James DeVeaux granted by the late President and Assistants.
Original grantee: John DeVeaux

Claimant's Name: Edward Davidson by Charles Watson
Acres: 50

Situation of lands: Lot in Savannah number 7 in the Third Tything Lower New Ward alias Reynolds Ward with Garden and Farm Lot formerly John Evans deceased.
Original grantee: None shown

Claimant's Name: Edward Davidson by Charles Watson
Acres: 50

Situation of lands: Lot in Savannah number 9 Fourth Tything of the same ward with Garden and Farm Lots granted him by thePresident and Assistants.
Original grantee: Edward Davidson

Claimant's Name: John Dudding by Keneth Baillie by Charles
                   Watson
Acres: 50

Situation of lands: At Newington granted by the late President and Assistants.
Original grantee: None shown

Claimant's Name: John Davis
Acres: 500

Situation of lands: On the north side at the head of Midway River granted by the Preisdent and Assistants July 1750 (?).
Original grantee: John Davis

Claimant's Name: John Davis Junr. by John Davis Senr.
Acres: 500

Situation of lands: On Skidoway Island by the President and Assistants December 1750.
Original grantee: John Davis Junr.

Claimant's Name: Michael Downer by Charles Watson
Acres: 50

Situation of lands: At Black Creek near Goshen formerly Murry's purchased by said Downer of Benjamin Sheftall.
Original grantee: John Murry

Claimant's Name: William Gerard DeBrahm by Charles Watson
Acres: 500

Situation of lands: About 7 miles west of the Town of Savannah granted him by the late Trustees.
Original grantee: William Gerard DeBrahm

Claimant's Name: William Gerard DeBrahm by Charles Watson
Acres: 137

Situation of lands: About 7 miles west of Savannah adjoining to 500 acres granted him by the President and Assistants.
Original grantee: William Gerard DeBrahm

Claimant's Name: Philip Delegal Junr.
Acres: 500

Situation of lands: On the fork of Little Ogechee from the President and Assistants December 21st 1747.
Original grantee: Philip Delegal Junr.

Claimant's Name: Philip Delegal Junr.
Acres: 300

Situation of lands: Upon Little Ogechee by purchase of James Thebault.
Original grantee: James Thebault

Claimant's Name: Philip Delegal Junr. for David Delegal his son
Acres: 100

Situation of lands: Upon on the north side of Great Ogechee from the President and Assistants November 9th 1752.
Original grantee: David Delegal

Claimant's Name: George Dunbar by Sir Patrick Houston Bart.
Acres: 500

Situation of lands: Illa Island in Savannah River given in exchange for 500 acres in Joseph's Town granted by the late Trustees in 1734.
Original grantee: George Dunbar

Claimant's Name: James Dixee
Acres: 200

Situation of lands: On the south branch of Little Ogechee River bounded south east of David Fox's land by allotment of the late President and Assistants.
Original grantee: James Dixee

Claimant's Name: George Dresler
Acres: 50

Situation of lands: Lot in Savannah number 10 in Vernon Tything Heathcote Ward with Garden and Farm Lot allotted by the late President and Assistants.
Original grantee: George Dresler

Claimant's Name: George Delegal Attorney for Philip Delegal Senr.
Acres: 500

Situation of lands: On the south branch of Little Ogechee from the late President and Assistants June 2nd 1752.
Original grantee: Philip Delegal Senr.

Claimant's Name: William Ewen
Acres: 200

Situation of lands: In Little Ogechee District adjoining west to Clement Martin on the north to Thomas Ellis and on all other sides by vacant lands by purchase of John Casper Walthour December 8th 1752.
Original grantee: John Casper Walthour

Claimant's Name: James Burnsides by William Ewen
Acres: 50

Situation of lands: Lot in Savannah number 3 in Tyrconnel Tything Derby Ward Farm Lot number 5 Garden Lot number 7 lying east.
Original grantee: None shown

Claimant's Name: James Burnsides by William Ewen
Acres: 400

Situation of lands: An island known by the name of Rotten Possum between Skidoway Island and late Coll. Stephens land on the river leading to Green Island.
Original grantee: None shown

Claimant's Name: Joseph Shubdrin
Acres: 50

Situation of lands: Bounding east Paul Finck south himself north and west vacant land from the late President and Assistants as heir to Daniel Subdrin (sic) his father deceased.
Original grantee: Daniel Shubdrin

Claimant's Name: Joseph Shubdrin
Acres: 50

Situation of lands: Bounding east Paul Finck south Daniel Shubdrin Junr. west vacant and north the first plantation from the late President and Assistants.
Original grantee: Joseph Shubdrin

Claimant's Name: Daniel Shubdrin Junr.
Acres: 50

Situation of lands: Bounding east Paul Finck south vacant and Peter Shubdrin west vacant north Joseph Shubdrin from the late Presidents and Assistants.
Original grantee: Daniel Shubdrin Junr.

Claimant's Name: Daniel Shubdrin Junr.
Acres: 2

Situation of lands: Garden on the east side of town bounding east George Bruckner south a large swamp west Paulus Zittrauer north the town from the late President and Assistants.
Original grantee: Daniel Shubdrin Junr.

Claimant's Name: Daniel Shubdrin Junr.
Acres: Town Lot

Situation of lands: One Town Lot in the 17th row and first division from the late President and Assistants.
Original grantee: None shown

Claimant's Name: John Peter Shubdrin
Acres: 50

Situation of lands: Bounding east Paul Finck and Anne Margaretta Feyrmuth (sic) south Nicolaus Shubdrin west vacant north Daniel Shubdrin Junr. from the late President and Assistants.
Original grantee: John Peter Shubdrin

Claimant's Name: John Peter Shubdrin
Acres: Town Lot

Situation of lands: One Town Lot in the 17 Row and first Division.
Original grantee: None shown

Claimant's Name: Nicolaus Shundrin (sic)
Acres: 50

Situation of lands: Bounding east Anna Margaretta Feyrmuth south John George Klein west vacant north John Peter Shundrin from the late President and Assistants.
Original grantee: Nicolaus Shubdrin

Claimant's Name: John Georg Klein
Acres: 50

Situation of lands: Bounding east Anna Margaretta Feyrmuth south Ludwig Weidman west John Rentz north Nicolaus Shubdrin from the late President and Assistants.
Original grantee: John Georg Klein

Claimant's Name: Ludwig Weidmann
Acres: 50

Situation of lands: Bounding east Anne Margaretta Feyrmuth south vacant west Jacob Kaupp north John Georg Klein.
Original grantee: None shown

Claimant's Name: Ludwig Weidmann
Acres: 25

Situation of lands: In the Town District bounding east and south vacant west Christopher Ortmann north the said creek which he bought of John Sheffler near Ebenezer Creek.
Original grantee: None shown

Claimant's Name: Paul Finck
Acres: 50

Situation of lands: Bounding east vacant south Anne Margaretta Feyrmuth west Daniel Shubdrin Junr. Joseph and John Shubdrin.
Original grantee: None shown

Claimant's Name: Anne Margaretta Feyrmuth
Acres: 50

Situation of lands: Bounding east and south vacant west John Peter and Nicolaus Shubdrin north Paul Finck.
Original grantee: None shown

Claimant's Name: Georg (sic) Fisher
Acres: 50

Situation of lands: Bounding east George Klein south Jacob Kaupp west and north vacant land.
Original grantee: None shown

Claimant's Name: Bartholomew Maik
Acres: 50

Situation of lands: Bounding east Ludwig Weidmann south Thomas Sweighoffer west vacant north John Rentz bought of Jacob Kaupp who left the colony.
Original grantee: None shown

Claimant's Name: Thomas Sweighoffer
Acres: 50

Situation of lands: Bounding east vacant south Balthazer Rieser west vacant north Jacob Kaupp.
Original grantee: None shown

Claimant's Name: Thomas Sweighoffer
Acres: None shown

Situation of lands: One Town Lot in the 11th Row and 2nd Division bound one side by Veit Landfelder.
Original grantee: None shown

Claimant's Name: Balthazer Rieser
Acres: 50

Claimant's Name: Balthazer Rieser
Acres: None shown

Situation of lands: One Town Lot in the 4th Row 2nd Division between Balthazer Metzger and David Eishberger and the Town Lot of his father in law Thomas Backer deceased in the 6th Row and 4th Division between John Maurer and Ursala Meyer.
Original grantee: None shown

Claimant's Name: John Georg Haid
Acres: 50

Situation of lands: Bounding east vacant south Jacob Dussing west John Georg Ziegler north Balthaser (sic) Rieser.
Original grantee: None shown

Claimant's Name: Jacob Dussing
Acres: 50

Situation of lands: Bounding east Balthazer Rieser and John Georg Haid south west and north John Georg Haid.
Original grantee: None shown

Claimant's Name: John Neidlinger
Acres: 50

Situation of lands: Bounding east and west vacant south Michael Weinkauff north Jacob Dussing.
Original grantee: None shown

Claimant's Name: John Neidlinger
Acres: None shown

Situation of lands: One Town Lot in the 17th Row and third Division.
Original grantee: None shown

Claimant's Name: Michael Weinkauff
Acres: 50

Situation of lands: Bounding east and west vacant south Jacob Mohr north John Neidlinger.
Original grantee: None shown

Claimant's Name: Ludwig Ernst
Acres: 50

Situation of lands: Bounding east the River Savannah south the Mill Lot west John Kappacher north Jacob Mohr.
Original grantee: None shown

Claimant's Name: Jacob Mohr
Acres: 50

Situation of lands: Bounding east and west vacant south Ludwig Ernst north Michael Weinjauff.
Original grantee: None shown

Claimant's Name: Ludwig Ernst
Acres: 2

Situation of lands: One Town Lot in the 27 (?) Row and 9th Division near Ursala Meyer - 2 acres Garden on the west side of the Town in the 2nd Row between Peter Arnsdorff and Bartholomew Rieser.
Original grantee: None shown

Claimant's Name: John Kappacher
Acres: 50

Situation of lands: Bounding east Ludwig Ernst and Mill Lot south west and north vacant land.
Original grantee: None shown

Claimant's Name: The Publick for an intended Grist Mill
Acres: 100

Situation of lands: Bounding east the Savannah River south Valentin Deppe west vacant north Ludwig Ernst.
Original grantee: None shown

Claimant's Name: Valentin Deppe
Acres: 50

Situation of lands: Bounding east the Savannah River south
Rupert Schrempff west Jacob Huber north Mill Lot.
Original grantee: None shown

Claimant's Name: Valentin Deppe
Acres: None shown

Situation of lands: One Town Lot in the 1st row the 3rd
division near Matthew Zettler.
Original grantee: None shown

Claimant's Name: Rupert Shrempff's widow
Acres: 50

Situation of lands: Bounding east the Savannah River south
Cunrad Frieskinger west Jacob Huber north Valentin Deppe.
Original grantee: None shown

Claimant's Name: Rupert Shrempff's widow
Acres: 2

Situation of lands: Garden bought of widow Lenhoffer
deceased in the west side of the Town 1st Row between John
Sheffter and Gabriel Bach.
Original grantee: None shown

Claimant's Name: Rupert Shrempff's widow
Acres: None shown

Situation of lands: One Town Lot in the first Row 2nd
Division near John Casper Wertsok bought of Thomas Bichler
deceased.
Original grantee: None shown

Claimant's Name: Jacon Huber
Acres: 50

Situation of lands: Bounding east Valentin Deppe and Rupert Shrempff south Georg Bollinger west John Miohler north vacant.
Original grantee: None shown

Claimant's Name: John Miohler
Acres: 50

Situation of lands: Bounding east Jacob Huber south John Georg Bollinger west Henry Ludwig Buntz north vacant.
Original grantee: None shown

Claimant's Name: John Georg Bollinger
Acres: 50

Situation of lands: Bounding east Cunrad Frickinger south vacant west John Georg Buntz north John Miohler and Jacob Huber.
Original grantee: None shown

Claimant's Name: Henry Ludwig Buntz
Acres: 50

Situation of lands: Bounding east John Miohler south John Georg Buntz west Christian Oechslin north ~~Henry Ludwig Buntz~~ Casper Heok.
Original grantee: None shown

Claimant's Name: John Georg Buntz
Acres: 50

Situation of lands: Bounding east John Georg Bollinger south vacant west Christian Oechslin north Henry Ludwig Buntz.
Original grantee: None shown

Claimant's Name: Christian Oechslin
Acres: 50

Situation of lands: Bounding east Henry Ludwig Buntz, south John Georg Buntz west Casper Heok north vacant.
Original grantee: None shown

Claimant's Name: Casper Heok
Acres: 50

Situation of lands: Bounding east Christian Oechslin south and north vacant west John Hangleiter.
Original grantee: None shown

Claimant's Name: Cunrad Frickinger
Acres: 50

Situation of lands: Bounding east the Savannah River south Christian Bidenback west John Georg Bollinger north Rupert Schrempff.
Original grantee: None shown

Claimant's Name: Christian Bidenback
Acres: 50

Situation of lands: Bounding east the Savannah River south John Georg Rau west vacant north Cunrad Frickinger.
Original grantee: None shown

Claimant's Name: Christian Bidenback
Acres: 50

Situation of lands: Bought of Christian Birch bounding east John Casper Wertsch south vacant west John Adam Treuttlin north Christoph Dellinger.
Original grantee: None shown

Claimant's Name: Urbanus Buntz
Acres: 50

Situation of lands: Bought of John Georg Rau bounding east the Savannah River south John Martyn Rheinlander west vacant north Christian Biddenback.
Original grantee: None shown

Claimant's Name: John Martyn Rheinlander
Acres: 50

Situation of lands: Bounding east the River Savannah south John Paul Franck west Matthew Biddenback, north John Georg Rau.
Original grantee: None shown

Claimants' Name: John Martyn Rheinlander
Acres: 2

Situation of lands: Garden on the west side of the Town in the third row between Peter Gruber and Rauner.
Original grantee: None shown

Claimant's Name: John Paul Franck
Acres: 50

Situation of lands: Bounding east the Savannah River south John Georg Pechtly west Matthew Biddenback north John Martyn Rheinlander.
Original grantee: None shown

Claimant's Name: Matthew Biddenback
Acres: 50

Situation of lands: Bounding east John Paul Franck and John Martyn Rheinlander south John Georg Meyer west and north vacant.
Original grantee: None shown

Claimant's Name: John Hangleiter
Acres: 50

Situation of lands: Bought of John Georg Pechtly bounding east River Savannah south John Georg Meyer west vacant north John Paul Franck.
Original grantee: None shown

Claimant's Name: John Hangleiter
Acres: 50

Situation of lands: Bought of John Georg Meyer bounding east the River, south Samuel Graves west the 2nd lot of the said Meyer north of John Georg Pechtly.
Original grantee: None shown

Claimant's Name: George Gruber
Acres: 50

Situation of lands: The second lot of John Georg Meyer bounding east the first lot of said Meyer ~~north of John Georg Pechtly~~ west John Casper Wertsch south and north vacant. NOTE: Crossed out in original
Original grantee: None shown

Claimant's Name: John Casper Wertsch
Acres: 50

Situation of lands: Bounding east George Gruber west Christian Birck south and north vacant.
Original grantee: None shown

Claimant's Name: John Casper Wertsch
Acres: None shown

Situation of lands: Two town lots one for himself in the 1st row and second division between Thomas Bichler and Nicolaus Cronberger - the second in the 4th division of said row between Theobald Keeffer and Christian Birck which he bought of John Georg Meyer.
Original grantee: None shown

Claimant's Name: John Adam Treuttlin
Acres: 50

Situation of lands: Bounding east Christian Birck south and west vacant north Wolffgang Mack.
Original grantee: None shown

Claimant's Name: Wolffgang Mack
Acres: 50

Situation of lands: Bounding east Christopher Dellinger south John Adam Treuttlin west and north vacant.
Original grantee: None shown

Claimant's Name: John Kunold
Acres: 50

Situation of lands: Bought of Christopher Dellinger bounding east vacant south Christian Birck west Wolffgang Mack north vacant.
Original grantee: None shown

Claimant's Name: Samuel Graves
Acres: 50

Situation of lands: Bounding east the River Savannah south Georg Meyer deceased west vacant north John Georg Meyer now possessed by John Hangleiter.
Original grantee: None shown

Claimant's Name: Samuel Graves
Acres: None shown

Situation of lands: One town lot bought of John Jacob Metzger in the 4th row 2nd division between Christian Leimberger and Balthaser Metzger deceased - the said Metzger's lot which he bought of said Metzger.
Original grantee: None shown

Claimant's Name: Matthias Meyer
Acres: 50

Situation of lands: Of his father George Meyer deceased bounding east the Savannah River south John Groll west vacant pine land north Samuel Graves.
Original grantee: None shown

Claimant's Name: Matthias Groll
Acres: 50

Situation of lands: Of his father John Groll deceased bounding east the river south John Georg Gnann west vacant north Matthias Meyer.
Original grantee: None shown

Claimant's Name: John Georg Gnann
Acres: 50

Situation of lands: Bounding east the river south John Jacob Metzger west vacant north John Groll.
Original grantee: None shown

Claimant's Name: John Jacob Metzger
Acres: 50

Situation of lands: Bounding east the river south Philip Metzger west John Shiele north John Georg Gnann.
Original grantee: None shown

Claimant's Name: John Jacob Metzger
Acres: None shown

Situation of lands: Two town lots one bought of Christian Hesster in the 3rd row 2nd division between Michael and Georg Rieser - the other bought of Samuel Graves in the vii row and 2nd division the last.
Original grantee: None shown

Claimant's Name: John Georg Bechtle
Acres: 50

Situation of lands: Bought of Philip Metzger deceased butting east the river south vacant swamp west Jacob Meyer north John Jacob Metzger.
Original grantee: None shown

Claimant's Name: John Shiele
Acres: 50

Situation of lands: Bounding east John George Bechtly south Jacob Meyer west vacant north John Georg Gnann.
Original grantee: None shown

Claimant's Name: Matthew Zettler
Acres: 100

Situation of lands: Bounding east a large cypress swamp south the same swamp west Michael Oechslin north Christopher Rottenberger and Jacob Meyer.
Original grantee: None shown

Claimant's Name: Matthew Zettler
Acres: 2

Situation of lands: Garden on the west side of the town in the first row between Rupert Kalcher and Simon Reutter. One town lot in the 1st row and 4 division.
Original grantee: None shown

Claimant's Name: Jacob Mayer
Acres: 50

Situation of lands: Bounding east John Georg Bechtle south Matthew Zettler west Christopher Rottenberger north John Shiele.
Original grantee: None shown

Claimant's Name: Christopher Rottenberger
Acres: 50

Situation of lands: Bounding east Jacob Mayer south and west Matthew Zettler north John Shiele.
Original grantee: None shown

Claimant's Name: Christopher Rottenberger
Acres: 2

Situation of lands: Garden on the west side of the town near old Ebzer (sic) Creek in the 4th row.
Original grantee: None shown

Claimant's Name: Christopher Rottenberger
Acres: 10

Situation of lands: Or 5 Gardens all joined to the first 2 acres bought them of Thomas Geswandel Gabriel Maurer Thomas Sweighoffer John Neidlinger and Samuel Graves.
Original grantee: None shown

Claimant's Name: Christopher Rottenberger
Acres: None shown

Situation of lands: One town lot in the vth row and 4th division the first near Georg Kogler.
Original grantee: None shown

Claimant's Name: Michael Oechslin
Acres: 50

Situation of lands: Bounding east Matthew Zettler south vacant swamp west Philip Paulitsch north George Deininger.
Original grantee: None shown

Claimant's Name: Georg Deininger
Acres : 50

Situation of lands: Bounding east vacant pine land south Michael Oechslin west Philip and John Martyn Paulitsch north vacant.
Original grantee: None shown

Claimant's Name: John Martyn Paulitsch
Acres: 50

Situation of lands: Bounding east Georg Deininger south Philip Paulitsch west Cunrad Rahn north vacant pine land.
Original grantee: None shown

Claimant's Name: John Gugell
Acres: 50

Situation of lands: Bought of John Georg Hunold bounding east Philip Paulitsch south old Ebenezer Creek west Martyn Soldner north Cunrad Rahn.
Original grantee: None shown

Claimant's Name: Cunrad Rahn
Acres: 50

Situation of lands: Bounding east John Martyn Paulitsch south John Gugell west Martyn Solener north vacant.
Original grantee: None shown

Claimant's Name: Martyn Dasher
Acres: 50

Situation of lands: Bought of Martyn Solener's widow bounding east Cunrad Rahn and John Gugel south old Ebenezer Creek west and north vacant.
Original grantee: None shown

Claimant's Name: Martyn Dasher
Acres: 2

Situation of lands: Garden on the west side of the Town in the IIId Row near Leonhard Kraus and vacant land.
Original grantee: None shown

Claimant's Name: Martyn Dasher
Acres: None shown

Situation of lands: One Town Lot in the IId row first division between John Kruse and Veit Landfelder the Garden and Town Lot bought of Michael Rieser, Senr. deceased.
Original grantee: None shown:

Claimant's Name: Martyn Dasher
Acres: 100

Situation of lands: About 4 miles from old Ebenezer on the first Bridge Branch.
Original grantee: None shown

Claimant's Name: The heirs of Reverend Mr. Christian Gronau deceased
Acres: 10

Situation of lands: Bounding east the Town of Savannah and Savannah River south and west the Gardens of Theobald Keeffer Christian Leimberger and Christopher Rottenberger north old Ebenezer Creek.
Original grantee: None shown

Claimant's Name: The Heirs of Reverend Mr. Christian Gronau deceased
Acres: None shown

Situation of lands: One Town Lot in the first row near the River Savannah the last lot in the 4th division near Christian Birck.
Original grantee: None shown

Claimant's Name: Rupert Kalcher's widow
Acres: 6

Situation of lands: Bought of John Martyn Kasmayer bounding east Christohper Rottenberger's Garden south and west vacant north John Smith.
Original grantee: None shown

Claimant's Name: Rupert Kalcher's widow
Acres: 2

Situation of lands: Garden on the west side of the town in the 1st row between Matthew Zettler and Rupert Sheiner deceased.
Original grantee: None shown

Claimant's Name: Rupert Kalcher's widow
Acres: None shown

Situation of lands: One Town Lot in the IIId row 4 division the first lot near Simon Reutter-one Town Lot bought of Simon Steiner's widow in the IId row and 2d division between George Sanfftleben and Leonard Krause.
Original grantee: None shown

Claimant's Name: John Smith
Acres: 50

Situation of lands: Bounding east John Martyn Kasmayer south vacant west Michael Kaberer north old Ebenezer Creek.
Original grantee: None shown

Claimant's Name: John Smith
Acres: 2

Situation of lands: Garden on the west side of the Town in the IId row between Bartholomew Rieser and John Pletter.
Original grantee: None shown

Claimant's Name: John Smith
Acres: None shown

Situation of lands: One Town Lot in the IV row first division between George Pechtly and Joseph Leitner.
Original grantee: None shown

Claimant's Name: Michael Haberer
Acres: 50

Situation of lands: Bounding east John Smith south and west vacant north old Ebenezer Creek.
Original grantee: None shown

Claimant's Name: Michael Haberer
Acres: None shown

Situation of lands: One Town Lot in the Vth row and 2d division between Christoph. Cramer and George Kocher.
Original grantee: None shown

Claimant's Name: Peter Hammer
Acres: 50

Situation of lands: Bought of William Dods bounding east Christopher Ortmann south vacant west his second plantation north old Ebenezer Creek.
Original grantee: None shown

Claimant's Name: Peter Hammer
Acres: 50

Situation of lands: Bounding east William Dods south
vacant west John Michael Hirsch north the said creek.
Original grantee: None shown

Claimants' Name: John Michael Hirsch
Acres: 100

Situation of lands: Bounding north east Peter Hammer north
west the said creek south west George Heckett east vacant.
Original grantee: None shown

Claimant's Name: George Heckett
Acres: 50

Situation of lands: Bounding east John Michael Hirsch
south and west vacant north old Ebenezer Creek.
Original grantee: None shown

Claimant's Name: Ursula Meyer widow
Acres: None shown

Situation of lands: One Town Lot of Veit Lemhoffer
deceased in the VI row and 4th division between Thomas
Bacher and Ludwig Ernst.
Original grantee: None shown

Claimant's Name: Christian Ernst Thilo
Acres: 2

Situation of lands: Garden on the east side of the Town
bounding east a large swamp south George Bruckner deceased
west the Town north Christian Riedelsperger.
Original grantee: None shown

Claimant's Name: Christian Ernst Thilo
Acres: None shown

Situation of lands: Town Lot in the fourth row first division near George Glamer bought of John Jacob Helfensteins widow.
Original grantee: None shown

Claimant's Name: Christian Ernst Thilo
Acres: None shown

Situation of lands: Town Lot in the said division between John Smith bought of John Georg Pechtly.
Original grantee: None shown

Claimant's Name: Christian Ernst Thilo
Acres: None shown

Situation of lands: Town Lot in the 5th row first division bought of Carl Sigmund Ott.
Original grantee: None shown

Claimant's Name: Christian Ernst Thilo
Acres: None shown

Situation of lands: Town Lot in the 6th row second division bought of Philip Metzger deceased.
Original grantee: None shown

Claimant's Name: Christian Ernst Thilo
Acres: None shown

Situation of lands: Town Lot in the 3d row third division near Paulus Zittrauer bought of Christopher Ortmann deceased.
Original grantee: None shown

Claimant's Name: Christian Birck
Acres: 50

Situation of lands: Bought of Thomas Bichler's widow bounding east a large sea proceeding from the Savannah River south Peter Arnsdorff west Veit Landfelder north vacant pine land.
Original grantee: None shown

Claimant's Name: Christian Birck
Acres: 2

Situation of lands: Garden bought of the said widow bounding east and north vacant south the said plantation west Veit Landfelder's Garden.
Original grantee: None shown

Claimant's Name: Veit Landfelder
Acres: 50

Situation of lands: Bounding east Christian Birck south Peter Arnsdorff west GeorgeBruckner deceased north his Garden and vacant pine land.
Original grantee: None shown

Claimant's Name: Veit Landfelder
Acres: 2

Situation of lands: Garden bounding south his plantation east Christian Birck west and north vacant pine land.
Original grantee: None shown

Claimant's Name: Frederica (sic) Bruckner
Acres: 100

Situation of lands: Bounding east Veit Landfelder south Martyn Lachner Junr. west Casper Clock and north vacant pine land.
Original grantee: None shown

Claimant's Name: Frederica Bruckner
Acres: 2

Situation of lands: Garden on the east side of the Town bounding south east a large swamp south west Daniel Shubdrin north west the Town north east Christian Ernst Thilo.
Original grantee: None shown

Claimant's Name: Frederica Bruckner
Acres: None shown

Situation of lands: One Town Lot in the IIId row and 3d division near Rupert Eishberger.
Original grantee: None shown

Claimant's Name: Christian Helser
Acres: 2

Situation of lands: Garden on the west side of the Town in the IIId row bounding east Peter Arnsdorff south a small road west Rupert Zittrauer now possessed by Peter Kohleison north vacant land.
Original grantee: None shown

Claimant's Name: Martyn Lackner Junr.
Acres: 50

Situation of lands: Bounding east Peter Arnsdorff south vacant pine land west John Casper Granwetter deceased north Veit Landfelder.
Original grantee: None shown

Claimant's Name: Martyn Lackner Junr.
Acres: 50

Situation of lands: On the west side of the long Bridge bought of Casper Clock bounding east George Bruckner south Salomo Zant west Urban Buntz north vacant pine land.
Original grantee: None shown

Claimant's Name: Martyn Lackner Junr.
Acres: None shown

Situation of lands: One Town Lot in the IId row first division the 4th between Michael Reiser Senr. and Rupert Schrempff.
Original grantee: None shown

Claimant's Name: Mary Catharina Cranwetter
Acres: 50

Situation of lands: From her father John Casper Cranwetter deceased bounding east Martyn Lackner south vacant west Salomo Zantt north Casper Clock.
Original grantee: None shown

Claimant's Name: Mary Catharina Clanwetter
Acres: None shown

Situation of lands: One Town Lot in the IVth row and third division the third near George Sweiger.
Original grantee: None shown

Claimant's Name: Salomo Zantt
Acres: 50

Situation of lands: Of his father's Bartholomew Zantt deceased bounding east John Casper Granwetter south vacant west George Glaner north Casper Clock.
Original grantee: None shown

Claimant's Name: Salomo Zantt
Acres: 2

Situation of lands: Garden and one Town Lot the Garden on the west side of the Town in the 2d row between Matthew Brandner and Andrew Resch's widow. The town lot in the V row and 4th division the fourth lot between Michael Sneider and George Eigel.
Original grantee: None shown

Claimant's Name: George Glaner
Acres: 50

Situation of lands: Bounding east Salomo Zantt south George Fowl west vacant north Urban Buntz.
Original grantee: None shown

Claimant's Name: George Glaner
Acres: None Shown

Situation of lands: One Town Lot in the IV row first division the fourth between John Jacob Helfenstin and Joseph Leitner.
Original grantee: None shown

Claimant's Name: George Fowl
Acres: 50

Situation of lands: Bounding east south and west vacant pine land north George Glaner.
Original grantee: None shown

Claimant's Name: John Rentz
Acres: 50

Situation of lands: Bought of Urbanus Buntz bounding east Casper Clock south George Glaner west and north vacant pine land.
Original grantee: None shown

Claimant's Name: John Rentz
Acres: 2

Situation of lands: Garden on the west side of the Town in the first row between Simon Reatter and Gabriel Bach bought of John George Meyer.
Original grantee: None shown

Claimant's Name: John Rentz
Acres: None shown

Situation of lands: Town Lot bought of Mr. Christian Ernst Thilo in the 3d row and 2d division the 5th lot near George Reiser.
Original grantee: None shown

Claimant's Name: John Ulrich Neidlinger
Acres: 50

Situation of lands: On said Bridge Creek bounding east south and north vacant pine land north George Niess.
Original grantee: None shown

Claimant's Name: George Niess
Acres: 50

Situation of lands: On said Bridge Creek bounding east John Ulrich Neidlinger west Michael Walliser south and north vacant pine land.
Original grantee:

Claimant's Name: Michael Walliser
Acres: 50

Situation of lands: On said Bridge Creek bounding east George Niess south west and north vacant.
Original grantee: None shown

Claimant's Name: Peter Arnsdorff
Acres: 50

Situation of lands: Bounding east the Savannah River south Joseph Leitner west Martyn Lachner Junr. north Veit Landfelder.
Original grantee: None shown

Claimant's Name: Peter Arnsdorff
Acres: 2

Situation of lands: Garden and 1 Town Lot, the Garden on the west side of the Town in the IId row between Frederick Willhelm Muller and Ludwig Ernst the Town Lot in the IId row 3d division the 2d between John Cornberger and David Krafft deceased.
Original grantee: None shown

Claimant's Name: Joseph Leitner
Acres: 32

Situation of lands: Granted to his wife Laurentz Andrew Arnsdorffs widow bounding east Savannah River south Mr. Theobald Keeffer west Martyn Lachner Junr. north Peter Arnsdorff.
Original grantee: None shown

Claimant's Name: Joseph Leitner
Acres: 2

Situation of lands: Garden on the west side of the Town in the 4th row between Matthew Burgsteiner and John Michael Muggizer.
Original grantee: None shown

Claimant's Name: Joseph Leitner
Acres: None shown

Situation of lands: One Twon Lot in the IV row first division between John Smith and Georg Glaner.
Original grantee: None shown

Claimant's Name: John Paul Miller
Acres: 50

Situation of lands: Bounding east and south Mr. John Flerl west Charles Flerl north Theobald Keeiffer.
Original grantee: None shown

Claimant's Name: John Paul Miller
Acres: 2

Situation of lands: Garden on the west side from his father Frederick Wilhelm Miller deceased in the IId row near Peter Arnsdorff and 1 Town Lot of his father in the V row 3 division the 5th near Peter Arnsdorff and 1 Town Lot of his father in the V row 3d division the 5th near Peter Kohleisen.
Original grantee: None shown

Claimant's Name: John Paul Miller
Acres: 2

Situation of lands: Garden and 1 Town Lot bought of John Sheffler the Garden in the first row west side of the Town between Simon Steiner and Veit Lemhoffer. The Town Lot in the IV row 3d division in the 5th near John Georg Sneider.

Original grantee: None shown

Claimant's Name: John Paul Miller
Acres: None shown

Situation of lands: 1 Town Lot of his brother Simon Miller deceased in the IV row 3d division the first near George Sweiger - another Town Lot bought on (sic) John Peter Kohleison in the Vth row 3d division the fourth between his father's lot and Matthew Burgsteiner.
Original grantee: None shown

Claimant's Name: John Flerl
Acres: 50

Situation of lands: Bounding east the River Savannah south Michael Reiser west Paul Miller and north Theobald Keeffer.
Original grantee: None shown

Claimant's Name: John Flerl
Acres: 50

Situation of lands: On the east side of the mill or Abercorn Creek in two different tracts one bounding by the north on the River Savannah; south Michael Rieser west by the River Savannah on the south by George Kogler on the east by Charles Flerl further addition ---
Original grantee: None shown

Claimant's Name: John Flerl
Acres: 2

Situation of lands: Garden on the west side of the Town in the fourth row the last Garden near Charles Sigmund Ott one Town Lot in the 2d row 2d division the 5th near Leonhard Krause.
Original grantee:

Claimant's Name: Charles Flerl
Acres: 50

Situation of lands: Bounding east Michael Rieser south and west vacant north Paul Miller.
Original grantee: None shown

Claimant's Name: Charles Flerl
Acres: 50

Situation of lands: Bounding on the North River Savannah south by John Cornberger east by Michael Reiser's addition west by Mr. John Flerl.
Original grantee: None shown

Claimant's Name: Charles Flerl
Acres: 2

Situation of lands: Garden in the 1 row between Thomas Bacher and Simon Steiner. Town Lot in the IId row 4th division the first.
Original grantee: None shown

Claimant's Name: Michael Rieser
Acres: 50

Situation of lands: Bounding east Savannah River south John Cronberger west Charles Flerl north John Flerl.
Original grantee: None shown

Claimant's Name: Michael Rieser
Acres: 50

Situation of lands: Bounded north by the said river south by John Cronberger east by a creek proceeding from the said river west by Charles Flerl.
Original grantee: None shown

Claimant's Name: Michael Rieser
Acres: 4

Situation of lands: Gardens one Garden of his father Bartholomew Rieser deceased and the other of his father in law Thomas Bacher deceased both on the west side of the Town the first in the 2d row between John Smith and Ludwig Ernst the other in the first row near Charles Flerl.
Original grantee: None shown

Claimant's Name: Michael Rieser
Acres: None shown

Situation of lands: One Town Lot of his father in the
III row 2 division the 2d between Christian Riedels-
perger and Christian Kessler.
Original grantee: None shown

Claimant's Name: John Cronberger
Acres: 100

Situation of lands: Of land 30 acres bounding east
Savannah River south George Kogler west Charles
Flerl north Michael Rieser. 70 acres upon the island bounding
north Charles Flerl and Michael Rieser south by a great
road east by a creek proceeding from the said Savannah
River west by George Kogler and Paul Littrauer.
Original grantee: None shown

Claimant's Name: John Cronberger
Acres: 2

Situation of lands: Garden on the west side of the Town
in the IIId row between Peter Reutter and Martyn Lachner, Sr.
Original grantee: None shown

Claimant's Name: John Cronberger
Acres: None shown

Situation of lands: Town Lot in the IId row and 2d division
the first near Peter Arnsdorff.
Original grantee: None shown

Claimant's Name: George Kogler
Acres: 50

Situation of lands: Bounding east the river south Paulus
Zittrauer west vacant pine land north John Cronberger.
Original grantee: None shown

Claimant's Name: George Kogler
Acres: 100

Situation of lands: Bought of the heirs of Viet (sic) Lemhoffer deceased bounding east vacant upon the island south Rupert Zimmerebner west vacant pine land north Gabriel Maurer now possesseth by Rupert Steiner.
Original grantee: None shown

Claimant's Name: George Kogler
Acres: None shown

Situation of lands: Town Lot in the V row 4th division the second between Michael Snieder and Christopher Rottenberger.
Original grantee: None shown

Claimant's Name: Paulus Zittrauer
Acres: 100

Situation of lands: Bounding east John Cronberger south Leonhard Krause west vacant pine land north George Kogler.
Original grantee: None shown

Claimant's Name: Paulus Zittrauer
Acres: 2

Situation of lands: Garden on the east side of the Town between Daniel Shubdrin and Christoph (sic) Cramer.
Original grantee: None shown

Claimant's Name: Paulus Zittrauer
Acres: None shown

Situation of lands: Town Lot in the IIId row 4th division the second between Christopher Ortman and Rupert Eishberger.
Original grantee: None shown

Claimant's Name: Leonhard Krause
Acres: 50

Situation of lands: Bounding east to his addition upon the island south Peter Kohleison west vacant pine land north Paulus Zittrauer.
Original grantee: None shown.

Claimant's Name: Leonhard Krause
Acres: 50

Situation of lands: Upon the island bounding east vacant land south Adam Stroub west by his first 50 acres and by Peter Kohleison and Rupert Eishberger north by a great road.
Original grantee: None shown

Claimant's Name: Leonhard Krause
Acres: 2

Situation of lands: Garden on the west side of the Town in the 3d row between Michael Rieser Senr. and Martyn Lachner Senr.
Original grantee: None shown

Claimant's Name: Leonhard Krause
Acres: None shown

Situation of lands: Town Lot in the IId row and 2d division the fourth between John Flerl and Simon Steiner.
Original grantee: None shown

Claimant's Name: Peter Kohleisen
Acres: 50

Situation of lands: Bought from Rupert Zittrauer deceased bounding east Leonhard Krause's addition south Rupert Eishberger west vacant pine land north Leonhard Krause.
Original grantee: None shown

Claimant's Name: Peter Kohleisen
Acres: 2

Situation of lands: Garden of the said Zittrauer on the west side of the Town in the 4th row between John Maurer and vacant Garden land.
Original grantee: None shown

Claimant's Name: Rupert Eishberger
Acres: 50

Situation of lands: Bounding east Leonhard Krause addition south Adam Stroub west vacant pine land north Peter Kohleisen
Original grantee: None shown

Claimant's Name: Rupert Eishberger
Acres: 2

Situation of lands: Garden on the west side of the Town in the second row between widow Resch and Rupert Zimmerebner.
Original grantee: None shown

Claimant's Name: Rupert Eishberger
Acres: None shown

Situation of lands: Town Lot in the IIId row 3d division the third between Paulus Zittrauer and George Bruckner.
Original grantee: None shown

Claimant's Name: Adam Stroub
Acres: 50

Situation of lands: Bounding east by his addition south John Pletter west pine land north Rupert Eishberger.
Original grantee: None shown

Claimant's Name: Adam Stroub
Acres: 50

Situation of lands: Bounding north by Leonhard Krause south by a small road east by vacant land west by himself John Pletter and John Maurer.
Original grantee: None shown

Claimant's Name: Adam Stroub
Acres: None shown

Situation of lands: Town Lot in the VIth row 3d division the second between vacant lots.
Original grantee: None shown

Claimant's Name: John Pletter
Acres: 50

Situation of lands: Bounding east Adam Stroub south John Maurer west vacant pine land north the said Adam Stroub.
Original grantee: None shown

Claimant's Name: John Pletter
Acres: 2

Situation of lands: Garden on the west side of the Town in the 2d row between John Smith and Matthew Brander.
Original grantee: None shown

Claimant's Name: John Maurer
Acres: 50

Situation of lands: Bounding east Adam Stroub south Matthew Brandner west pine land north John Pletter.
Original grantee: None shown

Claimant's Name: John Maurer
Acres: 2

Situation of lands: Town Lot and 2 acres Garden the Garden on the west side of Town in the IVth row between John Michael Muggizer and Rupert Zittrauer the Town Lot in the VIth row and 4th division the first near Thomas Bacher deceased.
Original grantee: None shown

Claimant's Name: Matthew Brander
Acres: 100

Situation of lands: Of land 50 acres bought of Andrew Grimmiger and 50 acres was granted to himself bounding east vacant south Christian Leimberger west vacant pine land north John Maurer.
Original grantee: None shown

Claimant's Name: Matthew Brandner
Acres: 2

Situation of lands: Garden in the west side of the Town in the IId row between John Pletter and Salomo Zantt.
Original grantee: None shown

Claimant's Name: Matthew Brandner
Acres: None shown

Situation of lands: Town Lot in the IIId row first division the 5th near Rupert Zimerebner.
Original grantee: None shown

Claimant's Name: Christian Leimberger
Acres: 100

Situation of lands: Of land 50 acres bought of Rupert Steiner the other granted to himself bounding east and west vacant south Thos Geswandel north Matthew Brandner.
Original grantee: None shown

Claimant's Name: Christian Leimberger
Acres: None shown

Situation of lands: Town Lot in the IV row 2d division the first near Jacob Mezger.
Original grantee: None shown

Claimant's Name: Thomas Gaswandel
Acres: 50

Situation of lands: Bounding east and west vacant land south Simon Reutter north Christian Leimberger.
Original grantee: None shown

Claimant's Name: Thomas Gaswandel
Acres: 2

Situation of lands: Garden on west side of Town granted his wife, Andrew Relch's widow in the IId row between Salomo Zantt and Rupert Eishberger.
Original grantee: None shown.

Claimant's Name: Thomas Gaswandel
Acres: None shown

Situation of lands: Town Lot in the IIId row first division the third between Rupert Zimmerebner and a vacant lot.
Original grantee: None shown

Claimant's Name: Simon Reutter
Acres: 50

Situation of lands: Bounding east and west vacant south George Kocher north Thomas Gaswandel.
Original grantee: None shown

Claimant's Name: Simon Reutter
Acres: 2

Situation of lands: Garden on the west side of the Town in the 1st row between John Georg Meyer and Matthew Zettler.
Original grantee: None shown

Claimant's Name: Daniel Remshardt
Acres: 50

Situation of lands: Bought of George Kocher bounding east the island south Rupert Steiner west vacant north Simon Reutter.
Original grantee: None shown

Claimant's Name: Daniel Remshardt
Acres: None shown

Situation of lands: Town Lot in the Vth row 2d division the 3d between Michael Haberer and John Georg Sneider.
Original grantee: None shown

Claimant's Name: Christian Steiner
Acres: 50

Situation of lands: Of his father Rupert Steiner deceased which he bought from Gabriel Maurer bounding east by his addition upon the island south Veit Lemhoffer now George Kogler belonging west vacant pine land north Daniel Remshardt.
Original grantee: None shown

Claimants' Name: Christian Steiner
Acres: 50

Situation of lands: On the island which bounding will appear by the plan of the surveyor Thomas Ellis.
Original grantee: None shown

Claimant's Name: Chrisitan Steiner
Acres: 2

Situation of lands: Garden on the west side of the Town in the first row between Rupert Kolcher and vacant land.
Original grantee: None shown

Claimant's Name: Christian Steiner
Acres: None shown

Situation of lands: Town Lot in the IId row 2d division the first near George Sanftleben.
Original grantee: None shown

Claimant's Name: Rupert Zimmereben
Acres: 75

Situation oflands: Of land 50 acres granted to him and 25 acres he bought of Martyn Lachner, Sr. who removed by consent of the late President and Assistants and the council bounding east by his further addition upon the island south the public mills west vacant pine land north Veit Lemhoffer now possessed by George Kogler.
Original grantee: None shown

Claimant's Name: Rupert Zimmerebner
Acres: 50

Situation of lands: On the island the bounding will appear in Mr. Ellis Plan.
Original grantee: None shown

Claimant's Name: Rupert Zimmerebner
Acres: 2

Situation of lands: Garden on the west side of the Town in the IId row between George Sanftleben and Rupert Eishberger.
Original grantee: None shown

Claimant's Name: Rupert Zimmerebner
Acres: None shown

Situation of lands: Town Lot in the IIId row first division the 4th between Thomas Gaswandel and Matthew Brandner.
Original grantee: None shown

Claimant's Name: The Publick
Acres: 75

Situation of lands: Of land for the grist and saw mills 50 acres bought of Joseph Leitner and 25 acres of Martyn Lachner, Sr. bounding east the further addition south Thomas Bichler west vacant north Rupert Zimmerebner.
Original grantee: None shown

Claimant's Name: The Publick
Acres: 50

Situation of lands: Upon the island granted by the late President and Assistants and Council as it will appear in the plan.
Original grantee: None shown

Claimant's Name: Reverend John Martyn Bolzius
Acres: 100

Situation of lands: Bought partly of Thomas Bichler deceased partly granted by the late President and Assistants of the Council bounding east vacant of the island south Matthew Burgsteiner's widow west vacant land north the Grist and Saw Mill Plantation.
Original grantee: None shown

Claimant's Name: Reverend John Martyn Bolzius
Acres: None shown

Situation of lands: Two Town Lots one he bought of John Martyn Rheinlander in the 1st row first division the 5th the other bought of George Sanftleben's widow in the IId row 2d division the second between Rupert Steiner and Simon Steiner.
Original grantee: None shown

Claimant's Name: Reverend John Martyn Bolzius
Acres: 2

Situation of lands: Garden of the said widow on the west side of the Town in the IId row between Rupert Zimmerebner and Jacob Schartner.
Original grantee: None shown

Claimant's Name: Matthew Burgsteiner's widow
Acres: 50

Situation of lands: Bounding east by the island south George Sweiger west vacant land north Thomas Bichler now the Reverend Mr. Bolzius.
Original grantee: None shown

Claimant's Name: Matthew Burgsteiner's widow
Acres: 2

Situation of lands: Garden on the west side of the Town in the IVth row between Joseph Leitner and vacant land.
Original grantee: None shown

Claimant's Name: Matthew Burgsteiner's widow
Acres: None shown

Situation of lands: Town Lot in Vth row 3d division the second between John Reutter and Peter Kohleisen.
Original grantee: None shown

Claimant's Name: Georg Sweiger
Acres: 50

Situation of lands: Bounding east by the island south Charles Sigmund Ott west pine land north Matthew Burgsteiner's widow.
Original grantee: None shown

Claimant's Name: Georg Sweiger
Acres: 2

Situation of lands: Garden on the west side of the Town in the IId row between Christian Leimberger and vacant land.
Original grantee: None shown

Claimant's Name: Georg Sweiger
Acres: None shown

Situation of lands: Town Lot in the IVth row 2d division between Simon Miller and John Casper Cranwetter.
Original grantee: None shown

Claimant's Name: Charles Sigmund Ott
Acres: 50

Situation of lands: Bounding east the said island south David Eishberger west vacant north George Sweiger.
Original grantee: None shown

Claimant's Name: Charles Sigmund Ott
Acres: None shown

Situation of lands: Garden on the west side of the Town in the 4th row near Mr. John Flerl.
Original grantee: None shown

Claimant's Name: David Eishberger
Acres: 50

Situation of lands: Bought of Henry Bishop first possessed by Simon Steiner deceased bounding east vacant on the island south George Dressler now possessed by Gabriel Maurer west vacant pine land north Charles Sigmund Ott.
Original grantee: None shown

Claimant's Name: David Eishberger
Acres: None shown

Situation of lands: Town Lot in the IVth row the 2d division the 5th lot near George Reiser.
Original grantee: None shown

Claimant's Name: Gabriel Maurer
Acres: 50

Situation of lands: Bought of George Dressler bounding east vacant on the island south Michael Reiser, Sr. deceased west vacant pine land north David Eishberger.
Original grantee: None shown

Claimant's Name: Gabriel Maurer
Acres: None shown

Situation of lands: Town Lot in the VIth row and 4th division the 5th.
Original grantee: None shown

Claimant's Name: Reverend Harman Henry Lemcke
Acres: 50

Situation of lands: Bought of Michael Reiser Sr. deceased bounding east on the said island south John Kruse deceased west David Eishberger north Gabriel Maurer.
Original grantee: None shown

Claimant's Name: Reverend Harman Henry Lemcke
Acres: 50

Situation of lands: Bought of the heirs of John Kruse bounding east the said island south John Gruber west Georg Eigell north Michael Reiser Sr.
Original grantee: None shown

Claimant's Name: Reverend Harman Henry Lemcke
Acres: 50

Situation of lands: Bought of David Eishberger bounding east Michael Reiser Sr. south George Eigell vacant pine land north Gabriel Maurer.
Original grantee: None shown

Claimant's Name: Reverend Harman Henry Lemcke
Acres: 4

Situation of lands: Two garden lots each of 2 acres the first bought of George Kogler on the east side of the Town near Mr. John Ludwig Meyer and vacant land the second bought of Christian Leimberger on the west side of the Town in the 1st row the first near John Reutter.
Original grantee: None shown

Claimant's Name: Reverend Harman Henry Lemcke
Acres: None shown

Situation of lands: Town Lot belonging to John Kruse's plantation in the V row the 3d division the first lot near John Reutter.
Original grantee: None shown

Claimant's Name: John Gruber, orphan of Peter Gruber, deceased
Acres: 50

Situation of lands: Bounding east on the island south John George Sneider west George Sanftleben north John Kruse now possessed by Mr. Lemcke.
Original grantee: None shown

Claimant's Name: John Gruber, orphan of Peter Gruber, deceased
Acres: 2

Situation of lands: Garden in the IIId row the 5th on the west side of the Town between Thomas Gaswandel and John Martyn Rheinlander.
Original grantee: None shown

Claimant's Name: John Gruber, orphan of Peter Gruber deceased
Acres: None shown

Situation of lands: Town Lot of his father in the IId row 4th division the fourth between Martyn Lachner Sr. and Martyn Hertzog deceased.
Original grantee: None shown

Claimant's Name: George Eigell
Acres: 50

Situation of lands: Bounding east John Kruse deceased south John Georg Sneider west Sebastian Fetzer north David Eishberger.
Original grantee: None shown

Claimant's Name: George Eigell
Acres: None shown

Situation of lands: Town Lot in the Vth row 4th division the fifth near Salomo Zantt.
Original grantee: None shown

Claimant's Name: Sebastian Fetzger
Acres: 50

Situation of lands: Bought of George Sanftleben's widow bounding east John Gruber south Christoph Cramer west vacant north Eigell.
Original grantee: None shown

Claimant's Name: Christoph Cramer
Acres: 50

Situation of lands: Bounding east John Georg Sneider south Mr. Christian Rabenhorst west vacant pine land north Sebastian Fetzger.
Original grantee: None shown

Claimant's Name: Christoph Cramer
Acres: 2

Situation of lands: Garden on the east side of the Town near Paulus Zittrauer.
Original grantee: None shown

Claimant's Name: Christoph Cramer
Acres: None shown

Situation of lands: Two Town Lots the first he bought of Rupert Schrempff deceased in the IId row 1st division the 5th near Martyn Lachner, Jr. the second in the Vth row 2d division the first near Michael Haberer.
Original grantee: None shown

Claimant's Name: John Georg Sneider
Acres: 50

Situation of lands: Bought of John George Held bounding east on the island south his father Michael Sneider west Christoph Cramer north Christian Rabenhorst.
Original grantee: None shown

Claimant's Name: John Georg Sneider
Acres: None shown

Situation of lands: Town Lot in the Vth row 2d division the 4th between John Sheffler and Daniel Remshard.
Original grantee: None shown

Claimant's Name: Michael Sneider
Acres: 50

Situation of lands: Bounding east on the said island south Christian Rabenhorst west Christian Rabenhorst north John Georg Sneider.
Original grantee: None shown

NOTE: The folowing is all crossed out.

~~Bounding east vacant north John Ludwig Meyer south vacant west David Unseldt.~~ - - - - -

Claimant's Name: John Ulrick Fetzer
Acres: 50

Situation of lands: Bounding east vacant north Mr. John Ludwig Meyer south vacant west David Unseldt.
Original grantee: None shown

Claimant's Name: Christian Reidelsperger
Acres: 120

Situation of lands: Bounding east on the Mill or Abercorn Creek south and west vacant land north partly John Ludwig Meyer partly vacant land.
Original grantee: None shown

Claimant's Name: Christian Reidelsperger
Acres: 80

Situation of lands: North vacant land granted him by the late President and Assistants of the Council bearing date 9 August 1754 but by neglect of Thomas Ellis not yet surveyed.
Original grantee: Christian Reidelsperger

Claimant's Name: Christian Reidelsperger
Acres: 2

Situation of lands: Garden on the east side of the Town between Christian Ernst Thilo and John Ludwig Meyer.
Original grantee: None shown

Claimant's Name: Christian Reidelsperger
Acres: None shown

Situation of lands: Town Lot in the IIId row 2d division the first near Michael Reiser.
Original grantee: None shown

Claimant's Name: Martyn Lachner, Sr.
Acres: 100

Situation of lands: Bounding east John Stahle and Jacob Moor at Goshen south the said Glebe west Balthasar Bacher north John Michael Weber.
Original grantee: None shown

Claimant's Name: Martyn Lachner, Sr.
Acres: 2

Situation of lands: Garden on the west side of the Town in the IIId row between Leonhard Krause and John Cornberger.
Original grantee: None shown

Claimant's Name: Martyn Lachner, Sr.
Acres: None shown

Situation of lands: Town Lot in the IId row 4th division the third between Simon Reutter and John Gruber.
Original grantee: None shown

Claimant's Name: Balthasar Bacher
Acres: 100

Situation of lands: Bounding east Martyn Lachner, Sr. south the said Glebe west vacant land north vacant.
Original grantee: None shown

Claimant's Name: John Michael Weber
Acres: 50

Situation of lands: Bought of George Reiser bounding east vacant south Martyn Lachner, Sr. west vacant north Veit Lachner.
Original grantee: None shown

Claimant's Name: Veit Lachner
Acres: 100

Situation of lands: Bounding east the back line of Abercorn south by vacant land and John Michael Weber west John Georg Sneider now by Lachner possessed north George Mackay.
Original grantee: None shown

Claimant's Name: Veit Lachner
Acres: None shown

Situation of lands: Town Lot in the VI row 3d division the first near Adam Stroub.
Original grantee: None shown

Claimant's Name: Veit Lachner
Acres: 50

Situation of lands: Bought of John George Sneider bounding east by his first 100 acres south west and north vacant pine land.
Original grantee: None shown

Claimant's Name: John Reutter, orphan of Peter Reutter deceased
Acres: 50

Situation of lands: Granted by the late President and Assistants but by neglect of Mr. Thomas Ellis not yet surveyed bounding east the back of the Glebe south north and west vacant pine land.
Original grantee: None shown

The clearest view of the whole settlement will fully appear from the general plan of the surveyor Mr. Thomas Ellis, who was ordered by the late President and Assistants of the Council the 15th November 1750 to return to the Council the buttings and boundings of all the lands granted to the inhabitants of Ebenezer and places adjacent.

Claimant's Name: James Heart per James Edward Powell
Acres: 500

Situation of lands: On the north side of Midway River between lands of Thomas Goldsmith and Nathaniel Watson by purchase from John Green allotted to him by the late President and Assistants April 5th 1750.
Original grantee: John Green

Claimant's Name: Jonathon Bryan
Acres: 500

Situation of lands: Granted by the late President and Assistants bounding south on the town line of Savannah east on Salters Creek north on the River Savannah and west on Bradleys Creek.
Original grantee: Jonathon Bryan

Claimant's Name: Jonathon Bryan
Acres: 500

Situation of lands: Bounding south on James Habersham Esqr. and west on Mr. van Brahm.
Original grantee: Jonathon Bryan

Claimants' Name: Jonathon Bryan
Acres: 500

Situation of lands: Bounding south on James Habersham Esqr. east on Joseph Bryan's land and west on Thomas Rasberry's land.
Original grantee: Jonathon Bryan

Claimant's Name: James Colvin by Sir Patrick Houstoun his attorney
Acres: 50

Situation of lands: Lot in the Town of Savannah number 1 in the first Tything Upper New Ward with a Garden Lot of five acres and a Farm Lot of forty-five acres granted by the late Trustees in 1735.
Original grantee: James Colvin

Claimant's Name: Henry Densler
Acres: 50

Situation of lands: On an island between Thunderbolt and Skidoway by warrant of the late President and Assistants.
Original grantee: Henry Densler

Claimant's Name: Henry Densler
Acres: 50

Situation of lands: In Vernonburgh as heir to his father.
Original grantee: None shown

Claimant's Name: Thomas Ellis
Acres: 50

Situation of lands: Lot in Town of Savannah number ten in Wilmington Tything Darby Ward with a Garden Lot and Farm Lot thereunto belonging in exchange with Richard Warren for a lot in the same town, etc.
Original grantee: None shown

Claimant's Name: Thomas Ellis
Acres: 300

Situation of lands: In the District of Little Ogechee adjoining lands of George Walthour and lands granted Henry William Parker which said tract was granted in 1751.
Original grantee: Thomas Ellis

Claimant's Name: Thomas Ellis
Acres: 50

Situation of lands: Lot of land on Skidoway Island adjoining north to land of William Becket purchased by said Ellis of Anthony Hancock.
Original grantee: Anthony Hancock

Claimant's Name: David Fox, Jr.
Acres: 400

Situation of lands: Situated on the south branch of Little Ogechee River from the late President and Assistants 31 August 1752.
Original grantee: David Fox, Jr.

Claimant's Name: Michael Germain
Acres: 5

Situation of lands: Town Lot in Savannah number 4 with the five acre lot belonging thereto.
Original grantee: None shown

Claimant's Name: Michael Germain
Acres: 50

Situation of lands: Town lot in Savannah number 8 this lot was granted to Isaac D. Vale who surrendered it for lot number 6 at Hampstead upon which Mr. Oglethorpe regranted it to Ann relict to Michael Germain who was (sic) his father with the forty-five and five acres thereunto belonging.
Original grantee: Isaac D. Vale

Claimant's Name: James Galache
Acres: 50

Situation of lands: Town Lot number 10 in the 4th Tything Upper New Ward Farm Lot number 3 in the same and Garden Lot number 78 lying east of the Town from the late President and Assistants.
Original grantee: James Galache

Claimant's Name: Charles Rogers
Acres: 44 7/8

Situation of lands: Farm Lot number 2 in the above Tything by purchase.
Original granree: Charles Rogers

Claimant's Name: Joseph Gibbons, Sr.
Acres: 500

Situation of lands: Adjoining to the west of Newington Village about six miles to the west of Savannah by the President and Assistants in June 1752.
Original grantee: Joseph Gibbons, Sr.

Claimant's Name: Joseph Gibbons, Jr.
Acres: 500

Situation of lands: Adjoining on the west end of Joseph Gibbons, Sr. land on the east lines of Mathew Mareve (?) and David Montaigut's land on the north line of William DeBrahm's land.
Original grantee: None shown

Claimant's Name: Benjamin Goldwire
Acres: 50

Situation of lands: Town Lot in Savannah number 1 Third Tything Upper New Ward Farm Lot number 7 near Hampstead Garden Lot number 90 east of the town purchased of Mr. James Campbell.
Original grantee: James Campbell

Claimant's Name: James Habersham, Esqr.
Acres: 500

Situation of lands: Situated on the north branch of Little Ogechee River bounding easterly of land of Noble Jones, Esqr. from the late President and Assistants July 9, 1751.
Original grantee: James Habersham

Claimant's Name: James Habersham, Esqr.
Acres: 50

Situation of lands: Town Lot number 6 in Wilmington Tything Darby Ward in Savannah Garden Lot number 52 and Farm Lot number 7 by purchase of the late William Stephens, Esqr. Attorney to Frances Watts widow and William Cox her son.
Original grantee: None shown

Claimant's Name: James Habersham, Esqr.
Acres: None shown

Situation of lands: Town Lot in Hardwicke number 32 from the late President and Assistants 13th June 1754.
Original grantee: James Habersham

Claimant's Name: James Habersham, Esqr. in trust for Joseph Habersham, his son
Acres: None shown

Situation of lands: Town Lot in Hardwicke number 33 from the late President and Assistants 13th June 1754.
Original grantee: Joseph Habersham

Claimant's Name: James Habersham, Esqr. in trust for James Habersham, his son
Acres: 500

Situation of lands: On the north branch of Little Ogechee River bounding southerly and easterly on lands of James Habersham, Sr. from the late President and Assistants 12 May 1752.
Original grantee: James Haberhsam, Jr.

Claimant's Name: Henry Hamilton by Charles Watson
Acres: 45

Situation of lands: Lot in the Town of Savannah number 4 in the Third Tything Lower New Ward alias Reynolds Ward with a Farm Lot thereunto belonging granted by the President and Assistants about 11 years ago.
Original grantee: Henry Hamilton

Claimant's Name: Henry Hamilton by Charles Watson
Acres: 100

Situation of lands: Lying at Midway bounded on both sides by lands called Peter Baillou's by the President and Assistants about 3 years ago.
Original grantee: Henry Hamilton

Claimant's Name: Jacob Holbrokk by Charles Watson
Acres: 5 1/8

Situation of lands: Lot in Savannah number 5 Vernon Tything Heathcote Ward with a Garden Lot in exchange with Anthony Gautier.
Original grantee: Anthony Gautier

Claimant's Name: Harris and Habersham
Acres: 100 feet

Situation of lands: Fronting the Bluff below the public wharf on which they have built a wharf laid out by the late President and Assistants by order of the late Trustees.
Original grantee: Harris and Habersham

Claimant's Name: Ralph Kilgore by Charles Watson
Acres: 250

Situation of lands: Lying above Augusta between two creeks there called Cayoke Creeks granted by the late President and Assistants to Thomas Red and purchased by the said Kilgore.
Original grantee: Thomas Kilgore

Claimant's Name: Thomas Lee by Charles Watson
Acres: 50

Situation of lands: Lot in Savannah number 1 in Holland
Tything Percival Ward with Garden and Farm Lot granted
him by the late President and Assistants in 1741.
Original grantee: Thomas Lee

Claimant's Name: Thomas Lee by Charles Watson
Acres: 89 6/8

Situation of lands: Two Farm Lots in Wilmington Tything
reserved by the late Trustees and commonly called Trust
Lots granted him by the late President and Assistants.
Original grantee: Thomas Lee

Claimant's Name: Thomas Lee by Charles Watson
Acres: 50

Situation of lands: Lot in Savannah number 8 in Moore
Tything Percival Ward with Garden and Farm Lot by title
from Ann the widow of John Kelly.
Original grantee: John Kelly

Claimant's Name: Thomas Lee by Charles Watson
Acres: 50

Situation of lands: On Skidoway Island number 6 in the
Old Village by gift from John Griffin his father-in-law
to whom the same was originally granted by the late
Trustees.
Original grantee: John Griffin

Claimant's Name: Matthew Mauve
Acres: 50

Situation of lands: Town Lot number 8 in Savannah the
first Tything Upper New Ward Garden Lot number 133
east Savannah Farm Lot number 8 granted by the Trustees
October 1739.
Original grantee: None shown

Claimant's Name: Matthew Mauve
Acres: 300

Situation of lands: Bounding south east of lands granted Mr. De Brahm south west of Mr. Pury's land and otherways bounds on vacant lands granted by the President and Assistants April 1753.
Original grantee: Matthew Mauve

Claimant's Name: Richard Milledge by Charles Watson
Acres: 50

Situation of lands: Lot in Town of Savannah number 6 Tyrconnel Tything Darby Ward with Garden and Farm Lot thereunto belonging by gift of his brother John Milledge who had it as heir to his brother Thomas Milledge eldest son and heir of Thomas Milledge their father deceased.
Original grantee: Thomas Milledge

Claimant's Name: Richard Milledge by Charles Watson
Acres: 44 7/8

Situation of lands: Farm Lot lying south of the Town of Savannah about two miles distance therefrom purchased by the said Richard of Thomas Parker.
Original grantee: None shown

Claimant's Name: Richard Milledge by Charles Watson
Acres: 44 7/8

Situation of lands: Farm Lot contiguous to the Farm Lot last mentioned purchased of Pickering Robinson, Esqr. in 1755.
Original grantee: None shown

Claimant's Name: Richard Milledge by Charles Watson
Acres: 44 7/8

Situation of lands: Farm Lot contiguous to the afore mentionedFarm Lots purchased of Mary Bowling spinster.
Original grantee: None shown

Claimant's Name: Richard Milledge by Charles Watson
Acres: 44 7/8

Situation of lands: Farm Lot contiguous as aforesaid purchased of James Tebeau.
Original grantee: None shown

Claimant's Name: Richard Milledge by Charles Watson
Acres: 89 6/8

Situation of lands: Two Farm Lots contiguous as aforesaid reserved by the late Trustees commonly known by the name of Trust Lots granted to said Milledge by the late President and Assistants.
Original grantee: Richard Milledge

Claimant's Name: Joseph Ottolenghe
Acres: 50

Situation of lands: Town Lot in Savannah number 2 in Sloper Tything Percival Ward Garden Lot number 93 east Farm Lot number 5 by warrant from the late President and Assistants.
Original grantee: None shown

Claimant's Name: Joseph Ottolenghe
Acres: 100

Situation of lands: Tract on Savannah River adjoining to the Glebe by the late President and Assistants.
Original grantee: Joseph Ottolenghe

Claimant's Name: Joseph Ottolenghe
Acres: 350

Situation of lands: Tract west of Savannah.
Original grantee: Joseph Ottolenghe

Claimant's Name: James Miller
Acres: 100

Situation of lands: Situated on the north branch of Little Ogeechee River bounding east of lands of James Habersham, Jr. by warrant from the late President and Assistants 7 December 1753.
Original grantee: James Miller

Claimant's Name: James Miller
Acres: None shown

Situation of lands: Town Lot number 6 the fourth Tything lower new ward with a Garden Lot date 4 April 1753.
Original grantee: None shown

Claimant's Name: Nicholas Miller
Acres: 89 6/8

Situation of lands: Two Trust Lots in the center of the fourth Tything Upper New Ward by warrant from the President and Assistants 6 April 1753.
Original grantee: Nicholas Miller

Claimant's Name: Nicholas Miller
Acres: 44 7/8

Situation of lands: Farm Lot in said Tything number 8 by purchase 24 May 1753.
Original grantee: Peter Joubert

Claimant's Name: Nicholas Miller
Acres: 45

Situation of lands: Town Lot and Farm Lot in said Tything number 7 by purchase 7 February 1755.
Original grantee: William Matthew

Claimant's Name: Clement Martin, Esqr.
Acres: 500

Situation of lands: North side of Little Ogechee River bounded on the south by the said river on the north with land granted to Jacob Walthour on the east with land granted to Newdigate Stephens on the west with land granted to John Farmur purchased from William Ewen.
Original grantee: William Ewen

Claimant's Name: Clement Martin, Esqr.
Acres: 500

Situation of lands: On the south side of the north branch of Newport River bounding north by the said river east by land allotted to William Martin west partly by land allotted to Thomas Carter and partly on vacant land allotted by the late President and Assistants to the said Clement.
Original grantee: Clement Martin

Claimant's Name: Clement Martin
Acres: 500

Situation of lands: On the south side of the north branch of Newport River bounded north by land allotted to Clement Martin on all other sides by vacant land allotted to William Martin.
Original grantee: William Martin

Claimant's Name: James Edward Powell
Acres: 500

Situation of lands: On Savannah River bounding easterly on lands of Robert Williams westerly on land of Cornelius Sandford and on vacant lands by deed of conveyance from Robert Williams.
Original grantee: None shown

Claimant's Name: James Edward Powell
Acres: 50

Situation of lands: Town lot number 60 by administration on the estate of Nathaniel Potticary who purchased it from the first grantee William Gough.
Original grantee: William Gough

Claimant's Name: James Edward Powell
Acres: 50

Situation of lands: Town Lot by purchase and was first granted to John Lindall.
Original grantee: John Lindall

Claimant's Name: James Edward Powell
Acres: 500

Situation of lands: On the north branch of St. Catherine's by allotment of the President and Assistants July 4, 1750.
Original grantee: James Edward Powell

Claimant's Name: George Peters
Acres: 50

Situation of lands: Town Lot in Savannah in Belitha Tything on the west side of town number 8 Farm Lot number 2 Garden Lot number 16 in the same Tything Heathcote Ward granted by the Trustees to his father in the year 1733.
Original grantee: None shown

Claimant's Name: James Parker
Acres: 50

Situation of lands: Town Lot in Savannah number 1 in Sloper Tything Percival Ward Garden Lot number 30 west Farm Lot number 6 by warrant from the late President and Assistants.
Original grantee: None shown

Claimant's Name: James Parker
Acres: 90

Situation of lands: Tract of land in the center of Sloper Tything by warrant from the late President and Assistants.
Original grantee: James Parker

Claimant's Name: Margaret Papot
Acres: 50

Situation of lands: Town Lot in Savannah number 10 in
Third Tything Upper New Ward Savannah Garden Lot number
20 east Farm Lot number 6 as relict of ~~James Papot~~ (sic)
Austin Weddell who had it from the late Honorable
Trustees in behalf of her self ~~Peter Papet~~(sic) Benjamin
Weddell her son ~~of said late deceased~~ (sic) by said late
Austin.
Original grantee: ~~James Papot~~ (sic) Austin Weddell

Claimant's Name: Margaret Papot
Acres: 50

Situation of lands: Town Lot number 10 in **Heathcote** (sic)
Sloper Tything ~~Upper New~~ (sic) Percival Ward Garden Lot
number 51 west Farm Lot number 9 in Savannah as relict
of James Papot who had it from the late Trustees in
behalf of her self and ~~Benjamin Weddell~~ (sic) Peter
Papot son of late James.
Original grantee: James Papot

Claimant's Name: Margaret Papot
Acres: 50

Situation of lands: Town Lot in Savannah number 4 first
Tything Lower New Ward Garden and Farm Lot thereto belonging in behalf of her son James Papot who had it
from the late Trustees.
Original grantee: None shown

Claimant's Name: Margaret Papot
Acres: 400

Situation of lands: On the head of the south branch of the
Little Ogeechee River as relict of said James Papot who
had it by warrant from late President and Assistants in
behalf of her self and son heir to the late James.
Original grantee: James Papot

Claimant's Name: Margaret Papot
Acres: 44 7/8

Situation of lands: Farm Lot number 8 in Sloper Tything Percival Ward by purchase from Abraham Bignon who had it from the late Trustees.
Original grantee: Abraham Bignon

Claimant's Name: Thomas Rasberry
Acres: 50

Situation of lands: Town Lot in Jekyl Tything in Savannah number 7 purchased from Sarah the wife of Timothy Breed of Charles Town daughter and heiress at law to said Hodges by indenture of lease and release 5 December 1751 in said Tything south east from the Town number 10 Garden Lot south east also from the Town number 36.
Original grantee: None shown

Claimant's Name: Thomas Rasberry
Acres: 89 6/8

Situation of lands: Two Trust Farm Lots in the center of Frederick Tything by warrant from the President and Assistants 13th November 1752.
Original grantee: Thomas Rasberry

Claimant's Name: Thomas Rasberry
Acres: 44 7/8

Situation of lands: Farm Lot number 3 in said Tything purchased from Peter Sliterman son in law to said Cross who obtained it by deed of gift.
Original grantee: Thomas Cross

Claimant's Name: Thomas Rasberry
Acres: 300

Situation of lands: On the south side of the north branch of Little Ogeechee River by warrant of the President and Assistants 6 April 1754 (?-torn).
Original grantee: Thomas Rasberry

Claimant's Name: William Russell
Acres: 50

Situation of lands: Town Lot number 6 in Jekyl Tything
Farm Lot 4 in said Tything Garden Lot number 26 south
east of the Town by purchase 16 February 1750.
Original grantee: Joseph Hughes

Claimant's Name: William Russell
Acres: 89 6/8

Situation of lands: Two Farm Lots in the center of the
above Tything warrant from the President and Assistants
4 April 1750.
Original grantee: William Russell

Claimant's Name: William Russell
Acres: 44 7/8

Situation of lands: Farm Lot number 6 in the above Tything
purchased 4 January 1749.
Original grantee: John Norton Wright

Claimant's Name: William Russell
Acres: 44 7/8

Situation of lands: Farm Lot number 2 in the above Tything
purchased 19 October 1750.
Original grantee: Sarah Milledge

Claimant's Name: William Russell
Acres: 44 7/8

Situation of lands: Farm Lot number 10 in the above
Tything purchased 1 April 1752.
Original grantee: Richard Hodges

Claimant's Name: William Russell
Acres: 44 7/8

Situation of lands: Farm Lot number 5 in the above
Tything purchased 1 January 1753.
Original grantee: Michael Germain

Claimant's Name: William Russell
Acres: 44 7/8

Situation of lands: Farm Lot number 1 in the above Tything purchased 14 March 1753.
Original grantee: John Penrose

Claimant's Name: William Russell
Acres: 44 7/8

Situation of lands: Farm Lot number 7 in the above Tything purchased 24 May 1753.
Original grantee: James Muse

N. B. The last mentioned six Farm Lots are part of 50 acres granted to the respective grantees. The above Russell was also possessed of 400 acres of land on the south end of Onslow Island by virtue of an allotment from the President and Assistants as also 100 acres on the main fronting the said island which he purchased of Gotlieb Haley which lands he sold to Doctor Lewis Johnson who will claim the same by virtue of the sale.

Claimant's Name: William Russell for the heirs of Joseph Hunter
Acres: 50

Situation of lands: Town Lot number 1 in Tyrconnel Tything Farm Lot number 3 in Tyrconnel Tything Garden Lot number 13 south east of the Town by purchase 24 September 1744.
Original grantee: John West

Claimant's Name: William Russell for the heirs of James Dormer who left him one of his Executors.
Acres: 50

Situation of lands: Town Lot number 4 in Wilmington Tything Farm Lot number 6 in Wilmington Tything Garden Lot number 61 east of the Town by an exchange for James Dormer's.
Original grantee: James Carwels

Claimant's Name: William Russell for David Brown of Charles
                  Town Power of Attorney
Acres: 50

Situation of lands: Town Lot number 2 in Moor's Tything
Farm Lot number 5 in Moor's Tything Garden Lot number 59
west of the Town by purchase 2 September 1749.
Original grantee: Robert Moore

Claimant's Name: William Russell for John Dobell of Charles
                  Town Power of Attorney
Acres: 50

Situation of lands: Town Lot number 10 in Laroche Tything
Farm Lot number 9 in Laroche Tything Garden Lot number 33
east of the Town by purchase 4 December 1748.
Original grantee: Henry Green

Claimant's Name: William Russell for William Grant of
                  Philadelphia Power of Attorney
Acres: 50

Situation of lands: Town Lot number 8 in the First
Tything of the Lower New Ward Farm Lot number 8 in
the First Tything Lower New Ward and Garden Lot number
93 west of the Town by purchase 23 July 1746.
Original grantee: Alexander Rantowle

Claimant's Name: William Elliott
Acres: 500

Situation of lands: On the north side of Great Ogechee
River fronting said river by warrant from the late
President and Assistants 8 November 1753.
Original grantee: William Elliott Jr.

Claimant's Name: William Elliott
Acres: None shown

Situation of lands: Lot in Hardwicke number 1.
Original grantee: William Elliott, Jr.

Claimant's Name: William Elliott for Charles West
Acres: 500

Situation of lands: On the south side of the Great Ogechee River adjoining Sterling Swamp bounding on the north east by John Harn's land and on all other sides on vacant land by warrant from the President and Assistants 8 November 1748.
Original grantee: Charles West

Claimant's Name: George Galphin
Acres: 500

Situation of lands: Vacant lands on all sides fronting upon Savannah River in Hallifax county and opposite Silver Bluff.
Original grantee: George Galphin

Claimant's Name: Lachlan McGillivray
Acres: 500

Situation of lands: On the head of branches of the Little Ogechee bounding north on Rodolph Purry and Alexander Wylly south on James Miller and all other sides on vacant land by warrant from the late President and Assistants.
Original grantee: Lachlan McGillivray

Claimant's Name: John Morel
Acres: 500

Situation of lands: To the west of Savannah bounded north by Pipemaker's Creek west by Newington and vacant land and on all other sides granted to Peter Morel deceased by the late President and Assistants June 3, 1752.
Original grantee: Peter Morel

Claimant's Name: John Morel
Acres: 50

Situation of lands: Town Lot in Tyrconnel Tything Derby Ward number 2 Derby-Ward (crossed out in original) together with a Farm and Garden Lot had in exchange of James Wilson for a Town Lot number 9 with Garden and Farm Lot in Holland's Tything Percival Ward granted by General Oglethorpe to John Morel 1738 or 1739.
Original grantee: None shown

Claimant's Name: John Morel for Peter Morel
Acres: None shown

Situation of lands: Lot of land in Abercorn Village number 4 purchased of Christian Dasher in 1748.
Original grantee: Christian Dasher

Claimant's Name: William Norton by Charles Watson
Acres: 50

Situation of lands: Lot in Savannah number 8 Vernon Tything Heathcote Ward with Garden and Farm Lot granted him by the late President and Assistants.
Original grantee: William Norton

Claimant's Name: William Norton by Charles Watson for his son Samuel
Acres: 50

Situation of lands: On Skidoway Island by gift of Lucy Mouse widow deceased.
Original grantee: None shown

Claimant's Name: John Pettigrew
Acres: 50

Situation of lands: In right of Catherine his wife claims 50 acres of land in the Township of Augusta granted by the late Trustees to Archibald McBain deceased which said Catherine is his only child.
Original grantee: Archibald McBain

Claimant's Name: John Pettigrew
Acres: 50

Situation of lands: In the same Township formerly granted to James Fraser deceased and purchased from him by George Galphin and John Spencer who sold it to the present claimant.
Original grantee: James Fraser

Claimant's Name: Christopher Ring
Acres: 50

Situation of lands: In the Village of Acton granted unto him by the late President and Assistants about the year 1744.
Original grantee: Christopher Ring

Claimant's Name: Christopher Ring for his father
Acres: 50

Situation of lands: In the same village granted at the same time and both run out in one tract.
Original grantee: None shown

Claimant's Name: John Steward
Acres: 50

Situation of lands: Town Lot number 7 first Tything Upper New Ward Garden Lot number 67 east and Farm Lot.
Original grantee: Donald Steward

~~Claimant's Name: Jon Van Beverhoudt by his father~~
~~Acres: 500~~

~~Situation of lands: Upon Bermuda Island by allottment of the late President and Assistants.~~
~~Original grantee: Johann Van Beverhoudt~~

~~Claimant's Name: Adrian Van Beverhoudt~~
~~Acres: 500~~

~~Situation of lands: Upon D⁰ by D⁰~~
~~Original grantee: Adriann Van Beverhoudt~~

N. B. All of the above is crossed out in the original

104.

Claimant's Name: Alexander Wylly
Acres: 500

Situation of lands: Nine miles west of Savannah bounding east of Rudoph (sic) Purry's land and on all sides vacant lands.
Original grantee: Alexander Wylly

Claimant's Name: Alexander Wylly
Acres: 50

Situation of lands: Town Lot number 9 in More Tything Percival Ward with Garden and Farm Lots purchased from William Blithman.
Original grantee: None shown

Claimant's Name: Michael Raddick
Acres: 50

Situation of lands: Between Skidoway River and Thunderbolt by the President and Assistants 8 August 1754.
Original grantee: Michael Raddick

Claimant's Name: Hugh Ross
Acres: 50

Situation of lands: Lot number 2 at Abercorn purchased of James Grant.
Original grantee: James Grant

Claimant's Name: Hugh Ross
Acres: 50

Situation of lands: Lot number 9 at Abercorn left him by will of James Fraser deceased.
Original grantee: James Fraser

Claimant's Name: Hugh Ross
Acres: 100

Situation of lands: Acres at Abercorn by the President and Assistants about 9 months ago.
Original grantee: Hugh Ross.

Claimant's Name: Hugh Ross
Acres: 50

Situation of lands: Town Lot in Savannah with the 5 acre and 45 acre lots granted to him by General Oglethorpe in 1738.
Original grantee: None shown

Claimant's Name: William Spencer
Acres: 500

Situation of lands: Situate in the District of Little Ogechee bounding westerly of lands of Francis Harris, Esqr. northerly on the Township of Savannah lands easterly on vacant lands and southerly of land of Henry William Parker by warrant from the late President and Assistants 4 July 1752.
Original grantee: William Spencer

Claimant's Name: William Spencer
Acres: 50

Situation of lands: Lot in Savannah number 6 Third Tything lately called the Upper New Ward now Anson Ward with Garden and Farm Lots allotted by the late President and Assistants 18 May 1745.
Original grantee: William Spencer

Claimant's Name: William Spencer
Acres: None shown

Situation of lands: Lot in Hardwicke on Great Ogechee River number 50 5 June 1754 allotted by the late President and Assistants.
Original grantee: William Spencer

Claimants' Name: Jere:(miah) Sliterman by Charles Watson
Acres: 50

Situation of lands: Lot in Savannah number 1 in Laroche Tything Heathcote Ward with a Garden and Farm Lot granted him by the late President and Assistants formerly William Francis's.
Original grantee: William Francis

Claimant's Name: Jere: Sliterman by Charles Watson
Acres: 89 6/8

Situation of lands: Tow Farm Lots in the same Tything and Ward commonly called Trust Lots granted him by the late President and Assistants in 1753.
Original grantee: Jere: Sliterman

Claimant's Name: Jere: Sliterman by Charles Watson
Acres: 44 7/8

Situation of lands: Garden and Farm Lots by gift of his mother-in-law Ann Emery widow.
Original grantee: None shown

Claimant's Name: William Seales
Acres: 50

Situation of lands: Lot in the Town of Savannah number 6 in Carpenter's Tything Decker Ward with Garden and Farm Lots by order of General Oglethorpe.
Original grantee: None shown

Claimant's Name: ~~Ann Steuart~~
Acres: ~~50~~

Situation of lands: ~~Town Lot in Savannah with Garden and Farm Lots by the late President and Assistants November 10, 1752.~~
Original grantee: ~~Ann Steuart~~

N. B. The above is crossed out in the original

Claimant's Name: David Snook by Charles Watson
Acres: 50

Situation of lands: Lot in Savannah number 2 in Eyles Tything Heathcote Ward with a Garden and Farm Lot granted him by the late Trustees.
Original grantee: David Snook

Claimant's Name: James White by David Snook by Charles Watson
Acres: 50

Situation of lands: Lot in Savannah number 4 in same Tything and Ward with Garden and Farm Lots granted said White by the late Trustees.
Original grantee: James White

Claimant's Name: David Snook for Richard Turner by Charles Watson
Acres: 50

Situation of lands: Lot in Savannah number 5 in Eyles' Tything Heathcote Ward with a Garden and Farm Lot granted to said Turner by the late Trustees.
Original grantee: Richard Turner

Claimant's Name: John Snook by Charles Watson
Acres: 89 6/8

Situation of lands: Two Farm Lots in Eyle's Tything reserved by the late Trustees and commonly called Trust Lots granted him by the late President and Assistants in 1752.
Original grantee: John Snook

Claimant's Name: Benjamin Sheftal by Charles Watson
Acres: 50

Situation of lands: Lot in Savannah number 4 in Heathcote Tything Decker Ward with a Garden and Farm Lot granted him by the late Trustees.
Original grantee: Benjamin Sheftal

Claimant's Name: Mordecai Sheftal by Charles Watson
Acres: 50

Situation of lands: In the Township of Vernonburgh purchased of Joseph Lathbury.
Original grantee: Joseph Lathbury

Claimant's Name: Benjamin Sheftal for Jacob Olivero
                   by Charles Watson
Acres: 50

Situation of lands: Lot in Savannah number 3 in Towers
Tything in Deckers Ward with a Garden and Farm Lot
granted said Olivero by the late Trustees.
Original grantee: Jacob Olivero

Claimant's Name: Peter Tondee by Charles Watson
Acres: 50

Situation of lands: Lot in Savannah number 10 in
Heathcote Tything Decker Ward with Garden and Farm Lots
as eldest son and heir of ----- Tondee his father
deceased who had it from the late Trustees.
Original grantee: -----Tondee

Claimant's Name: Peter Tondee by Charles Watson
Acres: 120

Situation of lands: Lying about three miles west of
Savannah granted him by the late President and Assistants
in 1752.
Original grantee: Peter Tondee

Claimant's Name: Stephen Tarian by Charles Watson
Acres: 50

Situation of lands: Lot in Savannah number 4 Vernon
Tything Heathcote Ward with Garden and Farm Lots
granted him by the late Trustees nineteen years ago.
Original grantee: Stephen Tarian

Claimant's Name: Charles Watson
Acres: 45

Situation of lands: Lot in Savannah number 4 Moore's
Tything Percival Ward with Farm and Garden Lot thereunto
belonging purchased of the co-heirs of Robert Haines
deceased.
Original grantee: Robert Haines

Claimant's Name: David Truan by Charles Watson
Acres: 89 6/8

Situation of lands: Two Farm Lots in Belitha Tything reserved by the late Trustees and commonly known as the Trust Lots granted him by the late President and Assistants in 1753.
Original grantee: David Truan

Claimant's Name: David Truan by Charles Watson
Acres: 44 7/8

Situation of lands: Farm Lot purchased of Giles Becu.
Original grantee: Giles Becu

Claimant's Name: Thomas Wilson by Charles Watson
Acres: 240

Situation of lands: Lying on the south side of Little Ogechee River granted him by the late President and Assistants and adjoining lands of Benjamin Wilson and Joseph Summers.
Original grantee: Thomas Wilson

Claimant's Name: Jeremiah Valaton by Charles Watson
Acres: 50

Situation of lands: Town Lot in Savannah number 3 in Vernon Tything Heathcote Ward with Garden and Farm Lot granted him by the late President and Assistants in 1742.
Original grantee: Jeremiah Valaton

Claimant's Name: Thomas Upton by Newdigate Stephens and
                   Charles Watson
Acres: 50 50

Situation of lands: Two Lots in the Town of Savannah number 6 and 7 in Moore Tything Percival Ward with each a Garden and Farm Lot thereto purchased of John Desborough of Charles Town in South Carolina and Ann his wife heretofore granted by the late Trustees.
Original grantee: John Desborough

Claimant's Name: Bartholomew Zouberbuhler
Acres: 500

Situation of lands: Situated on the east end of Argyle
Island bounding north on James DeVeaux and on all other sides
by the north and south branches of the River Savannah from
the President and Assistants 4 August 1750.
Original grantee: Bartholomew Zouberbuhler

Claimant's Name: Bartholomew Zouberbuhler
Acres: 100

Situation of lands: Situated between Joseph Watson and
William Francis on the River Savannah by purchase of
Jacob Waldbourger granted by the President and Assistants
November 11, 1752.
Original grantee: Jacob Waldbourger

Claimant's Name: Henry Yonge
Acres: 500

Situation of lands: On the Island of Skedoway bounding
north east on Warsaw River south of lands of Richard
Hazzard and north on the village lots of Skidoway by
warrant from the late President and Assistants the 5th
September 1753.
Original grantee: Henry Yonge

Claimant's Name: Henry Yonge
Acres: 37

Situation of lands: Small island in the marsh of Warsaw
River on the north east side bounding by the said river
and marshes of the same on all sides being short measure
of the foregoing tract by warrant from the late President
and Assistants 5 September 1753.
Original grantee: Henry Yonge

Claimant's Name: Francis Yonge by Henry Yonge
Acres: 500

Situation of lands: On the south side of Great Ogechee River bounding north east on Hugh Mackay's land east on John McLoud and on all other sides on vacant land by warrant from the late President and Assistants 4 October 1754 in right of his son Francis Yonge about 17 years of age.
Original grantee: Francis Yonge

Claimant's Name: Henry Yonge
Acres: 50

Situation of lands: A village lot the front of (7d ?) claimants' land to the north on Skidoway in right of his youngest son by the late President and Assistants.
Original grantee: None shown

Claimant's Name: Michael Bourgholter by Charles Watson
Acres: 450

Situation of lands: In the Village of Acton granted him by the late President and Assistants.
Original grantee: Michael Bourgholter

Claimant's Name: George Derrick by Charles Watson
Acres: 50

Situation of lands: In the same village by purchase from Simeon Leon.
Original grantee: Simeon Leon

Claimant's Name: Gasper Herback by Charles Watson
Acres: 50 50 50

Situation of lands: Granted by the late Trustees also 50 acres granted him by the late President and Assistants and fifty acres purchased of William Sheinhulst all in the same village.
Original grantee: Gasper Herback Gasper Herback
                  William Sheinhulst

Claimant's Name: Jacob Herback by Charles Watson
Acres: 50

Situation of lands: In the same village granted him by the late Trustees.
Original grantee: Jacob Herback

Claimant's Name: Simeon Gerin by Charles Watson
Acres: 50

Situation of lands: In the same village granted him by the late Trustees.
Original grantee: ~~Jacob Herback~~ Simeon Gerin

N. B. Crossed in the original

Claimant's Name: Rodolph Burghe by Charles Watson
Acres: 50

Situation of lands: In the same village granted as last mentioned.
Original grantee: Rodolph Burghe

Claimant's Name: Caul Rieter (In index = Paul Reitter)
Acres: 50

Situation of lands: In the same village purchased of John Tertler.
Original grantee: John Tertler

Claimant's Name: Jacob Danner by Charles Watson
Acres: 50

Situation of lands: In the Village of Acton granted him by the late Trustees.
Original grantee: Jacob Danner

Claimant's Name: Jacob Danner by Charles Watson
Acres: 50

Situation of lands: In the same village granted by the late President and Assistants.
Original grantee: Jacob Danner

Claimant's Name: George Burghold by Charles Watson
Acres: 50

Situation of lands: In the same village granted by the late President and Assistants.
Original grantee: George Burghold

Claimant's Name: Abraham Fry by Charles Watson
Acres: 50

Situation of lands: In the same village purchased by him of George Derrick.
Original grantee: George Derrick

Claimant's Name: Jacob Curtz by Charles Watson
Acres: 50

Situation of lands: In the same village granted him by the late Trustees.
Original grantee: Jacob Curtz

Claimant's Name: Christian Levenberger by Charles Watson
Acres: 50

Situation of lands: In the same village granted him as last mentioned.
Original grantee: Christian Levenberger

Claimant's Name: Nicholas Hanor by Charles Watson
Acres: 50

Situation of lands: In the same village granted him as last mentioned as eldest son and heir of Nicholas Hanor his father deceased.
Original grantee: Nicholas Hanor

Claimant's Name: George Uland by Charles Watson
Acres: 50

Situation of lands: In the same village had in exchange with Jacob Stroubler for a lot of like quantity in Vernonburgh.
Original grantee: Jacob Stroubler

Claimant's Name: George Uland by Charles Watson
Acres: 100

Situation of lands: In the same village granted him by
the late President and Assistants in 1754.
Original grantee: George Uland

Claimant's Name: Conrade Houver by Charles Watson
Acres: 50

Situation of lands: In the same village granted by the
late President and Assistants.
Original grantee: Conrade Houver

Claimant's Name: Christian Burgomaster
Acres: None shown

Situation of lands: In ditto granted by the President
and Assistants.
Original grantee: Christian Burgomaster

Claimant's Name: John Berrier (sic) by Charles Watson
Acres: 50

Situation of lands: In the Village of Vernonburgh granted
thirteen years since.
Original grantee: John Berrier (sic)

Claimant's Name: John Berrier by Charles Watson
Acres: 50

Situation of lands: In the same village granted by the late
President and Assistants a year since.
Original grantee: John Berrier

Claimant's Name: John Berrier by Charles Watson
Acres: 50

Situation of lands: In the same village purchased of Laurence
Reitnauer in the year 1749.
Original grantee: Laurence Reitnaurer

Claimant's Name: Jacob Berrier by Charles Watson
Acres: 50

Situation of lands: In the same Township of Vernonburgh granted him by the late President and Assistants about seven years ago.
Original grantee: Jacob Berrier

Claimant's Name: Gasper Snider by Charles Watson
Acres: 50

Situation of lands: In the same township granted by the late Trustees about thirteen years ago.
Original grantee: Gasper Snider

Claimant's Name: Gasper Snider by Charles Watson
Acres: 100

Situation of lands: In the same township late Adam Reinstettler deceased on the behalf of David Reinstettler an infant grandson of the said Gasper.
Original grantee: Adam Reinstettler

Claimant's Name: Matthias Coogle by Charles Watson
Acres: 50

Situation of lands: In the same township granted by the late President and Assistants about two years since.
Original grantee: Matthias Coogle

Claimant's Name: Matthias Coogle by Charles Watson
Acres: 50

Situation of lands: Purchased by him about two years since of Hans Jacob Matcher.
Original grantee: Hans Jacob Matcher

Claimant's Name: Theobald Keifer by Charles Watson
Acres: 50

Situation of lands: In the said township granted him by the late Trustees.
Original grantee: Theobald Keifer

Claimant's Name: David Keifer by Charles Watson
Acres: 50

Situation of lands: In the said townshop granted him by the late Trustees.
Original grantee: David Keifer

Claimant's Name: David and Frederick Keifer by Charles Watson
Acres: 50

Situation of lands: Each of them an undivided moiety as tenants in common of and in 50 acres of land in the said Township of Vernonburgh devised to them in and by the will of Anna Steinhaville proved the 7th December 1749.
Original grantee: Steinhaville (sic)

Claimant's Name: Adam Ordner by Charles Watson
Acres: 50

Situation of lands: In the said township granted by the late Trustees twelve years ago.
Original grantee: Adam Ordner

Claimant's Name: Adam Ordner by Charles Watson
Acres: 50

Situation of lands: In the same township granted by the late President and Assistants about one year since.
Original grantee: Adam Ordner

Claimant's Name: Jacob Nongazer by Charles Watson
Acres: 50

Situation of lands: In the same Township of Vernonburgh granted by the late Trustees twelve-years-age (sic) about twelve since.
Original grantee: Jacob Nongazer

Claimant's Name: Henry Nongazer by Charles Watson
Acres: 50

Situation of lands: In the same township as last mentioned.
Original grantee: Jacob Nongazer

Claimant's Name: Paul Hauvener's widow by Charles Watson
Acres: 50

Situation of lands: In the same township granted about twelve years since.
Original grantee: Paul Hauvener

Claimant's Name: David Fisher by Charles Watson
Acres: 50

Situation of lands: In the same township granted by the late ~~Trustees-about~~ (sic) President and Assistants about five years ago.
Original grantee: David Fisher

Claimant;s Name: Peter Dowle
Acres: 50

Situation of lands: In the same township granted by the late Trustees about twelve years since.
Original grantee: Peter Dowle

Claimant's Name: Samuel Hammond by Charles Watson
Acres: 50

Situation of lands: In the same township purchased by him of Joseph Folker.
Original grantee: Joseph Folker

Claimant's Name: George Uland by Charles Watson
Acres: 50

Situation of lands: In the same township on behalf of his daughter Elizabeth Barbara given to her by her grandmother Mariot Craven.
Original grantee: None shown

Claimant's Name: Matthias Reinstettler by Charles Watson
Acres: 50

Situation of lands: In the same township granted him about eleven years since by the late Trustees.
Original grantee: Matthias Reinstettler

Claimant's Name: Peter Young by Charles Watson
Acres: 50

Situation of lands: In the same township as only son and heir of Jerry Young his father deceased.
Original grantee: Jerry Young

Claimant's Name: Matthias Knapp by Charles Watson
Acres: 50

Situation of lands: In the same township as only-deceased heir (sic) formerly Daniel Deigler and purchased of David Debare by the said Matthias.
Original grantee: Daniel Deigler

Claimant;s Name: Martin Fenton by Charles Watson
Acres: 50

Situation of lands: In the same township purchased of Robert Houstoun.
Original grantee: Robert Houstoun

Claimant's Name: Martin Fenton by Charles Watson
Acres: 50

Situation of lands: In the same township purchased of David Marlow.
Original grantee: David Marlow

Claimant's Name: Walter Denny by Charles Watson
Acres: 50

Situation of lands: In the Township of Vernonburgh granted him as a discharged soldier.
Original grantee: Walter Denny

Claimant's Name: John Morel
Acres: 50

Situation of lands: In Holland Tything Percival Ward with the Garden and Farm Lots by warrant from James Ogelthorpe, Esqr. October 16, 1739.
Original grantee: None shown

Claimant's Name: John Todd, Jr., by Charles Watson Ex^d abt. 13th May 1757
Acres: 100

Situation of lands: Lying in the District of Newport in the Province of Georgia granted him by the late President and Assistants in 1754.
Original grantee: John Todd, Jr.

Claimant's Name: Duncan McGillivray by Charles Watson
Acres: 50

Situation of lands: In right of his wife in Goshen Village devised to his said wife by the will of John McKay her father deceased.
Original grantee: John McKay

Claimant's Name: William Payne
Acres: 500

Situation of lands: Purchased of Edmund Gray situate in the Point betwixt Savannah River and Little River about thirty miles above Augusta.
Original grantee: Edmund Gray

Claimant's Name: Charles Jordan
Acres: 50

Situation of lands: Lot in the Township of Augusta known by the number 35 purchased of Samuel Wright first granted to William Watkin's Taylor (tailor ?).
Original grantee: William Watkins

Claimant's Name: John Fitch
Acres: 50   50   (sic)

Situation of lands: Two fifty acre lots number 7 and number 8 in the Township of Augusta bounded north west by Martin Campbell southeast by the Town Common south west by Samuel Vening and north east by Savannah River formerly granted to James Mathes and John Grey by the late Trustees and since purchased of the said Mathes and Grey by John Cragg deceased and which said Finch (sic) hold in right of his wife, daughter of the said Cragg.
Original grantee: None shown

Claimants' Name: John Fitch
Acres: 50

Situation of lands: Lot number   in the Township of Augusta formerly granted to James Bubby and by him made over to Henry Overstreet and afterwards purchased of the said Overstreet by Hugh Oately of whom said Fitch purchased bounded south west by Cornelius Dohorty north west by George John Wisely north east by John Gloster south east by Peter Gates.
Original grantee: James Bubby

Claimant's Name: John Fitch
Acres: 50

Situation of lands: Situate on a branch running Bryer Creek about five miles to the southward of the said creek formerly an Indian Town now called Spring Groves bounded on all sides by vacant land granted by the President and Assistants in 1753.
Original grantee: John Fitch

Claimant's Name: Mary Bailey by Charles Watson
Acres: 50   50   (sic)

Situation of lands: Two fifty acre lots lying on an island called Tybee by deed of gift from James Hewitt to whom one of the said lots was granted by the late Trustees and the other descended to him as heir to his father.
Original grantee: James Ewitt (sic)   (Hewitt)

Claimant's Name: Jacob This
Acres: 50

Situation of lands: Fifty acres number 24 and a Town Lot in Vernonburgh by the late President and Assistants.
Original grantee: Jacob This

Claimant's Name: Jacob This
Acres: 50

Situation of lands: Ditto Lot in same town by ditto.
Original grantee: Jacob This

Claimant's Name: Jacob This for Hannah Dorothy This
Acres: 50

Situation of lands: Ditto lot in ditto number 23 by ditto to Valentine Bloom.
Original grantee: Valentine Bloom

Claimant's Name: Jacob Kusmaul
Acres: 50

Situation of lands: Lot number 2 at Goshen by warrant from the President and Assistants.
Original grantee: Jacob Kusmaul

Claimant's Name: William Clark by Edward Barnard Attorney
Acres: 50

Situation of lands: Lot in the Town of Augusta butting and bounding on the east side by lands of Doctor Fyffe and McBean Minoe on the north by lands of Lachlan McBean 500 acres and on the west by vacant land by an order of the President and Assistants.
Original grantee: William Clark

Claimant's Name: John Tinley by Edward Barnard Attorney
Acres: 50

Situation of lands: Lot number 1 in the Town of Augusta butting and bounding on the east by land of Mr. David Douglass on the south by land of James Dean and the west by Common Lands on the north the River Savannah granted him by General Oglethorpe.
Original grantee: John Tinley

Claimant's Name: John Tinley by Edward Barnard Attorney
Acres: 50

Situation of lands: Lot in Hamsted (sic) formerly belonging to Peter a Dutch man granted to said Tinley by General Oglethorpe in October 2, 1728 for four years servitude in the colony.
Original grantee: None shown

Claimant's Name: John Tinley by Edward Barnard Attorney
Acres: 50

Situation of lands: Lot 38 in the Town of Augusta butting and bounding on the east by land of Richard Lee on the south by vacant land on the west by land of Nicholas Murphey granted Thomas Webb soldier by the President and Assistants.
Original grantee: Thomas Webb

Claimant's Name: John Tinley by Edward Barnard Attorney
Acres: 50

Situation of lands: Lot number 32 butting and bounding on land of Mr. Visley and on the other side John Gloster granted to Thomas Giggs soldier by the President and Assistants.
Original grantee: Thomas Giggs

Claimant's Name: Michael Bourghalter, Jr. by Charles Watson
Acres: 50

Situation of lands: In the Village of Hampsted heretofore the estate of granted Waggener deceased him by the late Trustees.
Original grantee: Waggener Michael Bourghalter, Jr.

Claimant's Name: Michael Bourghalter by Charles Watson
Acres: 50

Situation of lands: In Hampsted Village granted him by the late Trustees.
Original grantee: Michael Bourghalter

Claimant's Name: ~~George Motts~~
Acres: ~~50~~

Situation of lands: ~~In the same village heretofore the estate formerly belonging to William Parker deceased.~~
Original grantee: ~~William Parker~~

The above crossed out in the original.

Claimant's Name: George Motts by Charles Watson
Acres: 50

Situation of lands: In the same village heretofore the estate of   Waggener deceased.
Original grantee: Waggener

Claimant's Name: David Keisler by Charles Watson
Acres: 50

Situation of lands: In the same village formerly belonging to William Parker deceased.
Original grantee: William Parker

Claimant's Name: David Kender
Acres: 50

Situation of lands: In Highgate Village granted him by the late Trustees.
Original grantee: David Kender

Claimant's Name: Simon Bouvier
Acres: 50

Situation of lands: In the village last mentioned granted him by the late Trustees.
Original grantee: Simon Bouvier

Claimant's Name: James Jansacke
Acres: 50

Situation of lands: In the village last mentioned granted him by the late Trustees twenty years since.
Original grantee: James Jansacke

Claimant's Name: Stephen Landree
Acres: 50

Situation of lands: In the same village as only son and heir of James Landree deceased.
Original grantee: James Landree

Claimant's Name: Robert Williams, Sr. by James Edward Powell
Acres: 500

Situation of lands: On Savannah River bounded easterly on lands granted to Patrick Tailfer and westerly on lands granted to John Williams south on vacant lands by grant from the Trustees.
Original grantee: Robert William, Sr.

Claimant's Name: Robert Williams, Sr. by James Edward Powell
Acres: 50

Situation of lands: Town Lot in Savannah as heir to the estate of James Williams.
Original grantee: James Williams

Claimant's Name: John Chapman by James Edward Powell
Acres: 500

Situation of lands: On Little Ogechee River adjoining adjoining (sic) to lands belonging to James Houstoun by warrant from General Oglethorpe.
Original grantee: John Chapman

Claimant's Name: Robert Williams, Jr.
Acres: 50

Situation of lands: Town Lot by gift of Robert Williams.
Original grantee: Robert Williams

Claimant's Name: Anthony Gautier
Acres: 50

Situation of lands: Town Lot number 6 in New Ward with 50 acres thereunto belonging grant of the Trustees in 1742.
Original grantee: Anthony Gautier

Claimant's Name: Lydia Dean for herself and Henry her son by Charles Watson
Acres: 50

Situation of lands: Town Lot in Savannah number ten in Eyles Tything Heathcote Ward with Garden and Farm Lots granted by the late Trustees.
Original grantee: None shown

Claimant's Name: William Newberry
Acres: 500

Situation of lands: Lying at a place called Withrington's Bluff upon the River Savannah purchased of Patrick Brown and granted to said Brown of the late President and Assistants.
Original grantee: Patrick Brown

Claimant's Name: James Parris by Charles Watson
Acres: 50

Situation of lands: Lot in the Township of Augusta where he now dwells.
Original grantee: None shown

Claimant's Name: John Smith
Acres: 500

Situation of lands: Lying south east from Savannah given by the late President and Assistants by warrant dated 6 May 1749 to the late William Parker obtained by purchase from his widow.
Original grantee: William Parker

Claimant's Name: John Smith by power of attorney from
                   James Wall
Acres: 500

Situation of lands: Situate on the Great Ogechee given him by the late President and Assistants.
Original grantee: James Wall

Claimant's Name: John Smith by power of attorney from
                   John Gordon
Acres: 500

Situation of lands: Situate on Red Bird Neck on said Ogechee by the late President and Assistants.
Original grantee: John Gordon

Claimant's Name: John Smith by power of attorney from
                   Thomas Horton
Acres: 500

Situation of lands: Situate on said Ogechee as administrator to Major Horton's Estate by the late President and Assistants.
Original grantee: Thomas Horton

Claimant's Name: John Smith by power of attorney from
                   Griffith Williams
Acres: 500

Situation of lands: On Red Bird Neck given by the late President and Assistants.
Original grantee: Griffith Williams

Claimant's Name: Smith and Gordon
Acres: None shown

Situation of lands: Lot in the Town of Savannah granted to Arthur Johnson being in the right made over to Smith and Gordon.
Original grantee: Arthur Johnson

Claimant's Name: Richard Cox, Sr.
Acres: 500

Situation of lands: On a point on the north side of Great Ogechee River opposite to lands formerly laid out for Captain James Mackay Mr. Bailey and Messrs. Sterling by the President and Assistants 6 February 1754.
Original grantee: Richard Cox, Sr.

Claimant's Name: Richard Cox, Jr.
Acres: 500

Situation of lands: Ditto by ditto.
Original grantee: Richard Cox, Jr.

Claimant's Name: James New
Acres: 500

Situation of lands: Situate in the District of Great Ogechee on the Poplar Swamp bounding north on lands of William Butler, Jr. east on Samuel New's land and on all other sides on vacant land by the late President and Assistants.
Original grantee: James New

Claimant's Name: Samuel New
Acres: 340

Situation of lands: Situate the District of Great Ogechee on Poplar Swamp bounding west on Mr. James New's land north on Baily's (sic) land and on all other sides on vacant land by the late President and Assistants 4 April 1754.
Original grantee: Samuel New

Claimant's Name: Samuel New
Acres: 160

Situation of lands: Situate on a point of land below the Town of Hardwicke bounding north on Great Ogechee River south on marshes of Red Bud (sic) and east on land called Jenys and Baker by the President and Assistants 6 February 1754.
Original grantee: Samuel New

Claimant's Name: Jonathon Bryan
Acres: 50

Situation of lands: Town Lot fronting on Bryan Street
Reynolds Ward second Tything 45 acre lot number 1 Reynolds
Ward and a 5 acre lot adjoining purchased of Hugh Anderson.
Original grantee: Hugh Anderson

Claimant's Name: Frederick Keifer
Acres: 50

Situation of lands: Town Lot in the Township of Vernonburgh
number 1 by the late President and Assistants November 2, 1744.
Original grantee: Frederick Keifer

Claimant's Name: Walter Fleming by Peter Baillou Ex^d per
                   att. 13th May 1757
Acres: 500

Situation of lands: On the Little Ogechee River near lands
belonging to Philip Delegal, Jr. granted by the late
President and Assistants.
Original grantee: Walter Fleming

Claimant's Name: David Montaigut by Charles Watson on behalf
                   of the heirs of Joshua Overend deceased
Acres: 50

Situation of lands: Lot in the Town of Savannah number 1
in Jekyl Tything Darby Ward with a Garden and Farm Lot
granted said Overend by the late Trustees.
Original grantee: Joshua Overend

Claimant's Name: John Martin Bolzius
Acres: 100

Situation of lands: In the Township of Ebenezer near the
Saw and Grist Mills bounding east on a large low island be-
yond the Mill Creek commonly called Abercorn Creek south of
widow Burgsteiner's plantation west of mere (sic) pine land
and north of Joseph Leitner's plantation now the property of
the said mill bought of Thomas Bickler deceased bought it (sic)
Original grantee: None shown

Claimant's Name: John Martin Bolzius
Acres: 500

Situation of lands: In the District of Joseph's Town bounding east of a large Savannah River Swamp south of the plantation of Mr. Lemcke west of all pine land and north of the limits of the village Goshen laid out by order of the late President and Council.
Original grantee: John Martin Bolzius

Claimant's Name: Elizabeth and Jane Evans by Charles Watson
Acres: 50

Situation of lands: Lot in the Town of Savannah number 7 in the Third Tything Lower New Ward alias Reynolds Ward with Garden and Farm Lots as daughters and coheirs of John Evans their father deceased.
Original grantee: John Evans

Claimant's Name: Elizabeth and Jane Evans by Charles Watson
Acres: 50

Situation of lands: Lot in the Town of Savannah number 3 in Carpenter's Tything Decker's Ward with a Garden and Farm Lot devised to her in and by the will of John Tisdale her (sic) grandfather.
Original grantee: None shown

Claimant's Name: John Elliott
Acres: 500

Situation of lands: North side of the South Swamp of Midway allotted by the President and Assistants July 11, 1752.
Original grantee: John Elliott

Claimant's Name: Gilbert Fyffe
Acres: 50

Situation of lands: In the Town of Augusta warrant from the President and Assistants butting and bounding on the west by land of Rotten (sic) and on the east by land of McBean Minor and on the north by the River Savannah on the south by vacant land.
Original grantee: Gilbert Fyffe

Claimant's Name: Margaret Fraser, widow
Acres: 500

Situation of lands: Margaret Fraser, widow of James Fraser of Augusta deceased claims the moyety (sic) or half part of all that tract or plantation of five hundred acres of land allotted by James Oglethorpe, Esqr.
Original grantee: James Fraser

Claimant's Name: Margaret Fraser, widow
Acres: None shown

Situation of lands: Also the house lot in the Town of Augusta with the dwelling house and appurtenances thereupon built for and during the term of her natural life as her dower according to the laws and customs of Georgia.
Original grantee: James Fraser

Claimant's Name: William Francis by Charles Watson
Acres: 50

Situation of lands: Lot in the Town of Savannah number 3 in Digby Tything Deckers Ward with a Garden and Farm Lot purchased of John Clark.
Original grantee: John Clark

Claimant's Name: William Francis by Charles Watson
Acres: 500

Situation of lands: Called the Grange lying on Savannah River about four miles above the Town of Savannah purchased of Thomas Bosomworth and Mary his wife in 1750.
Original grantee: None shown

Claimant's Name: William Francis by Charles Watson
Acres: 285

Situation of lands: Contiguous to the tract aforesaid purchased of Joseph Watson in 1749.
Original grantee: Joseph Watson

Claimant's Name: William Francis by Charles Watson
Acres: 100

Situation of lands: Lying westward of the Grange purchased of Henry Serjeant in 1752.
Original grantee: Henry Serjeant

Claimant's Name: William Francis by Charles Watson
Acres: 500

Situation of lands: On the south side of Little Ogechee River and bounding lands of William Elliott and James Papot granted by the late President and Assistants in 1748.
Original grantee: William Francis

Claimant's Name: William Francis by Charles Watson
Acres: 100

Situation of lands: Adjoining the five hundred acres last mentioned purchased of Peter Slyterman this present year 1755.
Original grantee: Peter Slyterman

Claimant;s Name: Penelope Fitzwalter
Acres: 50

Situation of lands: Town Lot number 10 in Frederick Tything Farm Lot number 5 in ditto a Garden Lot number 1 south east of the Town as relict of John Wright who had it from the late Trustees.
Original grantee: John Wright

Claimant's Name: Penelope Fitzwalter
Acres: 50

Situation of lands: Town Lot number 8 in Wilmington Tything Farm Lot 9 in Wilmington Tything a Garden Lot number 42 east of the town as relict of Joseph Fitzwalter who had it from the late Trustees.
Original grantee: Joseph Fitzwalter

Claimant's Name: Penelope Fitzwalter
Acres: 50

Situation of lands: Town Lot in Jekyl Tything Farm Lot number 6 in Jekyl Tything Garden Lot number 42 as mother of the late John Norton Wright who had it as above. NB. her son Wright sold the Farm Lot number 6 in Jekyl Tything to William Russell
Original grantee: John Norton Wright

Claimant's Name: Thomas Frazer
Acres: 50

Situation of lands: Lot number 5 at Vernonburgh granted by the late President and Assistants.
Original grantee: Thomas Frazer

Claimant's Name: Catherine Fleming
Acres: 50

Situation of lands: Town Lot number 8 in third Tything Upper New Ward Lot number 1 Garden Lot number 149 east granted to John Smith by him transferred August 31, 1750 to George Uland who transferd (sic) it January 8, 1754 to Walter and Catherine Fleming.
Original grantee: John Smith

Claimant's Name: Henry Fletcher
Acres: 50

Situation of lands: Lot number 3 in the District of Abercorn.
Original grantee: None shown

Claimant's Name: John Fox
Acres: 400

Situation of lands: Situate on the south branch of Little OgecheeRiver adjoining David Fox by warrant from the President and Assistants.
Original grantee: John Fox

Claimant's Name: Thomas Goldsmith
Acres: 500

Situation of lands: Called the Golden Grove on the north east side of Midway River granted by the President and Assistants the 12th May 1752.
Original grantee: Thomas Goldsmith

Claimant's Name: Thomas Goldsmith
Acres: 50

Situation of lands: Lot number 14 in the Town of Frederica bought of Doleman with 50 acres of land.
Original grantee: Doleman

Claimant's Name: Isaac Gibs (sic)
Acres: 50

Situation of lands: Town Lot in Abercorn number 1 the Farm Lot to ditto given by the Trustees.
Original grantee: Isaac Gibs

Claimant's Name: Philip Gibbs
Acres: 50

Situation of lands: Town Lot in Abercorn number 7 ditto Farm Lot given by ditto.
Original grantee: Philip Gibs (sic)

Claimant's Name: Isaac Gibbs Junr. (sic)
Acres: 50

Situation of lands: Joining Abercorn by warrant from the President and Assistants.
Original grantee: Isaac Gibs, Jnr. (sic)

Claimant's Name: Margaret Bailer by Isaac Gibs
Acres: 50

Situation of lands: Town Lot in Abercorn number 13 ditto a Farm Lot by warrant from the President and Assistants.
Original grantee: None shown

Claimant's Name: Thomas Antrobos by Isaac Gibs
Acres: 50.

Situation of lands: Town Lot in Abercorn number 13 ditto a Farm Lot given by General Oglehtorpe.
Original grantee: Thomas Antrobos

Claimant's Name: Walter Fox by Isaac Gibs
Acres: 50

Situation of lands: Town Lot in Wilmington Tything Darby Ward given by General Oglethorpe.
Original grantee: Walter Fox

Claimant's Name: James Garvis
Acres: 1

Situation of lands: Lot in the Town of Augusta number 9 bought of Thomas Goodale granted him by an order from the President and Assistants.
Original grantee: Thomas Goodale

Claimant's Name: John Goldwire by Charles Watson
Acres: 50

Situation of lands: On right of his wife Town Lot in Savannah number 4 in the Fourth Tything of the Lower New Ward alias Reynolds Ward with a Garden and Farm Lot granted by the late Trustees to Robert Redford deceased.
Original grantee: Robert Redford

Claimant's Name: Anthony Groobs
Acres: 100

Situation of lands: Bounding on the south west side by lands of Thomas Ross and on all other sides by vacant land warrant from the President and Assistants the 12th of January 1747.
Original grantee: Anthony Groobs

Claimant's Name: Edward Goodale by Thomas Ellis
Acres: 300

Situation of lands: Lying south of lands granted Walter Fleming and west of James Dixse on the south branch of Little Ogechee granted by the President and Assistants 1753.
Original grantee: Edward Goodale

Claimant's Name: William Gibbons
Acres: 360

Situation of lands: Situate joining Newington Village granted by the President and Assistants 1754.
Original grantee: William Gibbons

Claimant's Name: William Gibbons
Acres: 250

Situation of lands: Situate on the head of Little Ogechee granted by President and Assistants.
Original grantee: William Gibbons

Claimant's Name: Mungoe Graham by will from Pat Graham Esqr.
Acres: 450

Situation of lands: Near Pipemakers Creek on Savannah River by the late President and Assistants 28th April 1752.
Original grantee: Pat Graham, Esqr.

Claimant's Name: George Grass
Acres: 50

Situation of lands: On Black Creek in Josephs Town.
Original grantee: George Grass

Claimant's Name: John Gabel
Acres: 50

Situation of lands: Lot at Abercorn number 12.
Original grantee: John Gabel

Claimant's Name: John Gabel
Acres: 50

Situation of lands: Lot at Abercorn adjoing the above.
Original grantee: John Gabel

Claimant's Name: Francis Harris
Acres: 50

Situation of lands: Number 1 in Fredericks Tything Derby Ward Garden Lot number 14 east Farm Lot number 6 by purchase of Joseph Stanley who had it granted by the late Trustees.
Original grantee: Joseph Stanley

Claimant's Name: Francis Harris
Acres: 500

Situation of lands: On the head of the north branch of Little Ogechee by warrant from the late President and Assistants.
Original grantee: Francis Harris

Claimant's Name: Francis Harris for Thomas Harris
Acres: 500

Situation of lands: Tract adjoining the above tract by the late President and Assistants.
Original grantee: Thomas Harris

Claimant's Name: Thomas Egerton by Messrs. Harris and
                   Habersham
Acres: 50

Situation of lands: Town Lot in Savannah number 5 in More Tything Percival Ward Garden Lot number 17 west Farm Lot number 3 granted by the late Trustees.
Original grantee: Thomas Egerton

Claimant's Name: Thomas Jones by Messrs. Harris and Habersham
Acres: 50

Situation of lands: Town Lot in Savannah number 2 in Carpenters Tything Deckers Ward Garden Lot number 40 east Farm Lot number 5 by purchase of Rebecca the relict of Paul Cheesewright.
Original grantee: Charles Cheesewright

Claimant's Name: Pytt and Tuckwell by Messrs. Harris and Habersham
Acres: 50

Situation of lands: Town Lot in Savannah number 5 in the Second Tything Lower New Ward Garden Lot number 78 east Farm Lot number 3 granted to John Brownfield by the Trustees and by him sold to the said Pytt and Tuckwell.
Original grantee: John Brownfield

Claimant's Name: George Austin by Messrs. Harris and Habersham
Acres: 50

Situation of lands: Town Lot in Savannah number 8 in Laroche Tything Heathcote Ward Garden Lot number 36 (?) west Farm Lot number 2 granted to Henry Garret by the late Trustees and by him sold to the said George Austin.
Original grantee: Henry Garret

Claimant's Name: William Woodroffe by Messrs. Harris and Habersham
Acres: 50

Situation of lands: Town Lot in Savannah number 5 in Laroche Tything Heathcote Ward Garden Lot number 36 west Farm Lot number 8 granted by the late Trustees.
Original grantee: William Woodroffe

Claimant's Name: Elisha Foster by Messrs, Harris and
                   Habersham
Acres: 50

Situation of lands: Town Lot in Savannah number 9 Tower
Tything Decker Ward Garden Lot number 44 west Farm Lot
number 3 granted by the late Trustees.
Original grantee: Elisha Foster

Claimant's Name: Sir Patrick Houstoun Bart.
Acres: 500

Situation of lands: West by Little Ogechee River east by
Vernon River south by a creek leading from Little Ogechee
to Vernon River north by lands granted to James Houstoun
by grant from the Trustees dated 1st August 1733.
Original grantee: Sir Patrick Houstoun Bart.

Claimant's Name: Priscilla Dunbar by Sir Patrick Houston
Acres: 50

Situation of lands: Town Lot in Frederica number 3 in
Archers Ward by General Oglehtorpe 1738.
Original grantee: Priscilla Dunbar

Claimant's Name: George Houstoun
Acres: 450

Situation of lands: By the late President and Assistants
to Captain Raymond Demere November 3rd 1748.
Original grantee: Raymond Demere

Claimant's Name: Samuel Hutson
Acres: 400

Situation of lands: On Black Creek about eight miles
above Mount Pleasant bounded east by Savannah River and
on all sides by vacant land by grant from the President
and Assistants 8th November 1754.
Original grantee: Samuel Hutson

Claimant's Name: Robert Hutson
Acres: 100

Situation of lands: On Barton Branch about seven miles above Mount Pleasant bounded east by Savannah River and on all other sides by vacant land by grant from the President and Assistants 9th November 1754.
Original grantee: Robert Hutson

Claimant's Name: David Humbert Ex^d and att. 13th May 1757
Acres: 300

Situation of lands: Lying at a place called Turkey Cock Hill on the west side of Pipemakers Creek bounded north west on land of Joseph Raymond granted by the late President and Assistants in 1754.
Original grantee: David Humbert

Claimant's Name: John Hanner by Charles Watson Ex^d and
                   att. 19th May 1757
Acres: 100

Situation of lands: Lying on the south branch of Little Ogechee River adjoining lands there of John Raddick granted by the late President and Assistants.
Original grantee: John Hanner

Claimant's Name: John Harn by Charles Watson
Acres: 500

Situation of lands: Lying on the south side of Great Ogechee River granted him by the late President and Assistants in 1745.
Original grantee: John Harn

Claimant's Name: John Harn by Charles Watson
Acres: 100

Situation of lands: On the south side of the Great Ogechee River heretofore granted John Nevie.
Original grantee: John Nevie

Claimant's Name: John Harn by Charles Watson
Acres: 500

Situation of lands: On the same side of the said river purchased of Stephen Williams in the year 1753.
Original grantee: Stephen Williams

Claimant's Name: John Harn by Charles Watson
Acres: 300

Situation of lands: On the same side of the said river Ogechee purchased of Martin Fenton.
Original grantee: Martin Fenton

Claimant's Name: John Harn by Charles Watson
Acres: 400

Situation of lands: On Great Ogechee River aforesaid at a place called Sterlings Swamp purchased of Valentine Bostick.
Original grantee: Valentine Bostick

Claimant's Name: John Harn by Charles Watson
Acres: 500

Situation of lands: On behalf of his son William Harn a minor on the same river granted his said son by the late President and Assistants.
Original grantee: William Harn

Claimant's Name: James Haselfoot by Charles Watson
Acres: 500

Situation of lands: By Samuel Mercer claims one hundred fifty acres of land in the province not yet set out under a grant from the late Trustees bearing date 27th February 1733 and entered in the office of the auditor of the plantations.
Original grantee: James Haselfoot

Claimant's Name: John Hamm
Acres: 500

Situation of lands: Up the River Savannah bought of Mr. James McLaren.
Original grantee: James McLaren

Claimant's Name: John Hamm
Acres: 500

Situation of lands: Up the River Savannah situated south west of lands granted to John Ross and bounded north west by the Germans on Black Creek and Goshen granted by the late President and Assistants 1754.
Original grantee: John Hamm

Claimant's Name: John Hinlin
Acres: 50

Situation of lands: At the Black Creek bounding east to Lucas Moser to the south Matthias Seckinger to the west to John Hinuich to the north George Gress by the late President and Assistants.
Original grantee: John Hinlin

Claimant's Name: James Houstoun
Acres: 500

Situation of lands: West by Little Ogechee River east by Vernon River north by vacant lands south by lands granted to Sir Patrick Houstoun by grant of the late Trustees dated the 14th November 1733.
Original grantee: James Houstoun

Claimant's Name: John George Heinoy
Acres: 50

Situation of lands: On Black Creek and Josephs Town.
Original grantee: John George Heinoy

Claimant's Name: Frederick Helvenston
Acres: 50

Situation of lands: Lot in the district of Abercorn number 6
Original grantee: Frederick Helvenston

Claimant's Name: George Johnson by Charles Watson
Acres: 50

Situation of lands: Lot in Savannah number 3 in the Second Tything of the Upper New Ward alias Anson Ward with a Garden and Farm Lot granted him by the late President and Assistants about the year 1742.
Original grantee: George Johnson

Claimant's Name: William Johnston
Acres: 50

Situation of lands: Lot number 7 upon Skidoway Island.
Original grantee: William Johnston

Claimant's Name: Jacob Illy
Acres: 50

Situation of lands: On Black Creek in Josephs Town.
Original grantee: Jacob Illy

Claimant's Name: Richard Johnston
Acres: 400

Situation of lands: About four miles from Little River and thirty from Augusta namely 324 and 76 on the main granted to him by the late Trustees 24th December 1747.
Original grantee: Richard Johnston

Claimant's Name: Richard Johnston
Acres: 150

Situation of lands: At a place known by the name of Spirit Creek granted to James Derisou by the late President and Assistants which said Johnston has bought.
Original grantee: James Dourowzeau

Claimant's Name: Richard Johnston
Acres: None shown

Situation of lands: Lot in Augusta Township opposite to Rea (sic) and Barksdale.
Original grantee: None shown

Claimant's Name: Theobold Keiffer
Acres: 400

Situation of lands: Butting and bounding east on the River Savannah south on Mr. John Henry Grive's land and on all other sides on vacant land in Hallifax by warrant from the President and Assistants 11th December 1752.
Original grantee: Theobold Keiffer

Claimant's Name: Theobold Keiffer
Acres: 50

Situation of lands: Namely 32½ acres butting and bounding north east on the River Savannah north west Joseph Leitner south west on Paul Miller south east on vacant land 17½ acres north east on Joseph Leitner's south east on Paul Miller and on all other sides on vacant land in the name of his father-in-law Matthias Bacher deceased which he received from George Sanfleben in 1742 in exchange for his right first laid out by Hugh Ross and by order of the late President and Assistants to Thomas Ellis run over again and possession given to said Keiffer in 1751.
Original grantee: None shown

Claimant's Name: Theobold Keiffer
Acres: 2

Situation of lands: Garden Lot in the first row the second number on the north side.
Original grantee: None shown

Claimant's Name: Theobold Keiffer
Acres: None shown

Situation of lands: Town Lot in the Town of Ebenezer in the first row in the last division on the north side the second number bounding south on Charles Flerl north on John George Meyer.
Original grantee: None shown

Claimant's Name: Hugh Kennedy
Acres: 50

Situation of lands: Situated near a lagoon opposite to the
Two Sisters on Savannah River about eight miles below Mount
Pleasant bounding east the said lagoon south and west
vacant land north by my (sic) [his] brother William Kennedy by
warrant of the President and Assistants 9th August 1754.
Original grantee: Hugh Kennedy

Claimant's Name: William Kennedy
Acres: 50

Situation of lands: Situated near a large lagoon
opposite the Two Sisters on Savannah River about 8 miles
below Mount Pleasant bounding east the said large
lagoon south by his brother Hugh Kennedy west and north
by vacant land by warrant of ditto.
Original grantee: William Kennedy

Claimant's Name: Jacob Keibler by Charles Watson Ex^d and
                   Att. 13th May 1757
Acres: 50

Situation of lands: Lying in the Village of Goshen near
lands of Matthias West and John Staley granted about six
years ago by the late Presidents and Assistants.
Original grantee: None shown

Claimant's Name: Harman Henry Lemke
Acres: 500

Situation of lands: In the District of Josephs Town
bounding east on a large swamp on Savannah River south on
Mr. Hamm's plantation north on Rev^d Mr. Bolzius and west
of mere pine land by order of the late President and
Assistants.
Original grantee: Harman Henry Lemke

Claimant's Name: William Little by Charles Watson
Acres: 50

Situation of lands: Town Lot in Savannah number 7 in Tyrconnel Tything Darby Ward with a Garden Lot and Farm Lot as only son and heir of William Little his father deceased.
Original grantee: William Little, the father

Claimant's Name: Anthony LeBon by Charles Watson
Acres: 50

Situation of lands: In Newington Villege granted him by the late President and Assistants in 1750.
Original grantee: Anthony LeBon

Claimant's Name: Adrian Loyer
Acres: 50

Situation of lands: Town Lot number 9 in Belitha Tything Heathcote Ward with Garden and Farm Lot granted to his father Adrian Loyer deceased by the Trustees.
Original grantee: Adrian Loyer the father

Claimant's Name: Samuel Lion
Acres: 50

Situation of lands: Half Moon Bluff on Skidoway Island by the President and Assistants 1753.
Original grantee: Samuel Lions

Claimant's Name: Isaac Lines
Acres: 500

Situation of lands: At the head of Midway River allotment of the late President and Assistants 14th March 1749/50.
Original grantee: Isaac Lines

Claimant's Name: William Low for Alexander Low
Acres: 500

Situation of lands: On the south side of the south branch of Newport River by the late President and Assistants April 4th 1754.
Original grantee: Alexander Low

Claimant's Name: John Warnock for James Lenox
Acres: 50

Situation of lands: Town Lot in Township of Vernonburgh by the late President and Assistants.
Original grantee: James Lenox

Claimant's Name: George Lambreek
Acres: 50

Situation of lands: On Black Creek granted by the President and Assistants.
Original grantee: George Lambreek

Claimant's Name: John Stevens by James Mackay
Acres: 500

Situation of lands: On the south side of Great Ogechee River by the late President and Assistants 20th May 1752.
Original grantee: John Stevens

Claimant's Name: Hugh Mackay by James Mackay
Acres: 500

Situation of lands: On the south side of the Great Ogechee by the late President and Assistants 5th June 1752.
Original grantee: Hugh Mackay

Claimant's Name: Patrick Sutherland by James Mackay
Acres: 500

Situation of lands: On the north side of Sapola River by the late President and Assistants.
Original grantee: Patrick Sutherland

Claimant's Name: John Gray by James Mackay
Acres: 500

Situation of lands: On the north side of the Sapola River by the late President and Assistants.
Original grantee: John Gray

Claimant's Name: Captain James Mackay bought from Thomas Sumner
Acres: 50

Situation of lands: Town Lot in Frederica number 6 on the south side of Talbot Street with Garden and Farm Lots thereunto belonging granted by General Oglethorpe to William Allan 1736 and sold by him to Thomas Sumner.
Original grantee: William Allan

Claimant's Name: Captain James Mackay
Acres: 50

Situation of lands: Town Lot in Frederica number 6 north side of Talbot Street with Garden and Farm Lots granted by General Oglethorpe to Daniel Cannon 1736 bought of Joseph Cannon eldest son of Daniel.
Original grantee: Daniel Cannon

Claimant's Name: Captain James Mackay
Acres: 50

Situation of lands: Town Lot in Frederica number 15 in Traces Ward with Garden and Farm Lots granted by General Oglethorpe to Anna Stevens 1742.
Original grantee: Anna Stevens

Claimant's Name: Captain James Mackay
Acres: ~~50~~

Situation of lands: Town Lot in Hardwicke number 59 by the late President and Assistants ~~9th November 1743~~ 30th June 1754.
Original grantee: James Mackay

Claimant's Name: Captain James Mackay
Acres: 500

Situation of lands: On the south side of the Great Ogechee
River by General Oglethorpe 9th November 1748.
Original grantee: James Mackay

Claimant's Name: Lucas Moser
Acres: 50

Situation of lands: On Black Creek by purchase of John
~~granted~~ Sherehouse granted Nicklaus Helmly.
Original grantee: Nicklaus Helmly

Claimant's Name: William Mackintosh
Acres: 500

Situation of lands: On the south side of the north branch
of Newport River granted by the President and Assistants
in 1754.
Original grantee: William Mackintosh

Claimant's Name: John Mackintosh
Acres: 500

Situation of lands: On the south side of Sappola River
granted by the President and Assistants.
Original grantee: John Mackintosh

Claimant's Name: Roderick Mackintosh
Acres: 500

Situation of lands: On the north branch of Sappola River
granted by the President and Assistants in 1754.
Original grantee: Roderick Mackintosh

Claimant's Name: Donald Mackay, Jr.
Acres: 250

Situation of lands: On the south side of the north branch
of Newport River granted by President and Assistants in 1754.
Original grantee: Donald Mackay, Junr.

Claimant's Name: John McBean
Acres: 100

Situation of lands: Known by the name of the Second Swamp granted by the President and Assistants in 1753.
Original grantee: John McBean

Claimant's Name: George McDonald
Acres: 150

Situation of lands: At the head of a creek on the north side of Sapola River granted by the President and Assistants in 1754.
Original grantee: George McDonald

Claimant's Name: Donald Kennedy
Acres: 150

Situation of lands: On the north side of Sapola River granted by the President and Assistants in 1753.
Original grantee: Donald Kennedy

Claimant's Name: Angus Mackintosh
Acres: 100

Situation of lands: Adjoining the lands of Alexander Mackdonald granted by the President and Assistants in 1754.
Original grantee: Angus Mackintosh

Claimant's Name: Donald Mackay, Senr.
Acres: 150

Situation of lands: Situated at a place known by the name of Turkey Camp Swamp granted by the President and Assistants in 1754.
Original grantee: Donald Mackay Senr.

Claimant's Name: Donald McLeod son of John
Acres: 50

Situation of lands: Granted as a bounty to all disbanded soldiers from General Oglethorpe's Regiment.
Original grantee: John McLeod deceased

Claimant's Name: James Stewart
Acres: 50

Situation of lands: On the north branch of Sappola River granted by the President and Assistants in 1749.
Original grantee: John Stuart (sic)

Claimant's Name: George Kidd
Acres: 50

Situation of lands: On Cat Head Creek granted by the President and Assistants in 1749.
Original grantee: George Kidd

Claimant's Name: Donald McDonald
Acres: 50

Situation of lands: Granted as a disbanded soldier from General Oglethorpe's Regiment.
Original grantee: Norman McDonald

Claimant's Name: Donald McDonald
Acres: 50

Situation of lands: Town Lot in Darien with 50 acres of land belonging thereto.
Original grantee: Norman McDonald

Claimant's Name: Donald Ross
Acres: 50

Situation of lands: Granted as a disbanded soldier.
Original grantee: Donald Ross

Claimant's Name: William Mackay
Acres: 50

Situation of lands: Granted as a disbanded soldier.
Original grantee: William Mackay

Claimant's Name: William Mackay
Acres: 50

Situation of lands: Granted as a disbanded soldier.
Original grantee: George Douglass deceased

Claimant's Name: William Mackay
Acres: Town Lot in Darien with a fifty acre lot belonging thereto.
Original grantee: George Douglass deceased

Claimant's Name: James Munroe
Acres: 50

Situation of lands: Granted as a disbanded soldier.
Original grantee: James Munroe

Claimant's Name: David Miller
Acres: 50

Situation of lands: Granted as a disbanded soldier.
Original grantee: David Miller

Claimant's Name: John Mackay
Acres: 50

Situation of lands: Granted as a disbanded soldier.
Original grantee: John Mackay

Claimant's Name: John Mackay
Acres: 5

Situation of lands: Town Lot in Darien with five acres thereunto belonging.
Original grantee: John Mackay

Claimant's Name: Roderick McLeod
Acres: 50

Situation of lands: Granted as a disbanded soldier.
Original grantee: Roderick McLeod

Claimant's Name: John Grant
Acres: 50

Situation of lands: Granted as a disbanded soldier.
Original grantee: John Grant

Claimant's Name: William Munroe
Acres: 50

Situation of lands: Town Lot in Darien with 50 acres of land thereunto belonging.
Original grantee: William Munroe

Claimant's Name: Mordah McLeod
Acres: 50

Situation of lands: At a place known by the name of Cane Savannah granted by the President and Assistants in the year 1754.
Original grantee: Mordah McLeod

Claimant's Name: Ronald McDonald
Acres: 50

Situation of lands: One Town Lot in Darien
Original grantee: Ronald McDonald

Claimant's Name: Ronald McDonald
Acres: 50   50

Situation of lands: Two Town Lots in Darien left him by the decease of two freeholders there.
Original grantee: None shown

Claimant's Name: Donald Mackenzie
Acres: 50

Situation of lands: Granted as a disbanded soldier on the south side of Sappola River.
Original grantee: Donald Mackenzie

Claimant's Name: Peter Grant
Acres: 50

Situation of lands: Granted as a disbanded soldier on the south side of Sappola River bounded on the north by said river on the west by fifty acres granted him in behalf of his mother by the Presidents and Assistants in 1754.
Original grantee: Peter Grant

Claimant's Name: Gilbert Grant
Acres: None shown

Situation of lands: Town Lot in Darien granted him in the year 1744.
Original grantee: Gilbert Grant

Claimant's Name: Hugh Morrison
Acres: 150

Situation of lands: On the head of the Sappola River granted by the President and Assistants.
Original grantee: Hugh Morrison

Claimant's Name: John Mackintosh B
Acres: 500

Situation of lands: John Mackintosh B situated on the north east side of Sappola River bounding on the south by said river on the west by a fifty acre lot which he purchased from William Harper a disbanded soldier on all other sides by vacant lands by the President and Assistants 3rd October 1746.
Original grantee: William Harper

Claimant's Name: John Mackintosh B
Acres: 50 50 50

Situation of lands: Three lots in the Town of Darien with fifty acres of land belonging to each of the lots.
Original grantee: John Mackintosh B

Claimant's Name: John Mackintosh M
Acres: 500

Situation of lands: Granted by the President and Assistants in 1750 on Black Island which said island not containing the full quantity they granted the remainder in a place known by the name of Turkey Camp Swamp.
Original grantee: John Mackintosh M

Claimant's Name: John Mackintosh M
Acres: 50   50

Situation of lands: Two lots in Darien with fifty acres of land belonging to each said lot.
Original grantee: None shown

Claimant's Name: Hugh Clarke
Acres: 500

Situation of lands: By the President and Assistants in 1750 on the head of Sappola River.
Original grantee: Hugh Clarke

Claimant's Name: Hugh Clarke
Acres: 50

Situation of lands: Town Lot in Darien with fifty acres of land belonging thereto.
Original grantee: None shown

Claimant's Name: Donald Clarke
Acres: 500

Situation of lands: By the President and Assistants in 1750 on a branch of the Buffaloe Swamp known by the name of Catthead.
Original grantee: Donald Clarke

Claimant's Name: Donald Clarke
Acres: 50   50   50

Situation of lands: Three Town Lots in Darien with fifty acres of land belonging to each said lot.
Original grantee: None shown

Claimant's Name: Lachlan Mackintosh
Acres: 500

Situation of lands: Granted by the President and Assisttants in 1750 on the north branch of Newport River.
Original grantee: Lachlan Mackintosh

Claimant's Name: Angus Clarke
Acres: 500

Situation of lands: Granted by the President and Assistants in 1750 on the north side of the Sapola River.
Original grantee: Angus Clarke

Claimant's Name: George Mackintosh
Acres: 500

Situation of lands: Granted by the President and Assistants in 1753 on the head of Sapola River.
Original grantee: George Mackintosh

Claimant's Name: William Clarke
Acres: 500

Situation of lands: Granted by the President and Assistants in 1750 on the south side of Sapola River known by the name of Cedar Bluff.
Original grantee: William Clarke

Claimant's Name: Henry Calwell
Acres: 500

Situation of lands: Granted by President and Assistants in 1753 on the north east side of Sapola River known by the name of Calwell's Point.
Original grantee: Henry Calwell

Claimant's Name: Alexander Mackdonald
Acres: 150

Situation of lands: Granted by the President and Assistants in 1744 on the north side of Sapola River.
Original grantee: Alexander Mackdonald.

Claimant's Name: Alexander Mackdonald
Acres: 50

Situation of lands: Town Lot in Darien with fifty acres of land belonging thereunto.
Original grantee: Alexander Mackdonald.

Claimant's Name: Samuel Marcer by Charles Watson
Acres: 50

Situation of lands: Lot in the Town of Savannah number 9 in Hucks Tything Percival Ward with a Garden and Farm Lot thereunto belonging granted by the late Trustees.
Original grantee: Samuel Marcer

Claimant's Name: Samuel Marcer by Charles Watson
Acres: 450

Situation of lands: Lying on Vernon River known by the name of Horseforth adjoining lands of Mr. Newdigate Stephens called Bewlie of which said lands 300 acres were granted by the late Trustees about the year 1739 and the residue by the late President and Assistants in 1753.
Original grantee: Samuel Marcer

Claimant's Name: Samuel Marcer by Charles Watson for
                   Elizabeth his wife.
Acres: 50

Situation of lands: In right of Elizabeth his wife a lot in the Town of Savannah number 7 in the Second Tything Upper New Ward alias Anson Ward with Garden and Farm lots thereunto belonging devised to the said Elizabeth by will of William Cross her former husband dated 4th August 1737.
Original grantee: William Cross

Claimant's Name: Samuel Marcer by Charles Watson for
                   Elizabeth his wife
Acres: 50

Situation of lands: In right of Elizabeth his wife a lot in the Town of Savannah number 5 in the Third Tything of the Lower New Ward alias Reynolds Ward with Garden and Farm Lot thereunto belonging devised to said Elizabeth by the will of John Tisdale her late husband dated 2d May 1752.
Original grantee: John Tisdale

Claimant's Name: Samuel Marcer by Charles Watson for
                   Elizabeth his wife
Acres: 50

Situation of lands: In right of Elizabeth his wife a lot of land on the Island of Skidoway devised to her by will of said John Tisdale which premises were heretofore the estate of Charles Wheeler.
Original grantee: Charles Wheeler

Claimant's Name: Samuel Marcer by Charles Watson for
                   Elizabeth his wife
Acres: 50

Situation of lands: In right of Elizabeth his wife a lot of land on the Great Ogechee near to Fort Argyle granted to the said John Teasdale deceased by the late Trustees and devised to the said Elizabeth in and by the will last mentioned.
Original grantee: John Tisdale

Claimant's Name: Samuel Marcer for Elizabeth his wife
Acres: 50

Situation of lands: In right and for the life of Elizabeth his said wife the said Samuel Marcer claims a lot in the Town of Savannah number 1 Wilmington Tything Darby Ward with a Garden and Farm Lot thereunto belonging containing in the whole fifty acres of land devised to the said Elizabeth in and by the will last mentioned the reversion and inheritance of which premises in and by the said will is vested in John Tisdale son of the said deceased.
Original grantee: None shown

Claimant's Name: John Ludwig Meyer
Acres: 200

Situation of lands: Situated on the Mill or Abercorn Creek granted by the late President and Assistants in the year 1749 bounding towards east on the said creek towards south on Christian Riedelsperger and John Ulrich Fetzer towards west vacant pine land and towards north on Mr. David Krafft deceased.
Original grantee: John Ludwig Meyer

Claimant's Name: John Ludwig Meyer
Acres: 2

Situation of lands: Garden and Town Lot the Garden situated on the east side of the town between George Kogler and Christian Riedelsperger Town Lot in the IIId row first division the Ist lot.
Original grantee: None shown

Claimant's Name: Abraham Minis by Charles Watson
Acres: 50

Situation of lands: Lot in the Town of Savannah number 4 in Hucks Tything Percival Ward with Garden and Farm Lot granted by the late Trustees.
Original grantee: Abraham Minis

Claimant's Name: Minis Minis by Charles Watson
Acres: 50

Situation of lands: Lot in the Town of Savannah number 5 in the Second Tything Upper New Ward alias Anson Ward with Garden and Farm Lot granted him by the late Trustees.
Original grantee: Minis Minis

Claimant's Name: Esther Minis and Joseph Minis by Charles
                   Watson
Acres: 50

Situation of lands: Claim each of them as (Tenants in Common) an undivided moiety or half part of and in a lot in the Town of Savannah number 2 Vernon Tything Heathcote Ward with a Garden and Farm Lot thereunto belonging by gift from their Uncle Simeon Minis.
Original grantee: Simeon Minis

Claimant's Name: David Montaigut by Charles Watson
Acres: 50

Situation of lands: Lot in Savannah number 5 in the First Tything of the Lower New Ward alias Reynolds Ward with a Garden and Farm Lot as eldest son and heir of Samuel Montaigut deceased.
Original grantee: Samuel Montaigut

Claimant's Name: David Montaigut by Charles Watson
Acres: 500

Situation of lands: Lying about eight miles west of the Town of Savannah granted him by the late President and Assistants.
Original grantee: David Montaigut

Claimant's Name: Lewis Micher by Charles Watson Ex^d and att. 13th May 1757
Acres: 50

Situation of lands: Adjoining the lands of Newington Village and lands of Joseph Gibbons granted by the late President and Assistants.
Original grantee: Lewis Micher

Claimant's Name: Peter Manley by Charles Watson Ex^d and att. 13th May 1757
Acres: 50

Situation of lands: Lot in Savannah number 4 in Holland Tything Percival Ward with Garden and Farm Lot as heir of Henry Manley his father.
Original grantee: Henry Manley

Claimant's Name:　John Muir by Charles Watson Ex.^{d} and att. 13th May 1757
Acres:　50

Situation of lands:　Lot in Savannah number 8 in Jekyl Tything Darby Ward with Garden and Farm Lot as son and heir of James Muir his father deceased to whom the same was granted by the late Trustees.
Original grantee:　James Muir

Claimant's Name:　Richard Mellichamp by Charles Watson
Acres:　50

Situation of lands:　Town Lot in Savannah number 10 in Vernon Tything Heathcote Ward with Garden and Farm Lot granted him by the late Trustees.
Original grantee:　Richard Mellichamp

Claimant's Name:　John Mackay by Charles Watson
Acres:　94½

Situation of lands:　Lying on Little Ogechee adjoining lands of John Milledge being part of one hundred acres granted him by the late President and Assistants.
Original grantee:　John Mackay

Claimant's Name:　Patrick Mackay by Charles Watson
Acres:　50

Situation of lands:　Lot in Savannah number 5 in Digby Tything Decker Ward with Garden and Farm Lot by purchase from Thomas Ellis.
Original grantee:　None shown

Claimant's Name:　Patrick Mackay by Charles Watson
Acres:　640

Situation of lands:　At Joseph Town containing forty chains in front on the River Savannah and one hundred and sixty chains back.
Original grantee:　Patrick Mackay

Claimant's Name: Patrick Mackay by Charles Watson
Acres: 640

Situarion of lands: Tract of the same quantity adjoining thereto both which tracts were granted him (the one in his own name the other in the name of his brother John Mackay) by the late Trustees in 1734 and in January 1736 the claimant imported (on the ship called the Prince of Wales George Dunbar Commander) thirty white servants agreeable to the conditions stipulated by the said Trustees.
Original grantee: John Mackay

Claimant's Name: William Mackay ~~James Dean by Charles Watson~~
Acres: 50

Situation of lands: Town Lot in Savannah number 9 in Eyles Tything Heathcote Ward with Garden and Farm Lot formerly James Dean's and granted the said William by the late President and Assistants.
Original grantee: James Dean

Claimant's Name: William Mackay by Charles Watson
Acres: 50

Situation of lands: At Darian (sic) contained in a Town Lot Garden and Farm Lot as eldest son and heir of John Mackay deceased.
Original grantee: John Mackay

Claimant's Name: John Milledge by Charles Watson
Acres: 50

Situation of lands: Lot in the Town of Savannah number 1 in Hucks Tything Percival Ward with Garden and Farm Lot granted him by the late Trustees.
Original grantee: John Milledge

Claimant's Name: John Milledge by Charles Watson
Acres: 50

Situation of lands: Town Lot in Savannah number 5 in Belitha Tything Heathcote Ward with Garden and Farm Lot purchased of the widow of George Roan about six years ago.
Original grantee: George Roan

Claimant's Name: John Milledge by Charles Watson
Acres: 400

Situation of lands: On the south side of Little Ogechee River adjoining lands of Joseph Phillips granted him by the late President and Assistants.
Original grantee: John Milledge

Claimant's Name: John Milledge by Charles Watson
Acres: 5 3/4

Situation of lands: Adjoining the said four hundred acres purchased of John Mackay.
Original grantee: John Mackay

Claimant's Name: John Milledge by Charles Watson
Acres: 50

Situation of lands: In the Village of Acton devised the said John in and by the last will of Robert Fox deceased.
Original grantee: Robert Fox

Claimant's Name: John Milledge by Charles Watson
Acres: 50

Situation of lands: For and in the right of his wife lot in the Town of Savannah with Garden and Farm Lot granted his said wife (by the name of Ann Skidoway Smith) by the late President and Assistants.
Original grantee: Ann Skidoway Smith

Claimant's Name: John Milledge by Charles Watson
Acres: 50

Situation of lands: For and in the right of his wife a lot of land on the Island of Skidoway she the said Ann being the only daughter and heir of Thomas Smith deceased.
Original grantee: Thomas Smith

Claimant's Name: Laughlin McBean
Acres: 499   1

Situation of lands: Situate on the River Savannah butting and bounding to land of Mr. Thomas Goodale within a mile and a half of Fort Augusta with a Town Lot number 2 consisting of one acre by General Oglethorpe in 1737.
Original grantee: Laughlin McBean

Claimant's Name: Laughlin McBean
Acres: 100

Situation of lands: On the Great Kayuka Creek or Quioco Creek on the Cherokee Creek Path about fifteen miles distant from the Township of Augusta by the President and Assistants.
Original grantee: Laughlin McBean

Claimant's Name: Constance Mackintosh
Acres: 45   1

Situation of lands: In behalf of her son Henry on lot in the Town of Frederica known by the number 3 north with an acre lot and forty-five acres belonging to said Town Lot.
Original grantee: None shown

Claimant's Name: Constance Mackintosh
Acres: 50

Situation of lands: In behalf of her son John fifty acres granted him by General Oglethorpe in the year 1741 adjoining to the lands known by the name of Calwells Swamp.
Original grantee: None shown

Claimant's Name: Constance Mackintosh in behalf of her daughter Constance Calwell
Acres: 50

Situation of lands: One lot in the Town of Frederica purchased from Christopher Seymour and known in the plan of said town by number 15 south with fifty acres belonging thereto.
Original grantee: Christopher Seymour

Claimant's Name: Audley Maxwell
Acres: 500

Situation of lands: In the forks of Midway River butting north upon Nathan Taylor west upon Isaac Lines and south upon Audley Maxwell Junr. by warrant from the President and Assistants 16th December 1749.
Original Grantee: Audley Maxwell

Claimant's Name: Audley Maxwell for Audley Maxwell Junr.
Acres: 200

Situation of lands: Butting north upon the last mentioned tract and west upon Andrew Collins south upon Sam. Bacon and Captain Baillie by a warrant from the President and Assistants 27th November 1752.
Original grantee: Audley Maxwell Junr.

Claimant's Name: George Mackay
Acres: 70

Situation of lands: North west of Abercorn by warrant from the President and Assistants.
Original grantee: George Mackay

Claimant's Name: George Mackay
Acres: 50

Situation of lands: Joining the above lands by warrant from the President and Assistants.
Original grantee: Mary Gibbs now wife to Mackay

Claimant's Names: Lewis Mutteair
Acres: 200

Situation of lands: On the south side of the Great Ogechee River by warrant from the President and Assistants.
Original grantee: Lewis Mutteair

Claimant's Name: Lewis Mutteair
Acres: 100

Situation of lands: On the south side of Great Ogechee River granted by the President and Assistants to John Mathis Bashlaw and bought of him by the said Mutteair.
Original grantee: John Mathis Bashlaw

Claimant's Name: John Mitchell
Acres: 500

Situation of lands: South side of northernmost swamp of North Newport by allotment of the late President and Assistants July 11, 1752.
Original grantee: John Mitchell

Claimant's Name: Sarah Mitchell
Acres: 500

Situation of lands: A middle branch of North Newport by allotment of the late President and Assistants July 11, 1752.
Original grantee: Sarah Mitchell

Claimant's Name: Charles Mearn
Acres: 100

Situation of lands: On the south side of the Great Ogechee granted by the late President and Assistants.
Original grantee: Charles Mearns

Claimant's Name: John Philip Miller
Acres: 100

Situation of lands: South east from the Town of Savannah by warrant from the late President and Assistants 13th August 1753.
Original grantee: John Philip Miller

Claimant's Name: Henry Meyers
Acres: 50

Situation of lands: On the north side of Great Ogechee River bounded east lands granted Mr. John Willson and north of Mr. Richard J'on (Johnson?) granted by the late President and Assistants in 1752.
Original grantee: Henry Meyers

~~Laying on the north side of Great Ogechee River about three miles above the said fifty acres vacant on all sides~~. (Sic)

Claimant's Name: John Mearn
Acres: 100

Situation of lands: On the south side of Great Ogechee granted by the President and Assistants.
Original grantee: John Mearn

Claimant's Name: Peter Marauld
Acres: 50

Situation of lands: In Acton Township by the President and Assistants number 26.
Original grantee: Peter Marauld

Claimant's Name: Jonas Mick
Acres: 50

Situation of lands: Lot at Goshen number 7 by warrant from the President and Assistants.
Original grantee: Jonas Mick

Claimant's Name: Jacob More
Acres: 50

Situation of lands: Lot in Goshen number 18 by warrant from the President and Assistants.
Original grantee: Jacob More

Claimant's Name: Jacob More by purchase
Acres: 50

Situation of lands: Lot at Goshen number 1 granted to Melchior Muller by the President and Assistants.
Original grantee: Melchier Muller

Claimant's Name: George Noble
Acres: 100

Situation of lands: On Newport River joining Water Mellon Bluff granted by the President and Assistants 1754.
Original grantee: George Noble

Claimant's Name: Robert Noble
Acres: 100

Situation of lands: On Newport River at Water Mellon Bluff granted by the President and Assistants 1754.
Original grantee: Robert Noble

Claimant's Name: Daniel Nunes by Charles Watson
Acres: 50

Situation of lands: Lot in Savannah number 7 Carpenters Tything Decker Ward with Garden and Farm Lot granted him by the late Trustees.
Original grantee: Daniel Nunes

Claimant's Name: Daniel Nunes by Charles Watson
Acres: 50

Situation of lands: In the Town of Augusta lying between the lands of James Fraser and James Paris purchased by the said Nunes of Robert Vaughn.
Original grantee: Robert Vaughn

Claimant's Name: Daniel Nunes by Charles Watson for
                  Isaac Nunes Henricus
Acres: 50

Situation of lands: Lot in Savannah number 7 Digby Tything Decker Ward with Garden and Farm Lot granted by the late Trustees.
Original grantee: Isaac Nunes Henricus

Claimant's Name: Daniel Nunes by Charles Watson for
                  Abraham DeLeon
Acres: 50

Situation of lands: Lot in Savannah number 4 Towers Tything Decker Ward with Garden and Farm Lot granted by the late Trustees.
Original grantee: Abraham DeLeon

Claimant's Name: Daniel Nunes by Charles Watson for Abraham Molena
Acres: 50

Situation of lands: Lot in Savannah number 9 Heathcote Ward Tything Decker Ward with Garden and Farm Lot granted by the late Trustees.
Original grantee: Abraham Molena

Claimant's Name: John Osgood
Acres: 500

Situation of lands: On the north side of the north swamp of the Newport by allotment of the late President and Assistants July 11th 1752.
Original grantee: John Osgood

Claimant's Name: John Osgood
Acres: 300

Situation of lands: On the south side of Midway River in trust as the present Dissenting Minister.
Original grantee: Glebe

Claimant's Name: Josiah Osgood
Acres: 500

Situation of lands: On a middle branch of North Newport by allotment of the late President and Assistants July 11th 1752.
Original grantee: Josiah Osgood

Claimant's Name: Gasper Offstater
Acres: 117

Situation of lands: On an island about eight miles east south east of Savannah bounding south west on John Alther and on all other sides by creeks and marshes by warrant from the late President and Assistants 23rd March 1747.
Original grantee: Gasper Offstater

Claimant's Name: Gasper Offstater
Acres: None shown

Situation of lands: Town Lot in Savannah number 8 in Tower Tything by purchase of Ann Emery February 6th 1755.
Original grantee: None shown

Claimant's Name: Joseph Oakes
Acres: 300

Situation of lands: At a place called the Crooked Beaver Dams in Augusta District butting and bounding on the east by Laughlin McBean on the north by the fifty acre lots of Augusta and on all other sides by vacant lands by the President and Assistants.
Original grantee: Joseph Oakes

Claimant's Name: David Onseld
Acres: 50

Situation of lands: Near Abercorn Creek bound west on Ludwig Meyer's land.
Original grantee: David Onseld

Claimant's Name: John Price
Acres: 50

Situation of lands: Situated about one mile south east from the Town of Frederica and bounded on the back line of Captain Demere.
Original grantee: John Price

Claimant's Name: John Price for his wife
Acres: 50

Situation of lands: Lot in the Town of Frederica belonging to his wife which was widow of Henry Manly deceased granted to her and possession given her by Major William Horton.
Original grantee: None shown

Claimant's Name: Henry William Parker for his mother Ann Parker
Acres: 500

Situation of lands: On the north branch of the Little Ogechee River bounding on the said river and on lands belonging to Mr. Charles Watson and Captain Francis Harris in behalf of his mother Mrs. Ann Parker relict of Henry Parker Esqr. who had it by warrant from the late President and Assistants.
Original grantee: Henry Parker

Claimant's Name: Henry William Parker
Acres: 500

Situation of lands: Tract adjoining the above by warrant from the President and Assistants.
Original grantee: Henry William Parker

Claimant's Name: Henry William Parker for Joseph Parker his brother
Acres: 500

Situation of lands: Tract above the head of the said north branch adjoining the township lands and to lands belonging to Noble Wimberley Jones by warrant from the President and Assistants.
Original grantee: Joseph Parker

Claimant's Name: John Perkins
Acres: 500   50   50

Situation of lands: Situated on the Darien Salts and bounded on the east by a river flowing from Doboy on the south by two fifty acre lots which he purchased from two disbanded soldiers namely William Hill and William Dobins.
Original grantee: John Perkins   William Hill   William Dobins

Claimant's Name: John Perkins
Acres: 45   1

Situation of lands: Lot in the Town of Frederica number 25 south with an acre lot and forty five acres thereunto belonging formerly the property of Richard White deceased.
Original grantee: Richard White

Claimant's Name: Thomas Parker
Acres: 5 1/8

Situation of lands: Lot in the Town of Savannah in Tyrconnel Tything Darby Ward with a Garden Lot thereunto belonging as heir of Samuel Parker his brother.
Original grantee: Samuel Parker

Claimant's Name: Thomas Parker
Acres: 50

Situation of lands: Lot in the Town of Savannah number 3 in Hucks Tything Percival Ward with Garden and Farm Lot thereunto belonging under the same title.
Original grantee: Samuel Parker

~~An island between Vernon River and Little Ogeechee River~~

Claimant's Name: James Parris by Charles Watson
Acres: 350

Situation of lands: Lying at New Savannah (about twelve miles below Augusta) bounded north by Savannah River and west by land of William Gray granted him by the late President and Assistants.
Original grantee: James Parris

Claimant's Name: John Pye by Charles Watson
Acres: 50

Situation of lands: Lot in Savannah number 4 in Sloper Tything Percival Ward with Garden and Farm Lot formerly Waterman's.
Original grantee: Waterman's

Claimant's Name: John Pye by Charles Watson
Acres: 89 6/8

Situation of lands: Two Farm Lots in Hucks Tything
commonly called Trust Lots granted him by the late
President and Assistants.
Original grantee: John Pye

Claimant's Name: John Pye by Charles Watson
Acres: 200

Situation of lands: Near Highgate granted by the President
and Assistants in the year 1754.
Original grantee: John Pye

Claimant's Name: John Pye by Charles Watson for his wife
Acres: 50

Situation of lands: In right of his wife lot in Savannah
number 3 in Moore Tything Percival Ward with Garden and
Farm Lot formerly Robert Potter.
Original grantee: Robert Potter

Claimant's Name: Joseph Pruniere for his wife by Charles
                   Watson
Acres: 50

Situation of lands: In right of his wife a lot in
Savannah number 8 Carpenters Tything Deckers Ward with
Garden and Farm Lot formerly Peter Mallea's deceased
from the late Trustees.
Original grantee: Peter Mallea

Claimant's Name: John and Mary Penrose by Charles Watson
Acres: 50

Situation of lands: Henry Hamilton Benjamin Goldwire and
Richard Milledge the executors of John Penrose deceased on
the behalf of John and Mary Penrose infants the children of
the said deceased claim a lot in Savannah number 5 in Jekyl
Tything Darby Ward with Garden and Farm Lots granted the
deceased by the late Trustees.
Original grantee: John Penrose

Claimant's Name: John and Mary Penrose by Charles Watson
Acres: 50

Situation of lands: Lot in Savannah number 1 in Eyles Tything Heathcote Ward with Garden and Farm Lot purchased by the deceased of John Yoakley.
Original grantee: John Yoakley

Claimant's Name: John and Mary Penrose by Charles Watson
Acres: 300

Situation of lands: On Whitmarsh Island granted the said deceased by the late President and Assistants.
Original grantee: John Penrose

Claimant's Name: Thomas Palmer
Acres: 50

Situation of lands: Lot in Savannah number 7 in the Lower New Ward with Garden and Farm Lot.
Original grantee: Thomas Palmer

Claimant's Name: Thomas Palmer
Acres: 300

Situation of lands: At Thunderbolt on lease.
Original grantee: None shown

Claimant's Name: Jacob Portz
Acres: 50

Situation of lands: Lot at Goshen number 6.
Original grantee: Jacob Portz

Claimant's Name: John Quarterman
Acres: 500

Situation of lands: On the south side of the middle branch of Midway Swamp by allotment of the late President and Assistants July 11th 1752.
Original grantee: John Quarterman

Claimant's Name: James Rutherford by Charles Watson
Acres: 50

Situation of lands: Lot in Town of Savannah number 7 in Slopers Tything Percival Ward with Garden and Farm Lot thereunto belonging purchased of Solomon Delgrass son and heir of Francis Delgrass in March 1755.
Original grantee: Francis Delgrass

Claimant's Name: James Rutherford by Charles Watson
Acres: 50

Situation of lands: On behalf of Williamina (sic) Rutherford his daughter an infant a lot in the Town of Frederica with a Farm Lot thereunto belonging by deed of gift from Margaret Johnson widow 30th April 1755.
Original grantee: None shown

Claimant's Name: Christian Rabenhorst
Acres: 500

Situation of lands: In the District of Ebenezer situated partly upon the Main partly upon the island opposite on the Mill or Abercorn Creek bounding east of vacant land on the island south partly of Mr. David Krafft's plantation partly on the island and partly on the Main west of vacant pine land north of Michael Shneider and Christopher Cramer by the late President and Assistants 6th December 1753.
Original grantee: Christian Rabnehorst

Claimant's Name: Christian Rabenhorst for the heirs of
                  David Krafft deceased
Acres: 500

Situation of lands: In the District of Ebenezer about two miles below the Grist Mills on the said creek partly upon the Main partly on the island opposite bounding east of vacant land upon the said large island south on the island vacant on the Main Mr. John Ludwig Meyer and vacant pine land north of his own above mentioned 500 acres west of Mr. David Krafft deceased 5th June 1752.
Original grantee: David Krafft

Claimant's Name: Christian Rabenhorst for the heirs of
                  David Krafft deceased
Acres: None shown

Situation of lands: Town Lot granted to Mr. David Krafft
deceased under the Government of the Trustees and two
others which Mr. David Krafft purchased of John Pletter
deceased and of John Martin Rheinlander as the property
of his mother widow Rheinlander deceased.
Original grantee: None shown

Claimant's Name: Cunrad Rahn for his brother Casper Rahn
Acres: 100

Situation of lands: At Hallifax by warrant from the
President and Assistants 11th December 1752 bounding south
on land of Mr. Theobold Keeffer and all other sides vacant.
Original grantee: Casper Rahn

Claimant's Name: Sarah Rigby wife of Nicholas Rigby
                  by Charles Watson
Acres: 5 1/8

Situation of lands: Lot in the Town of Savannah number 2
in Jekyl Tything Darby Ward with a Garden Lot thereunto
belonging containing together 5 1/8 acres granted her by
the name of Sarah Milledge spinster by the late Trustees
about the year 1739.
Original grantee: None shown

Claimant's Name: John Raddick by Charles Watson
Acres: 100

Situation of lands: Lying on the south branch of Little
Ogechee River between lands of John Fox and Edward Carlton
granted him by the late President and Assistants.
Original grantee: John Raddick

Claimant's Name: Joseph Raymond by Charles Watson
Acres: 300

Situation of lands: At a place called Turkey Cock Hill on the west side of Pipemakers Creek bounded south east on David Humbert's land granted by the late President and Assistants in 1754.
Original grantee: Joseph Raymond

Claimant's Name: Thomas Red
Acres: 200

Situation of lands: Situate lying and being on Savannah River about fifteen miles above Augusta warrant from the President and Assistants 22d November 1751.
Original grantee: Thomas Red

Claimant's Name: Pickering Robinson Esq.
Acres: 500

Situation of lands: Called Rawcliff as per the Attorney General's Fiet. (sic)
Original grantee: Pickering Robinson Esq.

Claimant's Name: Pickering Robinson Esq. for Thomas Robinson
Acres: 500

Situation of lands: Called Mulberry Grove as per the Attorney General's Fiet.
Original grantee: Thomas Robinson

Claimant's Name: Pickering Robinson Esq. for Samuel Barker
Acres: 500

Situation of lands: Called Blendon as per the Attorney General's Fiet.
Original grantee: Samuel Barker

Claimant's Name: Pickering Robinson Esq.
Acres: None shown

Situation of lands: Town Lot number 95 at Hardwicke per the Attorney General's Fiet.
Original grantee: Pickering Robinson Esq.

Claimant's Name: Pickering Robinson Esq.
Acres: 50

Situation of lands: Town Lot in Savannah number 1 in the Second Tything Lower New Ward Farm Lot number 5 in the Second Tything Garden Lot number 80 east of the town granted by the late Trustees to Henry Lloyd and purchased of him.
Original grantee: Henry Lloyd

Claimant's Name: Pickering Robinson Esq.
Acres: 50

Situation of lands: Town Lot in Savannah number 10 in Tyrconnel Tything Farm Lot number 10 in Tyrconnel Tything Garden Lot number 6 east of the town granted by the late Trustees to Henry Close and purchased by him.
Original grantee: Henry Close

N. B. the Farm Lot number 5 in the Second Tything Lower New Ward sold to John Penrose.

N. B. The Farm Lot number 10 in Tyrconnel Tything sold to Richard Milledge.

Claimant's Name: Matthew Roche
Acres: 200

Situation of lands: Situate partly on Argyle Island between the lands of Mr. James DeVeaux and Mr. William Backshell and partly a small island of thirty acres in the River Savannah between the Islands of Onslow and Argyle from the President and Assistants.
Original grantee: Matthew Roche

Claimant's Name: George Riser
Acres: 50

Situation of lands: On Black Creek in Joseph's Town.
Original grantee: George Riser

Claimant's Name: Joseph Summers by Charles Watson
Acres: 50

Situation of lands: Lot in the Town of Savannah number 1 in Vernon Tything Heathcote Ward with Garden and Farm Lot thereunto belonging purchased of James Summers.
Original grantee: None shown

Claimant's Name: Joseph Summers by Charles Watson exd. and allowd. 11th May 1757
Acres: 300

Situation of lands: On the south side of Little Ogechee River adjoining lands of Richard Cooper granted by the late President and Assistants in 1747.
Original grantee: ~~Richard Cooper~~ Joseph Summers

Claimant's Name: Joseph Summers by Charles Watson exaied. and allowd. 11th May 1757
Acres: 270

Situation of lands: On the south side on the said Little River adjoining on one side to land of Joseph Phillips granted by the late President and Assistants in 1752.
Original grantee: Joseph Summers

Claimant's Name: Joseph Stanley for Elizabeth his wife
Acres: 50   50

Situation of lands: Joseph Stanley and Isabel his wife claim in right of the said Isabel the widow and relict of John Browne late of Savannah Gent. deceased all those two lots in the Town of Savannah number 9 and number 6 in Moors Tything Percival Ward with Garden and Farm Lots to each by conveyance from David Snook the Attorney of John Desborough to whom the premises were originally allotted by the Trustees.
Original grantee: John Desborough

Claimant's Name: Joseph Stanley
Acres: 100

Situation of lands: Lying on the township line joyning (sic) to number 10 Joseph Parker by the Honorable Council.
Original grantee: Joseph Stanley

Claimant's Name: Michael Swiser
Acres: 50

Situation of lands: Town Lot in Savannah number 218 with the lands annexed granted by the President and Council.
Original grantee: Michael Swiser

Claimant's Name: Gotlieb Staley
Acres: 50

Situation of lands: Lot number 8 at Goshen by purchase of Christopher Wisenbacker.
Original grantee: Christian Wisenbacker

Claimant's Name: Gotlieb Staley
Acres: 50

Situation of lands: Lot number 12 at Goshen by purchase of Michael Illy.
Original grantee: Michael Illy

Claimant's Name: John Sherriff
Acres: 50

Situation of lands: Being the 12th lot of Newington Village about six miles to the west of Savannah by allotment of the President and Assistants in March 1754.
Original grantee: John Sherriff

Claimant's Name: Mary
Acres: 50

Situation of lands: Lot number 1 situated in the Town of Newington granted unto George Rihsh deceased.
Original grantee: ~~Mary~~ George Rihsh

Claimant's Name: Peter Slyterman by Charles Watson
Acres: 5 1/8

Situation of lands: Lot in the Town of Savannah number 2 in Frederick Tything Darby Ward with a Garden Lot thereto purchased of Thomas Cross.
Original grantee: Thomas Cross

Claimant's Name: John Swinea by Charles Watson
Acres: 100

Situation of lands: On the Little Ogechee adjoining lands late of Peter Guirard and now of Henry Bourquin and bounded by lands of Philip Delegal granted him by the President and Assistants.
Original grantee: John Swinea

Claimant's Name: Mary Smith widow by Charles Watson
Acres: 50

Situation of lands: Lot in the Town of Frederica near the market with a Farm Lot thereunto belonging purchased from William Francis.
Original grantee: William Francis

Claimant's Name: Newdigate Stephens by Charles Watson
                    ex^d and ald. 11th May 1757
Acres: 500

Situation of lands: On Vernon River known by the name of Bewlie granted by the late Trustees to William Stephens Esq. his father deceased and the right of the said Newdigate by deed of gift from Thomas Stephens his brother.
Original grantee: William Stephens

Claimant's Name: Newdigate Stephens for Benedict Ball
                    by Charles Watson
Acres: 50

Situation of lands: Lot in Savannah number 2 in Heathcote Tything Decker Ward with Garden and Farm Lot granted by the late Trustees.
Original grantee: Benedict Ball

Claimant's Name: Edward Sumner
Acres: 500

Situation of lands: The south side of the south branch of Midway by allotment of the President and Assistants July 11th 1752.
Original grantee: Edward Sumner

Claimant's Name: Salomo Shad
Acres: 50

Situation of lands: Bought of Philipp Paulitsch in Bethany District or Bleu Bluff in the Township of Ebenezer bounding east Michael Oexlins widow south old Ebenezer Creek west John Gugell and north John Martyn Paulitsch.
Original grantee: Philipp Paulitsch

Claimant's Name: Richard Spencer
Acres: 500

Situation of lands: On the middle branch of North Newport by allotment of the late President and Assistants July 11th 1752.
Original grantee: Richard Spencer

Claimant's Name: John Stevens
Acres: 500

Situation of lands: South side of south branch of Midway and north side of north branch of Newport by allotment of the late President and Assistants July 11th 1752.
Original grantee: John Stevens

Claimant's Name: Andrew Seckinger
Acres: 50

Situation of lands: At the Black Creek joining east Mr. Lemcke to the south Mr. Hamm to west John Rass John Sherais by the late President and Assistants.
Original grantee: Andrew Seckinger

Claimant's Name: John Shave
Acres: 200

Situation of lands: On the north side of the south swamp of Midway by allotment of the late President and Assistants 6th August 1752.
Original grantee: John Shave

Claimant's Name: John Stehely Junr.
Acres: 50

Situation of lands: Lot at Goshen number 17
Original grantee: John Stehely Junr.

Claimant's Name: John Sherauss
Acres: 50

Situation of lands: On Black Creek in Josephs Town.
Original grantee: John Sheraus

Claimant's Name: Martin Burkhart
Acres: 50

Situation of lands: On Black Creek in Josephs Town.
Original grantee: Martin Burkhart

Claimant's Name: Andrew Schneider
Acres: 50

Situation of lands: On Black Creek in Josephs Town.
Original grantee: Andrew Schneider

Claimant's Name: George Sherauss
Acres: 50

Situation of lands: On Black Creek in Josephs Town.
Original grantee: George Sherauss

Claimant's Name: John Stehely
Acres: 50

Situation of lands: At Goshen number 5 by warrant from the President and Assistants.
Original grantee: John Stehely

Claimant's Name: Matthew Seckinger
Acres: 50

Situation of lands: On Black Creek in Josephs Town
Original grantee: Matthew Seckinger

Claimant's Name: Isaac Tripp by Charles Watson Exd. and all. 13th May 1757
Acres: 1/8

Situation of lands: In right of his wife a lot in Savannah number 6 in Holland Tything Percival Ward heretofore granted William Barbo her late husband deceased by the President and Assistants.
Original grantee: William Barbo

Claimant's Name: Thomas Tripp by Charles Watson
Acres: 50

Situation of lands: Lot in Savannah number 6 in Vernon Tything Heathcote Ward with Garden and Farm Lot granted by the late Trustees twenty years since.
Original grantee: Thomas Tripp

Claimant's Name: Thomas Tripp by Charles Watson
Acres: 89 1/8

Situation of lands: Two Farm Lots in the same Tything and Ward commonly called Trust Lots granted by the late President and Assistants in the year 1753.
Original grantee: Thomas Tripp

Claimant's Name: Thomas Tripp by Charles Watson
Acres: 50

Situation of lands: For and in behalf of the heirs of Thomas (Thomas has been added at a later time in pencil) Atwell deceased a lot in Savannah number 6 in Hucks Tything Percival Ward with Garden and Farm Lot granted by the late Trustees.
Original grantee: Atwell

Claimant's Name: John Francis Triboudet by Charles Watson
Acres: 50

Situation of lands: Lying in Newington Village purchased by him of Anthony Pagea to whom the same was granted by the President and Assistants.
Original grantee: Anthony Pagea

Claimant's Name: Jacob Truan by Charles Watson Exd. and
                 all. 13th May 1757
Acres: 50

Situation of lands: Lot in Savannah number 10 in Holland Tything Percival Ward with Garden and Farm Lot thereunto belonging granted him by the late Trustees about eighteen years ago.
Original grantee: Jacob Truan

Claimant's Name: John Tisdale by Charles Watson
Acres: 50

Situation of lands: Town Lot in Savannah number 5 in Carpenters Tything Deckers Ward with Garden and Farm Lot thereunto belonging devised the said John in and by the will of John Tisdale his father deceased.
Original grantee: John Tisdale

Claimant's Name: John Tisdale
Acres: 50

Situation of lands: The reversion expectant on the death of Elizabeth the wife of Samuel Marcer of and in a lot in the Town of Savannah number 1 in Wilmington Tything Darby Ward with Garden and Farm Lot therto belonging devised him in and by the will above mentioned.
Original grantee: None shown

Claimant's Name: James Tebeau by Charles Watson exaised and all. 11th May 1757
Acres: 1/8

Situation of lands: Lot in the Town of Savannah number 9 in Tyrconnel Tything Darby Ward as only son and heir of Daniel Tebeau his father deceased.
Original grantee: Daniel Tebeau

Claimant's Name: Peter DeTemple Exd. and all. 11th May 1757
Acres: 50

Situation of lands: On Skidoway Island at Half Moon Bluff granted by the President and Assistants.
Original grantee: Peter DeTemple

Claimant's Name: Edmund Tannatt
Acres: 500

Situation of lands: On the north side of Little Ogechee bought of Mr. Newdigate Stephens.
Original grantee: Newdigate Stephens

Claimant's Name: Edmund Tannatt
Acres: 500

Situation of lands: On the south side of a branch of Midway River granted by the late President and Assistants July 4, 1753.
Original grantee: Edmund Tannatt

Claimant's Name: Nathan Taylor Exd. and all. 11th May 1757
Acres: 500

Situation of lands: On a middle branch of Midway warrant from the President and Assistants June 11th 1752.
Original grantee: Nathan Taylor

Claimant's Name: Frederick Feutel
Acres: 50

Situation of lands: Lot at Goshen number 13 granted to Jacob Weisenbach by warrant from the President and Assistants.
Original grantee: Jacob Weisenbach

Claimant's Name: Frederick Feutel   purchased
Acres: 50

Situation of lands: At Goshen number 14 granted to George Bate by the President and Assistants.
Original grantee: George Bate

Claimant's Name: Jacob Casper Walthour
Acres: 145

Situation of lands: Situated in Little Ogechee District on the south adjoining Clement Martins land on the west John Farmur on the north Henry William Parker and on the east Thomas Ellis by warrant from the President and Assistants February 3d 1750.
Original grantee: Jacob Casper Walthour

Claimant's Name: Jacob Casper Walthour for John Casper
                  Walthour his father
Acres: 50

Situation of lands: Lot number 9 situated in the Village of Goshen by warrant from the President and Assistants 1748.
Original grantee: John Casper Walthour

Claimant's Name: Joseph Watson
Acres: 500

Situation of lands: Grantham Town confirmed to him by the Honorable Trustees.
Original grantee: Joseph Watson

Claimant's Name: Joseph Watson
Acres: 60

Situation of lands: Half the Trust Lot to the north to pay one years rent every 2t (?) years confirmed to him by the Honorable Trustees.
Original grantee: Joseph Watson

Claimant's Name: Joseph Watson
Acres: 35

Situation of lands: At Yamacraw confirmed by the Honorable Trustees.
Original grantee: Joseph Watson

Claimant's Name: Joseph Watson
Acres: 50

Situation of lands: Town lot purchased of the widow of Humphry Bright given to him by the Honorable Trustees.
Original grantee: Humphry Bright

Claimant's Name: Benjamin Wilson by Charles Watson
Acres: 300

Situation of lands: Lying on the south side of Little Ogechee River granted him by the late President and Assistants and adjoining lands of John Wilson.
Original grantee: Benjamin Wilson

Claimant's Name: John Wilson by Charles Watson Exd. and all. 11th May 1757
Acres: 300

Situation of lands: Lying on the south side of Little Ogechee River adjoining lands of William Wilson granted said John by the President and Assistants.
Original grantee: John Wilson

Claimant's Name: John Wilson by Charles Watson Exd. and all. 11th May 1757
Acres: 200

Situation of lands: Lying on the north side of Great Ogechee River granted him by the late President and Assistants and adjoining lands of Henry Meyers.
Original grantee: John Wilson

Claimant's Name: William Wilson by Charles Watson Exd. and all. 11th May 1757
Acres: 300

Situation of lands: Lying on the south side of Little Ogechee River adjoining lands of Richard Cooper which said lands were granted the said Wilson by the late President and Assistants.
Original grantee: William Wilson

Claimant's Name: Matthias West
Acres: 50

Situation of lands: In the Village of Goshen purchased by him of Frederic Triedling two years ago.
Original grantee: ~~Matthias West~~ Frederic Triedling

Claimant's Name: Matthias West
Acres: 50

Situation of lands: In the same village purchased by him of John Farly about six months ago.
Original grantee: None shown

Claimant's Name: Parmenus Way
Acres: 500

Situation of lands: At the head of the north branch of Midway River by allotment of the late President and Assistants July 11th 1752.
Original grantee: Parmenus Way

Claimant's Name: Thomas Way Exd. and all. 11th May 1757
Acres: 200

Situation of lands: On the southernmost swamp of North Newport River by the late President and Assistants August 1752.
Original grantee: Thomas Way

Claimant's Name: Edward Way
Acres: 500

Situation of lands: South side of the south swamp of Midway by allotment of the late President and Assistants July 11th 1752.
Original grantee: Edward Way

Claimant's Name: Nathaniel Way
Acres: 500

Situation of lands: On the south branch of Midway by allotment of the late President and Assistants, July 11th 1752.
Original grantee: Nathaniel Way

Claimant's Name: Samuel Way
Acres: 500

Situation of lands: On the north side of the south branch of Midway Swamp by allotment of the late President and Assistants July 11th 1752.
Original grantee: Samuel Way

Claimant's Name: Moses Way Exd. and all. 11th May 1757
Acres: 200

Situation of lands: On the southernmost swamp of North Newport by allotment of the late President and Assistants August 6th 1752.
Original grantee: Moses Way

Claimant's Name: John Wachter
Acres: 50

Situation of lands: In Acton Village as only son and heir of Joseph Wachter deceased.
Original grantee: Joseph Wachter

Claimant's Name: Joseph Wood
Acres: 200

Situation of lands: On the south side of Great Ogechee by allotment of the late President and Assistants.
Original grantee: Joseph Wood

Claimant's Name: Willoughbe West
Acres: 500

Situation of lands: On the south side of Great Ogechee near where Fort Argyle stood by allotment of the late President and Assistants.
Original grantee: Willoughbe West

Claimant's Name: George Winkler Exd. and all. 11th May 1757
Acres: 50

Situation of lands: At Goshen number 11 by allotment of the late President and Assistants.
Original grantee: George Winkler

Claimant's Name: Isaac Young by Charles Watson
Acres: 450

Situation of lands: Fronting on Savannah River and bounded east by a creek called Pipemakers grant by the late Preisdent and Assistants.
Original grantee: Isaac Young

Claimant's Name: Isaac Young by Charles Watson
Acres: 100

Situation of lands: Adjoining the aforesaid tract late his fathers deceased intailed on the said Isaac by deed.
Original grantee: Isaac Young Snr.

Claimant's Name: Isaac Young by Charles Watson
Acres: 50

Situation of lands: Lot in Savannah number 5 in the Fourth Tything of the Lower New Ward alias Reynolds Ward with a Garden Lot and Farm Lot granted him by the late Trustees.
Original grantee: Isaac Young

Claimant's Name: Isaac Young by Charles Watson
Acres: 44 7/8

Situation of lands: Farm Lot containing forty four acres and seven eighth purchased of William Clement in the year 1746.
Original grantee: William Clement

Claimant's Name: Isaac Young
Acres: 5

Situation of lands: Garden Lot containing five acres formerly Hainks purchased of Charles Watson and Ann his wife.
Original grantee: Hainks

Claimant's Name: Isaac Young
Acres: 50

Situation of lands: For Elizabeth Young his daughter a Lot in Savannah number 8 in the Fourth Tything of the Upper New Ward alias Anson Ward with a Garden and Farm Lot by deed of gift from Lucy Mouse widow deceased.
Original grantee: Lucy Mouse

Claimant's Name: Isaac Young
Acres: 50

Situation of lands: For Thomas Young his brother a Lot in Savannah in the Fourth Tything of the Lower New Ward alias Reynolds Ward with a Garden and Farm Lot granted by the late Trustees.
Original grantee: Thomas Young

Claimant's Name: Isaac Young
Acres: 250

Situation of lands: For John Young his brother on an island between Thunderbolt and Skidoway granted him by the late President and Assistants in 1754.
Original grantee: John Young

Claimant's Name: Isaac Young
Acres: 50

Situation of lands: For Sarah Coosey (sic) his sister the widow of William Cooksey deceased the said Isaac claims a Lot in Savannah number 9 Wilmington Tything Darby Ward with Garden and Farm Lot granted her late husband by the late Trustees.
Original grantee: William Cooksey

Claimant's Name: Mary Young widow
Acres: 50

Situation of lands: Town Lot in Savannah in Frederick Tything with Garden and Farm Lot as relict to Thomas Young who obtained it by allotment from James Oglethorpe Esqr. 1745 which she claims in behalf of her self and son William Young a minor.
Original grantee: Thomas Young

Claimant's Name: Mary Young
Acres: 50

Situation of lands: Town Lot in Savannah number 10 in the First Tything Upper New Ward with Garden and Farm Lot in behalf of her son Phillip Box now in South Carolina to whom it was allotted by James Ogelthorpe, Esqr.
Original grantee: Phillip Box

Claimant's Name: Henry Yonge for John Kelsall
Acres: 500

Situation of lands: On the island of Skidoway bounding north on Richard Hazzard east on Rumney Marsh and all other sides on vacant land by warrant from the President and Assistants 14th December 1749.
Original grantee: John Kelsall

Claimant's Name: Middleton Evans Exd. and all. 11th May 1757
Acres: 500

Situation of lands: On the south side of Midway granted by the late President and Assistants.
Original grantee: Middleton Evans

Claimant's Name: Sarah Jones
Acres: 200

Situation of lands: Adjoining to lands of Isaac Barksdale about 12 miles above Augusta on the River Savannah granted by the late President and Assistants to her late husband Richard Jones.
Original grantee: Richard Jones

Claimant's Name: Samuel Venning
Acres: 50

Situation of lands: Lot in the Township of Augusta purchased of Henry Overstreet joining to John Fitch and on the Bever (sic) Dam granted by General Oglethorpe to said Overstreet.
Original grantee: Henry Overstreet

Claimant's Name: Robert Baillie
Acres: 500

Situation of lands: Situate upon the north branch of Newport River bounding on lands granted to Mr. John Thompson and Captain Kenneth Baillie granted by the President and Assistants in 1754.
Original grantee: Robert Baillie

Claimant's Name: Thomas Clancey by Robert Baillie
Acres: 50   50

Situation of lands: Two Town Lots in Frederica granted to John Ashmore by General Oglethorpe with two fifty acre lots the number and tything unknown claimed by virtue of a Power of Attorney from said Ashmore Savannah.
Original grantee: John Ashmore

Claimant's Name: Edward Chapman in right of Jane his wife by Charles Watson
Acres: 50

Situation of lands: Town Lot in Savannah number 7 in Holland Tything Percival Ward with a Garden Lot and Farm Lot thereunto belonging granted by the late ~~President and Assistants~~ Trustees unto William Grigson the former husband of the said Jane.
Original grantee: William Grigson

Claimant's Name: Andrew Collins
Acres: 200

Situation of lands: At the head of Midway River allotment of the President and Council of the late Trustees.
Original grantee: Andrew Collins

Claimant's Name: Richard Dennison in right of his wife
                   relict of Peter McHugh by Thomas Ellis
Acres: 500

Situation of lands: On the north side of the north branch of Midway River at the time granted was vacant on all sides.
Original grantee: Peter McHugh

Claimant's Name: Thomas Green by Charles Watson
Acres: 500

Situation of lands: On behalf of his wife Ann the only child of Edward Jenkins deceased on an island called Jenkins Island which said lands were granted the said Edward Jenkins by the late Trustees about eighteen years ago.
Original grantee: Edward Jenkins

Claimant's Name: Jacob Helvenstein by Thomas Ellis
Acres: 100

Situation of lands: On the north side of Great Ogechee River adjoining to land granted to Mr. Jeremiah Helvenstine.
Original grantee: Jacob Helvenstine

Claimant's Name: Jeremiah Helvenstine by Thomas Ellis
Acres: 100

Situation of lands: On the north side of Great Ogechee
River adjoining to lands granted to Mr. John Willson
east of lands granted to Mr. Jacob Helvenstine on all
other sides vacant land.
Original grantee: Jeremiah Helvenstine

Claimant's Name: Robert Luden by Charles Watson
Acres: 50   50

Situation of lands: In right of Mary his wife claims two
lots in the Town of Frederica containing together one
hundred acres one of said lots came to the said Mary as
heir to John Harding her brother and the other descended
to her on the death and as only child of   Spencer her
mother.
Original grantee: None shown

Claimant's Name: John Todd Senr. by Charles Watson
                   exaised and all. 11th May 1757
Acres: 100

Situation of lands: In the District of Newport in the
Province of Georgia granted him by the late President and
Assistants in 1754.
Original grantee: John Todd Snr.

Claimant's Name: George Cuthbert
Acres: 500

Situation of lands: On the north side of the Great Ogechee
River by allotment of the President and Assistants 22d
August 1752.
Original grantee: George Cuthbert

Claimant's Name: George Cuthbert
Acres: None shown

Situation of lands: A Lot in Savannah number 35 by allotment of the President and Assistants 5th June 1754.
Original grantee: George Cuthbert

Claimant's Name: Daniel Cuthbert by George Cuthbert
Acres: 500

Situation of lands: On the River Savannah by grant from
the Trustees in the year 1734 to John Cuthbert of Drakin
to whom he is now heir.
Original grantee: John Cuthbert

Claimant's Name: Cuthbert Gordon   (Gordon Cuthbert ?)
Acres: 500

Situation of lands: On Augustins Creek by allotment of
the President and Assistants the 4th April 1753.
Original grantee: Cuthbert Gordon

Claimant's Name: Nathaniel Hunting by Messrs. Harris and
                  Habersham in trust
Acres: 300

Situation of lands: Bounding south of Mr. John Davis'
land on Skidoway Island.
Original grantee: Nathaniel Hunting

Claimant's Name: Catherine Mullryne
Acres: 500

Situation of lands: Called Kelkenny upon a river or creek
of the same name claimed by Catherine Mullryne purchased
of John Hutchinson to whom possession was given and a survey
made by Henry Yonge the 17th April 1749.
Original grantee: John Hutchinson

Claimant's Name: Mary Mullryne
Acres: 500

Situation of lands: Called Fair Groves on the north side
of Midway River claimed by Mary Mullryne purchased of James
Williams to whom possession was given and a survey made by
Henry Yonge the 15th day of March 1754.
Original grantee: James Williams

Claimant's Name: John Mullryne
Acres: 500

Situation of lands: Called Concordia on the south side of
Midway River claimed by John Mullryne to whom possession
was given and a survey made by Henry Yonge the 11th day
of March 1754.
Original grantee: John Mullryne

Claimant's Name: John McCloud Exd. and all. 11th May 1757
Acres: 100

Situation of lands: On the south side of Great Ogechee
River allotted by the late President and Assistants.
Original grantee: John McCloud

Claimant's Name: John Burton by John MacClellan
Acres: 50

Situation of lands: Lot in Savannah number 203 situate in
the Upper New Tything of Savannah aforesaid with Garden
and Farm Lot thereunto belonging.
Original grantee: John Burton

Claimant's Name" William Burton by John MacClellan
Acres: 50

Situation of lands: Lot in Savannah number 205 situate
in the Upper New Tything of Savannah aforesaid with Garden
and Farm Lot thereunto belonging.
Original grantee: William Burton

Claimant's Name: William Buchanan
Acres: 500

Situation of lands: Claims on the Main opposite to the
Island Doboy in the neighborhood of Darian (sic) allotted
him by the late President and Assistants the 21st December
1747.
Original grantee: William Buchanan

Claimant's Name: Edward Barnard for Robert Germany
Acres: 200

Situation of lands: Claims two hundred acres of land situated at a place known by the name of Michaels Creek about ten miles above Augusta bounded on all sides by vacant land and granted by the late President and Assistants.
Original grantee: Robert Germany

Claimant's Name: Edward Barnard for John Germany
Acres: 200

Situation of lands: Claims two hundred acres of land situated on Savannah River about four miles above the mouth of Broad River at a place known by the name of Cladon Mount bounded north by Savannah River and on all other sides by vacant land granted by the late President and Assistants.
Original grantee: John Germany

Claimant's Name: Edward Barnard for Alexander Germany
Acres: 200

Situation of lands: Claims two hundred acres of land situated on the head of Little Cayoika Creek at a place known by the name of Green Bryer and about 15 miles back from Savannah bounded on all sides by vacant lands granted by the late President and Assistants.
Original grantee: Alexander Germany

Claimant's Name: Edward Barnard for Gilbert Fyffe Jnr.
Acres: 50

Situation of lands: Mary Fyffe widow of Gilbert Fyffe lately deceased in behalf of her eldest son Gilbert Fyffe Jnr. claims one Town Lot containing fifty acres in the Township of Augusta number 5 bounded north west by Pat: Clark south east by William Spencer north east by Savannah River south west by William Clark granted to her late husband Gilbert Fyffe by the late President and Assistants 15th January 1755.
Original grantee: Gilbert Fyffe

Claimant's Name: Edward Barnard for Jacob Hensler
Acres: 400

Situation of lands: Claims four hundred acres of land situated in the District of Halifax bounded north by John Myers east by Savannah River south and west by vacant land granted by the late President and Assistants 11th day of September 1755.
Original grantee: Jacob Hensler

Claimant's Name: Edward Barnard for Jacob Greiner, Andrew
                    Greiner, and John Casper Greiner
Acres: 100   100   100

Situation of lands: Jacob Greiner, Andrew Greiner and John Casper Greiner claims one hundred acres of land each situated in the District of Halifax bounded east by Savannah River north by Jacob Hensler south and west by vacant land granted by the late President and Assistants 11th day of September 1755.
Original grantee: Jacob Greiner, Andrew Greiner, and John
                    Casper Greiner

Claimant's Name: Edward Barnard for John Goldwire
Acres: 50

Situation of lands: Claims one fifty acres lot in the Township of Augusta number 20 bounded north by Ambrose Barr east and west by David Douglass Esqr. and south by Samuel Elsoner granted by the late President and Assistants in the year 1747.
Original grantee: John Goldwire

Claimant's Name: Edward Barnard for Ann Hopkins widow of
                    Christopher Hopkins
Acres   500

Situation of lands: Claims five hundred acres of land situate in the District of Halifax on the River Savannah about two miles north west of Bryer Creek and bounded otherways by vacant land granted to the said Christopher Christopher (sic) Hopkins her late husband by the President and Assistants the 7th October 1750.
Original grantee: Christohper Hopkins

Claimant's Name: Edward Barnard for John Casper Hirshman,
                   Casper Hirshman and John Casper Hirshman
Acres: 100   100   50

Situation of lands: John Casper Hirshman claims one hundred acres of land, Casper Hirshman one hundred acres and John Casper Hirshman fifty acres situated in the District of Halifax bounded east by the River Savannah north by Lucas Mosses (sic) and all other sides by vacant lands now known by the name of Deer Point granted by the late President and Assistants 11th day of September 1755.
Original grantee: John Casper Hirshman, Casper Hirshman, and John Casper Hirshman

Claimant's Name: Edward Barnard for Jacob Greiner
Acres: 200

Situation of lands: Claims two hundred acres of land situated in the District of Halifax bounded north by William McDonal (sic) east by Savannah River south and west by vacant land granted by the President and Assistants 11th day of September 1755.
Original grantee: Jacob Greiner

Claimant's Name: Edward Barnard for Thomas Red
Acres: 50

Situation of lands: Claims one fifty acre lot in the Township of Augusta number 21 bounding northwest by the Town Common south east by John Goldwire north east by James Deane and south west by Patt: Clark formerly to Ambrose Barr by the late President and Assistants purchased by the above Thomas Red.
Original grantee: Ambrose Barr

Claimant's Name: Edward Barnard for Thomas Hickambottom
Acres: 100

Situation of lands: Claims one hundred acres of land situate at a place known by the name of Lotts Hole about five miles above Augusta and three miles back from Savannah River bounded on all sides by vacant land granted by the late President and Assistants.
Original grantee: Thomas Hickambottom

Claimant's Name: Edward Barnard for Charles Jordan
Acres: 50   50

Situation of lands: Claims two fifty acre lots in the
Township of Augusta number 5 and number 34 bounded south
east by Lachlan Macbean north west by David Douglass Esqr.
north east by Samuel Elsoner south by Joseph Oaks and
formerly granted by the late President and Assistants to
John Etherinton and William Watkins and since purchased
by the above Charles Jordan as by deed of sale will appear.
Original grantee: John Etherington   William Watkins

Claimant's Name: John Graham Attorney for John Thompson
Acres: 500

Situation of lands: Claims five hundred acres of land situate on the north side of Newport River near a place called
Water Mellon Bluff granted the 8th February 1754 by the
President and Assistants of the late Trustees.
Original grantee: John Thompson

Claimant's Name: Andrew Walker
Acres: 50

Situation of lands: Claims a Town Lot in Savannah number
6 in the Second Tything in Anson Ward and 50 acres of land
granted by the Honorable Trustees.
Original grantee: None shown

Claimant's Name: Daniel Meyers
Acres: 50

Situation of lands: A Town Lot in Frederica number 22 in
Archer Ward a Garden Lot containing 5 acres and a Farm Lot
of 45 acres granted by the Honorable Trustees.
Original grantee: Henry Meyers

Claimant's Name: Martin Campbell for Richard Kent
Acres: 500

Situation of lands: Of land on Wilmington Island a lot in Savannah granted by the late President and Assistants.
Original grantee: Richard Kent

Claimant's Name: None given
Acres: 50

Situation of lands: And 50 acres of land left by will to Richard Kent by one Collins.
Original grantee: Collins

Claimant's Name: Noble Jones Esqr. claims in behalf of Sophia wife of William Williamson
Acres: 50   50   400

Situation of lands: A Town Lot number 4 in Frederica Tything Darby Ward with Garden and Farm Lot making in whole 50 acres. A Town Lot number 1 First Tything Reynolds Ward with Garden and Farm Lot making 50 acres. Acres of land on Augustine Creek.
Original grantee: Thomas Causton

Claimant's Name: William Barkshall
Acres: 500

Situation of lands: On Argyle Island on the River Savannah bounding north on John Rae and south on vacant land.
Original grantee: None shown

Claimant's Name: Christopher Ortman
Acres: 50

Situation of lands: Christopher Ortman number 5 in the Third Tything Second Ward at Ebenezer.
Original grantee: Christopher Ortman

Claimant's Name: Nicholas Cronanburgh
Acres: 200

Situation of lands: On Savannah River a mile below Purisburgh.
Original grantee: None shown

Claimant's Name: John George Zeigler
Acres: 50

Situation of lands: Of land bounding east Bath. Reiser and John George Haid south west and north vacant pine land.
Original grantee: John George Zeigler

Claimant's Name: John Kelsall
Acres: 500

Situation of lands: Situated on the Island of Skidoway bounding on lands of Richard Hazzard to the north and to the south on lands of John Davis.
Original grantee: John Kelsall

Claimant's Name: Joseph Goodby
Acres: 400

Situation of lands: Claims situate on the south side of Newport River bounding all sides by vacant land.
Original grantee: Joseph Goodby

Claimant's Name: James Read
Acres: 500

Situation of lands: Claims situate on the north side of Great Ogechee purchased of ~~James Read~~ Richard J'on (Johnson).
Original grantee: Richard J'on

Claimant's Name: David Cunningham as attorney
Acres: 50

Situation of lands: Claims a Town Lot in Savannah.
Original grantee: None shown

Claimant's Name: Joseph Stanley in behalf etc.
Acres: None shown

Situation of lands: A Town Lot number 7 Hucks Tything - a Town Lot number 3 La Roche Tything - a Town Lot number 5 Hucks Tything.
Original grantee: Hugh Fraser Isaac King Crook James Turner

Claimant's Name: Henry Yonge
Acres: 300

Situation of lands: Of land on Midway River by ~~purchase~~ conveyance from the Provost Marshall formerly the estate of Peter Baillou.
Original grantee: None shown

Claimant's Name: Sarah Jones
Acres: 200

Situation of lands: Of land near Uchee Island about 16 miles above Fort August (sic).
Original grantee: Richard Jones her late husband

Claimant's Name: Cornelius Dougherty
Acres: 499

Situation of lands: Of land situate in the Town of Augusta.
Original grantee: None shown

Claimant's Name: Benjamin Wilson Exd. and all. 11 May 1757
Acres: 300

Situation of lands: Benjamin Wilson 300 acres of land on the south side of Little Ogechee joining east on Joseph Summerour.
Original grantee: None shown

Claimant's Name: Thomas Wilson
Acres: 240

Situation of lands: Of land on the south side of Little Ogechee River ~~join~~ bounding south of lands of Benjamin Wilson.
Original grantee: Thomas Wilson

Claimant's Name: Nicholas Cronenburgh
Acres: None given

Situation of lands: A Town Lot in Ebenezer number 3 in the Eight Tything east of the contor sheet.
Original grantee: Nicholas Cronenburgh

Claimant's Name: Andrew Walset
Acres: None shown

Situation of lands: A Town Lot in Frederica number 23 in the south division of the Town joyning east on Henry Meyers and west on Archibald Sinclair.
Original grantee: None shown

Claimant's Name: Andrew Walset
Acres: 5

Situation of lands: Acre Lot number 3 and 45 acre lot in the 4th Tything number 2.
Original grantee: None shown

Claimant's Name: George Delegal
Acres: 500

Situation of lands: 500 acres of land on Little Ogechee joining to the northward of Mr. John DeVeaux and the eastward of Philip Delegal, Jnr.
Original grantee: None shown

Claimant's Name: Alexander Baillie allowed 6th April 1757
Acres: 100

Situation of lands: 100 Acres of marsh on Midway River Adjoining Probert (sic) Howard and Baillies Island granted by the late President and Assistants.
Original grantee: None shown

Claimant's Name: Henry Bourquin allowed 3d May 1757
Acres: 500

Situation of lands: Land lying on the east side of Little Ogechee purchased of John Farmur and called Churbury bounded by lands heretofore of William Ewen and now of Clement Martin Esqr. on the one side and by lands of the said Henry purchased of Charles Watson on the other.
Original grantee: None shown

INDEX

The name of each claimant and the name of the person for whom the land was claimed is in capital letters. Other names such as neighbors, relatives and place names are not. Names of original grantees are not capitalized.

A

Abercorn, 5, 84, 103, 105, 134, 135, 137, 165
Abercorn Creek, 65, 82, 129, 159, 170, 175
Abercorn District, 133, 142
Acton, 104, 112, 113, 163, 167, 190
Adlionby, 10
Aglionby, 12
Allan, William, 148
Allen, Mathew, 28
ALTHER, JOHN, 1
Alther, John, 1, 170
ANDERSON, ELIZABETH, 1
Anderson, Hugh, 129
Anderson, James, 1
ANDERSON, JOHN, 1
Anson Ward, 106, 143, 157, 159, 192, 203
ANTROBOS, THOMAS, 135
Antrobos, Thomas, 135
Archer Ward, 139, 203
Argyle Fort, 158
Argyle Island, 35, 111, 178, 204
Arnsdorff, Laurentz Andrew, 63
ARNSDORFF, PETER, 63
Arnsdorff, Peter, 44, 58, 59, 60, 63, 64, 67
ARTHUR, FRANCIS, 1
Arthur, Francis, 1
Ashmore, John, 194
Atwell ---, 185
Atwell, Thomas, 185
Augusta, 6, 7, 8, 20, 22, 23, 27, 28, 30, 31, 32, 90,
    103, 120, 121, 122, 123, 126, 131, 135, 143, 144,
    164, 168, 170, 172, 177, 194, 199, 200, 201, 202,
    203, 206
Augusta Common, 201, 202
Augusta District, 170
Augustins Creek, 197, 204
AUSTIN, GEORGE, 138
Austin, George, 138

209.

B

Bach, Gabriel, 45, 62
BACHER, BALTHASAR, 83
Bacher, Balthaser, 83
Bacher, Matthias, 144
Bacher, Thomas, 57, 66, 71
Backer, Thomas, 43
Backshell, William, 178
BACON, SAMUEL, 15
Bacon, Samuel, 15, 165
BAILER, MARGARET, 135
Bailey ---, 128
BAILEY, JOHN, 18
BAILEY, MARY, 121
Bailey, Mr., 128
BAILEY, THOMAS, 11
Bailey, Thomas, 11
BAILLIE, ALEXANDER, 207
Baillie, Captain, 165
BAILLIE, KENETH, 18, 19
Baillie, Keneth, 18, 36
Baillie, Keneth, Jr., 19
Baillie, Captain Kenneth, 194
BAILLIE, ROBERT, 194
Baillie, Robert, 194
Baillies Island, 207
BAILLOU, ISAAC, 4
BAILLOU, JAMES, 4
Baillou, John, 5
BAILLOU, PETER, 4, 5, 6,
Baillou, Peter, 35, 90, 206
Baker ---, 128
BAKER, BENJAMIN, 16
Baker, Benjamin, 16
Baker, Elizabeth, 15
BAKER, RICHARD, 16
Baker, Richard, 16
BAKER, WILLIAM, 15
Baker, William, 15
BALL, BENEDICT, 181
Ball, Benedict, 181
Ballew, John, 5
Barbados, 18
Barbo, William, 11, 35, 184
BARKER, JOSEPH, 17
Barker, Joseph, 17

B

BARKER, SAMUEL, 177
Barker, Samuel, 177
BARKSDALE, ISAAC, 19
Barksdale, Isaac, 19, 194
BARKSDALE AND RAE, 19
Barksdale and Rae, 144
BARKSHALL, WILLIAM, 204
BARNARD, EDWARD, 7, 8, 199, 200, 201, 202, 203
Barnard, Edward, 122, 123
BARNARD, JOHN, 9, 10, 12, 13
Barnard, John, 9
BARNARD, TIMOTHY, 9
Barr, Ambrose, 8, 27, 200, 201
Barton Branch, 140
Bashlaw, John Mathis, 166
Bassett, Natt, 7
Bassett, Thomas, 7
Bate, George, 187
BATE, JOHN CASPER, 19
Bate, John Casper, 19
Bateman, Elizabeth, 33
Bateman, Robert, 33
Beacham, John, 24
Beaver Dam, 194, 202
BECHTLE, JOHN GEORG, 51
Bechtle, John Georg, 52
Bechtly, John George, 51
Becket, William, 87
BECKETT, THOMAS, 17
Beckett, Thomas, 17
BECKETT, WILLIAM, 17
Beckett, William, 17
Becu, Giles, 110
Begling, Richard, 32
Belitha Tything, 4, 96, 110, 146, 163
BELL, WILLIAM, 2
BELTZ, SIGMUND, 16
Beltz, Sigmund, 16
BENNETT, JOHN, 16
Bennett, John, 1, 16
BENNISON, RICHARD, 6
Bennison, Richard, 6
Bermuda Island, 104
BERRIER, JACOB, 116
Berrier, Jacob, 116

B

BERRIER, JOHN, 115
Berrier, John, 115
Bethany District, 182
Bewlie, 157, 181
Bichler, Thomas, 45, 49, 58, 75, 76
Bickler, Thomas, 129
BIDENBACK, CHRISTIAN, 47
Bidenback, Christian, 47
BIDENBACK, MATTHEW, 48
Bidenback, Matthew, 48
Bignon, Abraham, 4, 98
BIRCK, CHRISTIAN, 58, 59
Birck, Christian, 47, 49, 50, 55, 59
Bishop, Henry, 78
Black, David, 14
Black Creek, 14, 37, 136, 139, 142, 143, 147, 149, 178, 182, 183, 184
Black Island, 155
Blendon, 177
Bleu Bluff, 182
Blithman, William, 105
Bloom, Valentine, 122
BOBBY, JAMES, 20
Bobby, James, 20
BODELL, LEONARD, 2
Bodell, Leonard, 2
BOLLINGER, JOHN GEORG, 46
Bollinger, John Georg, 46, 47
BOLTON, ROBERT, 6, 7
Bolton, Robert, 7
BOLZIUS, JOHN MARTIN, 2, 75, 76, 129, 130
Bolzius, John Martin, 3, 76, 130, 145
BOREMAN, MICHEL, 13, 14
Boreman, Michel, 14
Bosomworth, Mary, 131
Bosomworth, Thomas, 131
Bostick, Valentine, 141
Bourdeaux, 12
BOURGHALTER, MICHAEL, 112, 124
Bourghalter, Michael, 112, 124
BOURGHALTER, MICHAEL, JR., 123
Bourghalter, Michael, Jr., 123
BOURQUIN, BENEDICT, 13
Bourquin, Benedict, 12, 13

B

BOURQUIN, HENRY, 8, 12, 207
Bourquin, Henry, 12, 13, 181, 207
BOUVIER, SIMON, 124
Bouvier, Simon, 124
BOWLING, MARY, 13
Bowling, Mary, 92
Bowling, Timothy, 13
Box, Philip, 193
BRADDOCK, DAVID CUTLER, 3
Braddock, David Cutler, 3, 26
BRADLEY, JAMES, 12
BRADLEY, WILLIAM, 10, 12
Bradley, William, 9
BRADLEY, WILLIAM, JR., 13
Bradleys Creek, 85
BRANDER, MATTHEW, 71, 72
Brander, Matthew, 61, 71, 72, 75
Breed, Sarah, 98
Breed, Timothy, 98
Bridge Branch, 54
Bridge Creek, 62, 63
Brier Creek, 20
Bright, Humphrey, 4, 188
BRITON, JOHN PETER, 3
Briton, John Peter, 4
Broad River, 28, 199
Brooks, Francis, 29
BROOKS, JAMES, 28, 29
Broughton Street, 21
BROWN, DAVID, 101
Brown, Patrick, 126
BROWN, PATRICK; CLARK, DANIEL; AND McGILLIVRAY, LACHLAN,
Brown, Patt, 7
Browne, Isabel, 179
Browne, John, 179
Brownfield, John, 138
BROWNJOHN, BENJAMIN, 2
Brownjohn, William, 2
Bruckner, George, 40, 57, 59, 60, 70
BRUCKNER, FREDERICA, 59
BRYAN, JONATHON, 85, 129
Bryan, Jonathon, 85, 86
Bryan, Joseph, 16, 86
Bryan Street, 129
Bryer Creek, 121, 200

B

Bubby, James, 121, 200
BUCHANAN, WILLIAM, 198
Buchanan, William, 198
Buffalo Swamp, 155
BUNTZ, HENRY LUDWIG, 46
Buntz, Henry Ludwig, 46
BUNTZ, JOHN GEORG, 46
Buntz, John Georg, 46, 47
Buntz, Urban, 60, 61, 62
BUNTZ, URBANUS, 47
BURGHE, RODOLPH, 113
Burghe, Rodolph, 113
BURGHOLD, GEORGE, 114
Burghold, George, 114
BURGOMASTER, CHRISTIAN, 115
Burgomaster, Christian, 115
Burgsteiner, Matthew, 64, 65, 76, 77
BURGSTEINER, MATTHEW, WIDOW OF, 76, 77
Burgsteiner, widow, 129
BURKHART, MARTIN, 183
Burkhart, Martin, 183
Burmuda Island, 18
BURNLEY, SAMUEL, 15
Burnley, Samuel, 15
BURNSIDES, JAMES, 39
Burtley, John, 31
Burtley, Richard, 10
BURTON, JOHN, 198
Burton, John, 198
BURTON, WILLIAM, 198
Burton, William, 198
BUTLER, ELISHA, 14
Butler, Elisha, 14
BUTLER, JAMES, JR., 10
Butler, James, Jr., 10
BUTLER, JOSEPH, 14, 15
Butler, Joseph, Jr., 15
BUTLER, JOSEPH, SR., 14
BUTLER, SHEM, 15
Butler, Shem, 15
BUTLER, THOMAS, 10
Butler, Thomas, 10
BUTLER, WILLIAM, 8, 10, 11, 14
Butler, William, 8, 14
Butler, William, Jr., 128

C

Cadman, John, 12
CALWELL, CONSTANCE, 164
CALWELL, HENRY, 156
Calwell, Henry, 156
Calwells Point, 156
Calwells Swamp, 164
CAMPBELL, JAMES, 21
Campbell, James, 8, 88
CAMPBELL, MARTIN, 203
Campbell, Martin, 121
CAMPBELL, MARTIN AND MACARTIN, FRANCIS, 22
CAMPHER, CHRISTIAN, 25
Campher, Christian, 25
CAMUSE, ANTHONY, 22
Camuse, Anthony, 22
Cane Savannah, 153
Cannon ---, 23
Cannon, Daniel, 148
Cannon, Joseph, 148
Cannon, Marmaduke, 23
CARLTON, EDWARD, 24
Carlton, Edward, 24, 176
Carpenter Tything, 5, 21, 107, 130, 138, 168, 173, 185
CARR, WILLIAM, 29
Carr, William, 29
CARTER, THOMAS, 25
Carter, Thomas, 25, 95
Causton, Thomas, 204
Carwels, James, 100
CARY, JANE, 22
CARY, JOHN, 22
Cat Head Creek, 151, 155
Cayoke Creek, 90
Cedar Bluff, 156
CHAPMAN, EDWARD, 194
CHAPMAN, JANE, 194
CHAPMAN, JOHN, 125
Chapman, John, 125
Charles Town, 98, 101, 110
Cheesewright, Charles, 138
Cheesewright, Paul, 138
Cheesewright, Rebecca, 138
Cherokee Path, 164
Churburg, 207
Cladon Mount, 199

C

CLANCEY, THOMAS, 194
CLARK, DANIEL; BROWN, PATRICK; AND McGILLIVRAY, LACHLAN, 20
Clark, John, 131
Clark, Pat, 8, 199, 201
CLARK, PATRICK, 27, 28
Clark, Patrick, 27, 28
CLARK, WILLIAM, 122
Clark, William, 27, 199, 122
CLARKE, ANGUS, 156
Clarke, Angus, 156
CLARKE, DONALD, 155
Clarke, Donald, 155
CLARKE, HUGH, 155
Clarke, Hugh, 155
CLARKE, WILLIAM, 156
Clarke, William, 156
CLEMENT, WILLIAM, 29
Clement, William, 192
CLEMENTS, WILLIAM, 29
Clements, William, 29, 30
CLIFTON, WILLIAM, 21
Clock, Casper, 59, 60, 61, 62
Close, Henry, 178
Coffee, John, 2
COFFEY, FRANCES, 25, 30
COFFEY, JOHN, 26
Coles, Joseph, 32
Colkins, John, 5
Colkins, Jonathon, 5
Collins ---, 204
COLLINS, ANDREW, 195
Collins, Andrew, 165, 195
COLLINS, THOMAS, 26
Collins, Thomas, 27
Collins Creek, 10
COLVIN, JAMES, 86
Colvin, James, 86
Concordia, 198
Contor Sheet, 207
COOGLE, MATTHIAS, 116
Coogle, Matthias, 116
Cooksey, William, 193
Coonoche River, 17, 26
COOPER, RICHARD, 26
Cooper, Richard, 3, 26, 179, 189

C

Coosey, Sarah, 193
Cornberger, John, 63, 66, 67, 83
CORNECK, JAMES, 27
Cornell, George, 22
Council, The, 14, 15, 76, 82, 85, 179
COX, RICHARD, 128
Cox, Richard, 128
COX, RICHARD, SR., 127
Cox, Richard, Sr., 128
Cox, William, 89
Cragg, John, 121
CRAMER, CHRISTOPH, 81
Cramer, Christoph, 56, 58, 81, 175
Cranwetter, John Casper, 61, 77
CRANWETTER, MARY CATHARINA, 60, 61
Craven, Mariot, 118
CRIETER, JOHN, 28
Crieter, John, 28
CRONANBURGH, NICHOLAS, 204, 206
Cronanburgh, Nicholas, 207
CRONBERGER, JOHN, 67
Cronberger, John, 67, 68
CRONBERGER, NICHOLAS, 3
Cronberger, Nicholas, 3, 49
Crook, Isaac King, 205
Crooked Beaver Dams, 170
Cross, Thomas, 98, 181
Cross, William, 157
Crosswell, Benjamin, 27
CUBBEDGE, GEORGE, 30
Cubbedge, George, 30
CUBBEDGE, JOHN, 24, 25, 30
Cubbedge, John, 24
Cubbedges Creek, 25
CUNNINGHAM, DAVID, 28, 29, 205
Cunningham, David, 28
CUPPER, PETER, 30
CURTZ, JACOB, 114
Curtz, Jacob, 114
CUTHBERT, DANIEL, 197
CUTHBERT, GEORGE, 196
Cuthbert, George, 23, 24, 196
CUTHBERT, GORDON, 197
Cuthbert, George, 197
Cuthbert, John, 197

D

DANNER, JACOB, 113
Danner, Jacob, 113
Darien, 151, 152, 153, 154, 155, 156, 157, 162, 198
Darien Salts, 171
DASHER, CHRISTIAN, 30
Dasher, Christian, 103
DASHER, MARTYN, 54
DAVIDSON, EDWARD, 36
Davidson, Edward, 36
DAVIS, CALEB, 9, 10
DAVIS, JOHN, 36
Davis, John, 36, 197, 205
DAVIS, JOHN, JR., 36
Davis, John, Jr., 37
Davis, John, Sr., 36
Davis, William, 202
DEAN, HENRY, 126
DEAN, JAMES, 31, 162
Dean, James, 123, 162, 201
DEAN, LYDIA, 126
Dean, Mrs., 31
DeBare, David, 119
DeBrahm, Mr., 92
DeBrahm, William, 16, 88
DEBRAHM, WILLIAM GERARD, 37
DeBrahm, William, Gerard, 37
Deckers Ward, 5, 9, 10, 33, 107, 108, 109, 130, 131, 138, 139, 161, 168, 169, 173, 181, 185
Deer Point, 201
Deigler, Daniel, 119
DEININGER, GEORG, 53
Deininger, Georg, 53
DELEGAL, DAVID, 38
Delegal, David, 38
DELEGAL, GEORGE, 38, 207
Delegal, Philip, 8, 13, 181
DELEGAL, PHILIP, JR., 37, 38
Delegal, Philip, Jr., 37, 129, 207
DELEGAL, PHILIP, SR., 38
Delegal, Philip, Sr., 38
DELEON, ABRAHAM, 168
DeLeon, Abraham, 169
Delgrass, Francis, 175
Delgrass, Solomon, 175
Dellinger, Christoph, 47, 50

D

Demere, Captain, 170
DEMERE, RAYMOND, 30
Demere, Raymond, 139
DEMETRE, ANN, 32, 33, 34
DEMETRE, DANIEL, 34
Demetre, Daniel, 34
DENNISON, RICHARD, 195
DENNY, WALTER, 119
Denny, Walter, 119
DENSLER, HENRY, 86
Densler, Henry, 86
DEPPE, VALENTIN, 45
Deppe, Valentin, 44, 45, 46
Derby Ward, 5, 13, 21, 22, 32, 33, 86, 89, 92, 103, 129, 135, 137, 146, 158, 161, 172, 173, 176, 181, 185, 186, 193, 204
Derisou, James, 143
DERRICK, GEORGE, 112
Derrick, George, 114
De Saint Julien, Elizabeth, 95
Desborough, Ann, 10
Desborough, John, 110, 179
DE TEMPLE, PETER, 186
DeTemple, Peter, 186
DEVEAUX, JAMES, 35
Deveaux, James, 35, 36, 111, 178
DEVEAUX, JAMES, JR., 35
Deveaux, James, Jr., 35
Deveaux, James, Sr., 35
DEVEAUX, JOHN, 36
Deveaux, John, 36, 207
Dickensons Neck, 23, 34
Digby Tything, 9, 21, 131, 161, 168
Dissenting Minister, 169
District of Halifax, 200, 201
District of Newport, 196
DIXEE, JAMES, 38
Dixee, James, 38
Dixse, James, 136
DOBELL, JOHN, 101
Dobins, William, 171
Doboy Island, 171, 198
Dods, William, 56, 57
Dohorty, Cornelius, 121
Doleman ---, 134

D

DORMER, JAMES, 100
Dormer, James, 100
DOUGHERTY, CORNELIUS, 206
Douglass ---, 9
DOUGLASS, DAVID, 20, 31, 32
Douglass, David, 31, 32, 123, 200, 203
Douglass, George, 152
Douglass, John, 32
Dourowzeau, James, 143
DOWLE, PETER, 118
Dowle, Peter, 118
DOWNER, MICHAEL, 37
Drakin, 197
DRESLER, GEORGE, 38
Dresler, George, 38
Dressler, George, 78
DUDDING, JOHN, 36
DUNBAR, GEORGE, 38
Dunbar, George, 38, 162
DUNBAR, PRISCILLA, 139
Dunbar, Priscilla, 139
DUSSING, JACOB, 43
Dussing, Jacob, 43

E

Ebenezer, 28, 54, 85, 129, 144, 182, 204, 207
Ebenezer Creek, 41, 52, 53, 54, 55, 56, 57, 182
Ebenezer District, 175
EGERTON, THOMAS, 137
Egerton, Thomas, 138
Eigel, George, 61
Eigell ---, 81
EIGELL, GEORGE, 80
Eigell, George, 79
Eighth Tything, 207
EISHBERGER, DAVID, 78
Eishberger, David, 43, 77, 78, 79, 80
EISHBERGER, RUPERT, 70
Eishberger, Rupert, 60, 68, 69, 70, 72, 75
ELLICOTT, JOHN, 130
Ellicott, John, 130
ELLIOTT, WILLIAM, 101, 102
Elliott, William, 132
Elliott, William, Jr., 101

E

Ellis, Mr., 75
ELLIS, THOMAS, 86, 87
Ellis, Thomas, 16, 39, 74, 82, 85, 87, 136, 144, 161, 187
Elsoner, Samuel, 200, 203
Emery, Ann, 107, 170
ERNST, LUDWIG, 44
Ernst, Ludwig, 44, 57, 63, 66
Etherington, John, 203
EVANS, ELIZABETH AND JANE, 130
EVANS, JANE AND ELIZABETH, 130
Evans, John, 36, 130
EVANS, MIDDLETON, 193
Evans, Middleton, 1, 194
EWEN, WILLIAM, 39
Ewen, William, 39, 95, 207
Ewitt, James, 121
Eyles Tything, 107, 108, 126, 162, 174

F

Fair Groves, 197,
Farly, John, 189
Farmur, John, 8, 95, 187, 207
FENTON, MARTIN, 119
Fenton, Martin, 141
FETZER, JOHN ULRICH, 82
Fetzer, John Ulrich, 159
FETZGER, SEBASTIAN, 80
Fetzger, Sebastian, 80, 81
FEUTEL, FREDERICK, 186, 187
FEYRMUTH, ANNE, MARGARETTA, 42
Feyrmuth, Anne, Margaretta, 40, 41
Finch---, 121
FINCK, PAUL, 41
Finck, Paul, 39, 40, 42
First Tything, 2, 6, 9, 86, 91, 97, 101, 104, 160, 193, 204
FISHER, DAVID, 118
Fisher, David, 118
FISHER, GEORG, 42
FITCH, JOHN, 121
Fitch, John, 121, 194, 202
Fitzwalter, Joseph, 133
FITZWALTER, PENELOPE, 132, 133
FLEMING, CATHERINE, 133

F

Fleming, Catherine, 133
FLEMING, WALTER, 129
Fleming, Walter, 129, 133, 136
FLERL, CHARLES, 65, 66
Flerl, Charles, 64, 65, 66, 67, 144
FLERL, JOHN, 65
Flerl, John, 64, 66, 69, 78
FLETCHER, HENRY, 133
Folker, Joseph, 118
Fort Argyle, 158, 191
Fort Augusta, 164, 206
FOSTER, ELISHA, 139
Foster, Elisha, 139
Fourth Tything, 2, 29, 36, 88, 94, 135, 191, 192, 207
FOWL, GEORGE, 62
Fowl, George, 61
Fox, David, 38, 134
FOX, DAVID, JR., 87
Fox, David, Jr., 87
FOX, JOHN, 133
Fox, John, 134, 176
Fox, Robert, 163
FOX, WALTER, 135
Fox, Walter, 13, 135
FRANCIS, WILLIAM, 131, 132
Francis, William, 106, 111, 132, 181
FRANCK, JOHN PAUL, 48
Franck, John Paul, 48
Fraser, Hugh, 205
Fraser, James, 7, 104, 105, 131, 168
FRASER, MARGARET, 131
FRAZER, THOMAS, 133
Frazer, Thomas, 133
Frederica, 23, 30, 33, 134, 139, 148, 164, 170, 171, 172, 175, 181, 194, 196, 203, 207
Frederick Tything, 21, 32, 98, 132, 137, 181, 193, 204
FRICKINGER, CUNRAD, 47
Frickinger, Cunrad, 46, 47
Frieskinger, Cunrad, 45
Frisby, Abraham, 18
FRY, ABRAHAM, 114
Fyffe, Docotr, 122
FYFFE, GILBERT, 130
Fyffe, Gilbert, 27, 131, 199
FYFFE, GILBERT, JR., 199
Fyffe, Gilbert, Jr., 199
Fyffe, Mary, 199

G

GABEL, JOHN, 137
Gabel, John, 137
Gable, John, 28
GALACHE, JAMES, 87
Galache, James, 88
GALPHIN, GEORGE, 102
Galphin, George, 102, 104
Garrett, Henry, 138
GARVIS, JAMES, 135
GASWANDEL, THOMAS, 72, 73
Gaswandel, Thomas, 75, 80
Gates, Peter, 27, 121
GAUTIER, ANTHONY, 126
Gautier, 90, 126
Georgia, 196
GERIN, SIMEON, 113
Gerin, Simeon, 113
Germain, Ann, 87
GERMAIN, MICHAEL, 87
Germain, Michael, 87, 99
Germans, the, 142
German Village, 30
GERMANY, ALEXANDER, 199
Germany, Alexander, 199
GERMANY, JOHN, 199
GERMANY, ROBERT, 199
Germany, Robert, 199
Geswandel, Thomas, 53, 72, 73
Gibbons ---, 26
Gibbons, Joseph, 160
GIBBONS, JOSEPH, JR., 88
GIBBONS, JOSEPH, SR., 88
Gibbons, Joseph, Sr., 88
GIBBONS, WILLIAM, 136
Gibbons, William, 136
GIBBS, ISAAC, JR., 134
Gibbs, Isaac, Jr., 134
Gibbs, Mary 165
GIBBS, PHILIP, 134
Gibbs, Philip, 134
GIBS, ISAAC, 134
Gibs, Isaac, 134, 135
Giggs, Thomas, 123
GILBERT, ROBERT, 21
Gilbert, Robert, 21

G

Glamer, George, 58
GLANER, GEORGE, 61
Glaner, George, 61, 62, 64
Glebe, 83, 84, 85, 93, 169
Gloster, John, 121, 123
GNANN, JOHN GEORG, 51
Gnann, John Georg, 51
Goff, Samuel, 33
Golden Grove, 134
GOLDSMITH, THOMAS, 134
Goldsmith, Thomas, 85, 134
GOLDWIRE, BENJAMIN, 88
Goldwire, Benjamin, 8, 31, 173
GOLDWIRE, JOHN, 135, 200
Goldwire, John, 201
GOODALE, EDWARD, 136
Goodale, Edward, 136
Goodale, Thomas, 23, 135, 164
GOODBY, JOSEPH, 205
Goodby, Joseph, 205
GORDON, CUTHBERT, 197
Gordon, Cuthbert, 197
GORDON AND SMITH, 127
GORDON, JOHN, 127
Gordon, John, 127
Gore, William, 6
Goshen, 13, 14 19, 30, 37, 83, 120, 122, 130, 142, 145, 167, 174, 180, 183, 184, 187, 189, 191
Gough, William, 95
GRAHAM, ANN, 23, 24
GRAHAM, JOHN, 21, 203
GRAHAM, MUNGOE, 136
GRAHAM, PAT, 136
Graham, Pat, 136
Graham, Patrick, 23, 24
Grange, The, 131, 132
GRANT, GILBERT, 154
Grant, Gilbert, 154
Grant, James, 105
GRANT, JOHN, 153
Grant, John , 153
GRANT, PETER, 154
Grant, Peter, 154
GRANT, WILLIAM, 101
Grantham Town, 187

G

Granwetter, John Casper, 60, 61
GRAVES, SAMUEL, 50
Graves, Samuel, 49, 50, 51, 53
Gray, Edmund, 120
GRAY, JOHN, 148
Gray, John, 148
Gray, William, 172
Gready, John, 5, 35
Great Ciokee Creek, 20
Great Kayuka Creek, 164
Great Ogechee District, 128
Great Ogechee River, 8, 10, 14, 17, 38, 101, 102, 106, 112, 127, 128, 140, 141, 147, 149, 158, 165, 166, 167, 189, 191, 195, 196, 198, 205
Green, Ann, 195
Green, Henry, 101
Green, John, 85
GREEN, THOMAS, 195
Green Bryer, 199
Green Island, 39
GREINER, ANDREW, 200
Greiner, Andrew, 200
GREINER, JACOB, 200, 201
Greiner, Jacob, 200
GREINER, JOHN CASPER, 200
Greiner, John Casper, 200
Gress, George, 142
Grey, John, 121
Griffin, John, 91
Grigson, Jane, 195
Grigson, William, 195
Grimmiger, Andrew, 71
Grist Mill, 75, 129, 175
Grist and Saw Mill Plantation, 76
Grive, John Henry, 144
Groll, John, 50, 51
GROLL, MATTHIAS, 50
GRONAU, CHRISTIAN, 54, 55
GROOBS, ANTHONY, 135
Groobs, Anthony, 136
GROSS, GEORGE, 136
Gross, George, 136
GRUBER, GEORGE, 49
Gruber, George, 49
GRUBER, JOHN, 79, 80

G

Gruber, John, 79, 81, 83
Gruber, Peter, 48
GUGELL, JOHN, 53
Gugell, John, 54, 182
Guirard, Peter, 8, 181

H

HABERER, MICHAEL, 56
Haberer, Michael, 73, 81
HABERSHAM AND HARRIS, 90
Habersham and Harris, 90, 137, 138, 139
HABERSHAM, JAMES, 88, 89
Habersham, James, 85, 86, 89
Habersham, James, Jr., 94
HABERSHAM, JOSEPH, 89
Habersham, Joseph, 89
HAID, JOHN GEORG, 43
Haid, John Georg, 43, 205
Haines, Robert, 109
Hainks ---. 192
Haley, Gotlieb, 100
Half Moon Bluff, 17, 146, 186
Halifax, 144, 176
Halifax County, 102
HAMILTON, HENRY, 90
Hamilton, Henry, 90, 173
HAMM, JOHN, 141, 142
Hamm, John, 142
Hamm, Mister, 145, 182
HAMMER, PETER, 56, 57
Hammer, Peter, 57
HAMMOND, SAMUEL, 118
Hampstead, 87, 88, 123, 124
Hancock ---, 5
Hancock, Anthony, 87
HANGLEITER, JOHN, 48
Hangleiter, John, 47, 50
HANNER, JOHN, 140
Hanner, John, 140
HANOR, NICHOLAS, 114
Hanor, Nicholas, 114
Harding, John, 196
Hardwicke, 8, 17, 24, 89, 101, 106, 128, 148,

H

Hargrove, John, 19
HARN, JOHN, 140, 141
Harn, John, 102, 140
Harn, William, 141
Harper, William, 154
HARRIS AND HABERSHAM, 90
Harris and Habersham, 90, 137, 138, 139
HARRIS, FRANCIS, 18, 137
Harris, Francis, 106, 137, 171
Harris, William, 33
HARRIS, WILLIAM THOMAS, 34
Harris, William Thomas, 34
HASELFOOT, JAMES, 141
Haselfoot, James, 141
HAUVENER, PAUL, WIDOW OF, 118
Hauvener, Paul, 118
Hawkins, Doctor, 30
Haynes, William, 33
Hazzard, Richard, 111, 193, 205
HEART, JAMES, 85
Heathcote Tything, 24, 33, 97, 108, 109, 169, 181
Heathcote Ward, 4, 33, 38, 90, 96, 103, 106, 107, 108, 109,
    110, 126, 138, 146, 160, 161, 162, 163, 174, 179, 184
HECKETT, GEORGE, 57
Heckett, George, 57
HEINOY, JOHN GEORGE, 142
Heinoy, John George, 142
Held, John George, 81
Helfenstein, John Jacob, 58, 62
HELSER, CHRISTIAN, 60
HELVENSTEIN, JACOB, 195
Helvenstein, Jacob, 195, 196
HELVENSTEIN, JEREMIAH, 196
Helvenstein, Jeremiah, 195, 196
HELVENSTON, FREDERICK, 142
Helvenston, Frederick, 142
Hencock, John, 5
HENRICUS, ISAAC NUNES, 168
Henricus, Isaac Nunes, 168
HENSLER, JACOB, 200
Hensler, Jacob, 200
HEOK, CASPER, 47
Heok, Casper, 46, 47
HERBACK, GASPER, 112
Herback, George, 112

H

HERBACK, JACOB, 112
Herback, Jacob, 113
Hertzog, Martyn, 80
Hesster, Christian, 51
Hewitt, James, 121
HICKAMBOTTOM, THOMAS, 201
Hickambottom, Thomas, 201
Highgate, 124, 173
High Road, 30
Hill, Thomas, 7
Hill, William, 171
HINLIN, JOHN, 142
Hinlin, John, 142
Hinuick, John, 142
HIRSCH, JOHN MICHAEL, 57
Hirsch, John Michael, 57
Hirsham, John Casper, 201
HIRSHMAN, CASPER, 201
Hirshman, Casper, 201
HIRSHMAN, JOHN CASPER, 201
Hirshman, John Casper, 201
Hodges ---, 98
Hodges, Richard, 99
Hoffsetter, Gasper, 1
HOLBROKK, JACOB, 90
Holland Tything, 10, 35, 91, 103, 120, 160, 184, 185, 195
Holmes ---. 2
Holzendorf, Doctor, 30
HOPKINS, ANN, 200
Hopkins, Christopher, 200
Horseforth, 157
HORTON, THOMAS, 127
Horton, Thomas, 127
Horton, Major William, 171
HOUSTON, JAMES, 142
Houston , James, 125, 139, 142
HOUSTOUN, GEORGE, 139
HOUSTOUN, SIR PATRICK, BART., 139
Houstoun, Sir Patrick, Bart., 86, 139, 142
Houstoun, Robert, 119
HOUVER, CONRADE, 115
Houver, Conrade, 115
Howarth, Probart, 19, 207
HUBER, JACOB, 45
Huber, Jacob, 44, 46

H

Huck Tything, 2, 21, 157, 159, 162, 172, 173, 185, 205
Hughes, Joseph, 99
Hughes, William, 33
HUMBERT, DAVID, 140
Humbert, David, 140, 177
Hunold, John Georg, 53
HUNTER, JOSEPH, 100
HUNTING, NATHANIEL, 197
Hunting, Nathaniel, 197
Hutchinson, John, 197
HUTSON, ROBERT, 140
Hutson, Robert, 140
HUTSON, SAMUEL, 139
Hutson, Samuel 139

I

Illa Island, 38
ILLY, JACOB, 143
Illy, Jacob, 143
Illy, Michael, 180
Indian Town, 121

J

JANSACKE, JAMES, 125
Jansacke, James, 125
Jekyl Tything, 98, 99, 129, 133, 161, 173, 176
Jenkins, Edward, 195
Jenkins Island, 195
Jenys ---, 128
Johnson, Arthur, 127
JOHNSON, GEORGE, 143
Johnson, George, 143
Johnson, Doctor Lewis, 100
Johnson, Margaret, 175
JOHNSON, RICHARD, 143
Johnson, Richard, 143, 167, 205
JOHNSTON, WILLIAM, 143
Johnston, William, 143
J'on, Richard, 167, 205
Jones, N. W., 2, 3
JONES, NOBLE, 204
Jones, Noble, 89
Jones, Noble Wimberley, 171

J

Jones, Richard, 194, 206
JONES, SARAH, 194, 206
JONES, THOMAS, 138
JONES, WILLIAM, 202
Jones, William, 202
JORDAN, CHARLES, 120, 203
Jordan, Charles, 203
Josephs Town, 24, 30, 38, 136, 142, 143, 145, 161, 178, 183, 184
Josephs Town District, 130
Joubert, Peter, 94

K

Kaberer, Michael, 56
Kacher, Rupert, 52
KALCHER, RUPERT, 55
KAPPACHER, JOHN, 44
Kappacher, John, 44
Kasmayer, John Martyn, 55, 56
Kaupp, Joseph, 41, 42
Keeffer, Theobald, 49, 55, 63, 64, 65, 176
KEIBLER, JACOB, 145
KEIFER, DAVID, 117
Keifer, David, 117
KEIFER, DAVID AND FREDERICK, 117
KEIFER, FREDERICK, 129
Keifer, Frederick, 129
KEIFER, FREDERICK AND DAVID, 117
KEIFER, THEOBALD, 116
Keifer, Theobald, 116
KEIFFER, THEOBOLD, 144
Keiffer, Theobold, 144
KEISLER, DAVID, 124
Kelkenny, 197
Kelly, Ann, 91
Kelly, John, 91
KELSALL, JOHN, 193, 205
Kelsall, John, 193, 205
KENDER, DAVID, 124
Kender, David, 124
KENNEDY, DONALD, 150
Kennedy, Donald, 150
KENNEDY, HUGH, 145
Kennedy, Hugh, 145

K

Kennedy, John, 30
KENNEDY, WILLIAM, 145
Kennedy, William, 145
KENT, RICHARD, 203
Kent, Captain Richard, 9, 204
Kessler, Christian, 67
KIDD, GEORGE, 151
Kidd, George, 151
KILGORE, RALPH, 90
Kilgore, Thomas, 90
Klein, George, 42
KLEIN, JOHN GEORG, 41
Klein, John Georg, 41
KNAPP, MATTHIAS, 119
Kocher, George, 56, 73
KOGLER, GEORGE, 67, 68
Kogler, George, 53, 65, 67, 68, 74, 79, 159
Kohleison, John Peter, 65
KOHLEISON, PETER, 69
Kohleison, Peter, 60, 64, 68, 69, 70, 77
Kolcher, Rupert, 74
KRAFFT, DAVID, 175, 176
Krafft, David, 63, 159, 175, 176
KRAUSE, LEONHARD, 68, 69
Krause, Leonhard, 54, 55, 65, 68, 69, 70, 83
Kruse, John, 54, 78, 79, 80
KUNOLD, JOHN, 50
KUSMAUL, JACOB, 122
Kusmaul, Jacob, 122

L

Lachner ---, 84
LACHNER, MARTYN, SR., 83
Lachner, Martyn, Sr., 67, 69, 74, 75, 80, 84
LACHNER, VIET, 84
Lachner, Viet, 84
Lackner, Martyn, 61
LACKNER, MARTYN, JR., 60
Lackner, Martyn, Jr., 59, 63, 81
LAMBREEK, GEORGE, 147
Lambreek, 147
LANDFELDER, VIET, 59
Landfelder, Viet, 42, 54, 58, 59, 60, 63
Landree, James, 125

L

LANDREE, STEPHEN, 125
Lane, Hugh, 17
Langley, George, 5
Laroche Tything, 11, 33, 101, 106, 138, 205
Lathbury, Joseph, 108
Lebanon, 35
LEBON, ANTHONY, 146
LeBon, Anthony, 146
Lee, Richard, 27, 123
LEE, THOMAS, 91
Lee, Thomas, 91
LEIMBERGER, CHRISTIAN, 72
Leimberger, Christian, 50, 55, 71, 72, 77, 79
LEITNER, JOSEPH, 63, 64
Leitner, Joseph, 56, 62, 63, 75, 76, 129, 144
LEMCKE, REVEREND HARMAN HENRY, 78, 79, 145
Lemcke, Reverend Harman Henry, 145
Lemcke, Mister, 80, 130, 182
Lemhoffer, Widow, 45
Lemhoffer, Viet, 57, 64, 68, 74
LEMKE, REVEREND HARMAN, 3
LENOX, JAMES, 147
Lenox, James, 147
Leon, Simon, 112
LEVENBERGER, CHRISTIAN, 114
Levenberger, Christian, 114
Lindall, John, 96
LINES, ISAAC, 146
Lines, Isaac, 146, 165
LION, SAMUEL, 146
Lion, Samuel, 146
LITTLE, WILLIAM, 145, 146
Little, William, 146
Little Cayoika Creek, 199
Little Cyoka Creek, 202
Little Ogechee District, 39, 87, 106, 187
Little Ogechee River, 3, 8, 12, 13, 18, 24, 26, 35, 36, 37, 38, 87, 89, 94, 95, 97, 98, 102, 110, 125, 129, 132, 134, 136, 137, 139, 140, 142, 161, 163, 171, 176, 179, 181, 186, 188, 189, 190, 206, 207
Little River, 120, 143
Littrauer, Paul, 67
Lloyd, Henry, 178
Long Bridge, 60
Long Island, 18

M

MAYER, JACOB, 52
Mayer, Jacob, 52
McBain, Archibald, 103
McBEAN, JOHN, 150
McBean, John, 150
McBEAN, LAUGHLIN, 164
McBean, Laughlin, 122, 164, 170, 203
McBean, Minor, 131
McCLOUD, JOHN, 198
McCloud, John, 198
McDonal, William, 201
McDONALD, DONALD, 151
McDONALD, GEORGE, 150
McDonald, George, 150
McDonald, Norman, 151
McDONALD, RONALD, 153
McGILLIVRAY, DUNCAN, 120
McGILLIVRAY, LACHLAN, 102
McGillivray, Lachlan, 102
McGILLIVRAY, LACHLAN, BROWN, PATRICK, AND CLARK, DANIEL, 20
McHugh, Peter, 11, 195
McKay, John, 120
McKINTOSH, RODERICK, 23
McKintosh, Roderick, 23
McLaren, James, 142
McLEOD, DONALD, 150
McLeod, John, 150
McLEOD, MORDAH, 153
McLeod, Mordah, 153
McLEOD, RODERICK, 152
McLeod, Roderick, 152
McLoud, John, 112
MEADOWS, RICHARD, 202
Meadows, Richard, 202
MEARN, CHARLES, 166
Mearn, Charles, 166
MEARN, JOHN, 167
Mearn, John 167
MEARS, WILLIAM, 21
Mears, William, 21
Meddows, Richard, 202
MELLICHAMP, RICHARD, 161
Mellichamp, Richard, 11, 161
Mercer, Samuel, 141

M

Metzger, Balthazer, 43, 50
Metzger, Jacob, 72
METZGER, JOHN JACOB, 51
Metzger, John Jacob, 50, 51
Metzger, Philip, 51, 58
Meyer, Georg, 50
Meyer, Jacob, 51, 52
Meyer, John George, 48, 49, 50, 62, 73, 144
MEYER, JOHN LUDWIG, 159
Meyer, John Ludwig, 79, 82, 83, 159, 175
Meyer, Ludwig, 170
MEYER, MATTHIAS, 50
Meyer, Matthias, 51
MEYER, URSULA, 57
Meyer, Ursula, 43, 44
MEYERS, DANIEL, 203
MEYERS, HENRY, 166
Meyers, Henry, 189, 203, 207
Micheals Creek, 199
MICHER, LEWIS, 160
Micher, Lewis, 160
MICK, JONAS, 167
Mick, Jonas, 167
Midway, 6, 90
Midway Narrows, 30
Midway River, 1, 5, 8, 10, 11, 15, 16, 18, 24, 25, 26, 27, 30, 36, 85, 130, 134, 146, 165, 169, 182, 186, 189, 194, 195, 197, 198, 206, 207
Midway Swamp, 174
Mill Creek, 28, 32, 65, 82, 129, 159, 175
MILLEDGE, JOHN, 162, 163
Milledge, John, 5, 92, 161, 162, 163
MILLEDGE, RICHARD, 92, 93
Milledge, Richard, 92, 173, 178
Milledge, Sarah, 99, 176
Milledge, Thomas, 92
MILLER, DAVID, 152
Miller, David, 152
Miller, Frederick Wilhelm, 64
MILLER, JAMES, 93, 94
Miller, James, 94, 102
MILLER, JOHN PAUL, 64, 65
MILLER, JOHN PHILIP, 166
Miller, John Philip, 166
MILLER, NICHOLAS, 94

M

Miller, Nicholas, 94
Miller, Paul, 65, 144
Miller, Simon, 65, 77
Millichamps, Thomas, 10
Mill Lot, 44, 45
MINIS, ABRAHAM, 159
Minis, Abraham, 159
MINIS, ESTHER, 159
MINIS, JOSEPH, 159
Minis, Simeon, 160
Minoe, McBean, 122
MIOHLER, JOHN, 46
Miohler, John 46
MITCHELL, JOHN, 166
Mitchell, John, 166
MITCHELL, SARAH, 166
Mitchell, Sarah, 166
MOHR, JOHN, 44
Mohr, John, 44
MOLENA, ABRAHAM, 169
Molena, Abraham, 169
MONTAIGUT, DAVID, 129, 160
Montaigut, David, 88, 160
Montgaigut, Samuel, 160
Mooney, Thomas, 28
Moor, Jacob, 83
Moore, Robert, 101
Moore Tything, 11, 91, 101, 105, 109, 110, 138, 173, 179
MORE, JACOB, 167
More, Jacob, 167
MOREL, JOHN, 102, 103, 120
Morel, John, 103
MOREL, PETER, 103
Morel, Peter, 102
MORRISON, HUGH, 154
Morrison, Hugh, 154
MOSER, LUCAS, 149
Moser, Lucas, 142
Mosses, Lucas, 201
MOTTS, GEORGE, 124
Mount Pleasant, 139, 140, 145
Mouse, Ann, 29
Mouse, Lucy, 103, 192
Muggizer, John Michael, 71
Muggizer, Michael, 64

M

Muir, James, 161
MUIR, JOHN, 161
Muir, John, 161
Mulberry Grove, 177
Muller, Frederick Wilhelm, 63
Muller, Melchier, 167
MULLRYNE, CATHERINE, 197
Mullryne, Catherine, 197
MULLRYNE, JOHN, 198
Mullryne, John, 198
MULLRYNE, MARY, 197
Mullryne, Mary, 197
MUNROE, JAMES, 152
Munroe, James, 152
MUNROE, WILLIAM, 153
Munroe, William, 153
Murphy, Nicholas, 27, 123
Murry ---, 37
Murry, John, 37
Muse, James, 100
Mutteair ---, 166
MUTTEAIR, LEWIS, 165
Mutteair, Lewis, 10, 14, 165
Myers, John 200

N

NEIDLINGER, JOHN, 43
Neidlinger, John, 44, 53
NEIDLINGER, JOHN ULRICH, 62
Neidlinger, John Ulrich, 63
Ness River, 3
Nevie, John, 140
NEW, JAMES, 128
New, James, 128
NEW, SAMUEL, 128
New, Samuel, 128
NEWBERRY, WILLIAM, 126
Newington, 2, 4, 36, 88, 102, 136, 146, 160, 180, 185
Newport District, 120
Newport River, 25, 29, 32, 34, 95, 147, 149, 156, 168, 169, 194, 203, 205
New Savannah, 172
New Village Skidoway, 7
New Ward, 126

N

NIESS, GEORGE, 63
Niess, George, 62, 63
NOBLE, GEORGE, 168
Noble, George, 168
NOBLE, ROBERT, 168
Noble, Robert, 168
NONGAZER, HENRY, 117
NONGAZER, JACOB, 117
Nongazer, Jacob, 117, 118
North Newport River, 15, 166, 169, 182, 189
North Newport Swamp, 15, 16
NORTON, WILLIAM, 103
Norton, William, 103
NUNES, DANIEL, 168, 169
Nunes, Daniel, 7, 168

O

OAKES, JOSEPH, 170
Oakes, Joseph, 170, 203
Oaks, Joseph, 27, 203
Oately, Hugh, 121
O'Brien, Kenedy, 20
OECHSLIN, CHRISTIAN, 46
Oechslin, Christian, 46, 47
OESCHLIN, MICHAEL, 53
Oeschlin, Michael, 52, 53
Oexlins, Michael, 182
OFFSTATER, GASPER, 169, 170
Offstater, Gasper, 170
Oglethorpe, General, 20, 23, 24, 27, 30, 33, 103, 106, 107,
    123, 125, 135, 139, 148, 149, 150, 151, 164, 194
Oglethorpe, James, 20, 22, 23, 31, 32, 120, 131, 193
Oglethorpe, Mister, 87
Old Skidoway Village, 91
OLIVERO, JACOB, 109
Olivero, Jacob, 109
ONSELD, DAVID, 170
Onseld, David, 170
Onslow Island, 100, 178
ORDNER, ADAM, 117
Ordner, Adam, 117
Ormston, Thomas, 30
ORTMANN, CHRISTOPHER, 204
Ortmann, Christopher, 41, 56, 58, 68, 204

O

OSGOOD, JOHN, 169
Osgood, John, 169
OSGOOD, JOSIAH, 169
Osgood, Josiah, 169
Ott, Carl Sigmund, 58
OTT, CHARLES SIGMUND, 77
Ott, Charles Sigmund, 65, 77, 78
OTTOLENGHE, JOSEPH, 93
Ottolenghe, Joseph, 93
Overend, Joshua, 129
OVEREND, JOSHUA, HEIRS OF, 129
Overstreet, Henry, 121, 194

P

Pagea, Anthony, 185
Palmer, Richard, 35
PALMER, THOMAS, 174
Palmer, Thomas, 174
Papot, James, 3, 97, 132
Papot, Jeremiah, 22
PAPOT, MARGARET, 97
Papot, Peter, 97
Paris, James, 168
PARKER, ANN, 171
Parker, Ann, 171
Parker, Henry, 8, 171
PARKER, HENRY WILLIAM, 171
Parker, Henry William, 87, 106, 171
PARKER, JAMES, 96
Parker, James, 96
PARKER, JOHN, 11
Parker, John, 11
PARKER, JOSEPH, 171
Parker, Joseph, 171, 179
Parker, Samuel, 172
PARKER, THOMAS
Parker, Thomas, 92
Parker, William, 124, 126
Parker, William Henry, 187
PARRIS, JAMES, 126, 172
Parris, James, 172
PAULITSCH, JOHN MARTYN, 53
Paulitsch, John Martyn, 53, 54, 182
Paulitsch, Philip, 53, 182

P

PAYNE, WILLIAM, 120
Pechtly, George, 56
Pechtly, John Georg, 48, 49, 58
Penrose, John, 100, 173, 174, 178
PENROSE, JOHN AND MARY, 173, 174
Penrose, Mary, 173
PENROSE, MARY AND JOHN, 173, 174
PENSYRE, SAMUEL, 21
Pensyre, Samuel, 22
Percival Ward, 2, 4, 10, 21, 22, 35, 91, 93, 96, 97, 98,
    103, 105, 109, 110, 120, 138, 157, 159, 160, 162, 172,
    173, 175, 179, 184, 185, 195
PERKINS, JOHN, 171, 172
Perkins, John, 171
Peter, a Dutchman, 123
PETERS, GEORGE, 96
Pettigrew, Catherine, 103
PETTIGREW, JOHN, 103
Philadelphia, 101
Phillips, Joseph, 18, 163, 179
Pipemakers Creek, 102, 136, 140, 177, 191
Plessing Leonard, 14
PLETTER, JOHN, 71
Pletter, John, 56, 70, 71, 72, 176
Plumb Park, 5
Poplar Swamp, 14, 128
Ports, Philip, 13
PORTZ, JACOB, 174
Portz, Jacob, 174
Potter, Robert, 173
Potticary, Nathaniel, 95
POWELL, JAMES EDWARD, 95, 96
Powell, James Edward, 85, 96, 125
Pratt, Thomas, 33
President and Assistants, 1, 2, 3, 4, 6, 7, 8, 9, 10, 11, 12,
    13, 14, 15, 16, 17, 18, 19, 22, 23, 24, 25, 26, 27, 28,
    29, 30, 31, 32, 34, 35, 36, 37, 38, 39, 40, 41, 74, 75
    76, 82, 85, 86, 87, 88, 89, 90, 91, 92, 93, 94, 95, 96,
    97, 98, 99, 100, 101, 102, 103, 104, 105, 106, 107, 109,
    110, 111, 112, 113, 114, 115, 118, 120, 121, 122, 123,
    126, 127, 128, 129, 130, 131, 132, 133, 134, 135, 136,
    137, 139, 140, 141, 142, 143, 144, 145, 146, 147, 148,
    149, 150, 151, 153, 154, 155, 156, 157, 159, 160, 161,
    162, 163, 164, 165, 166, 167, 168, 169, 170, 171, 172,
    173, 174, 175, 176, 177, 178, 180, 181, 182, 183, 184,

P

    186, 187, 189, 190, 191, 193, 194, 197, 198, 199, 200,
    201, 202, 203, 204, 207
President and Council, 32, 130, 180, 195
PRICE, JOHN, 170
Price, John, 170
Prince of Wales Ship, 162
Provost Marhsall, 206
PRUNIERE, JOSEPH, 173
PUBLICK FOR AN INTENDED GRIST MILL, 44
PUBLICK FOR GRIST AND SAW MILLS, 75
Public Mills, 74
Public Wharf, 90
Purisburgh, 3, 204
Purry, Rodolph, 102, 105
Pury, Mister, 92
PYE, JOHN, 172, 173
Pye, John, 173
PYTT AND TUCKWELL, 138

Q

QUARTERMAN, JOHN, 174
Quarterman, John, 174
Quioco Creek, 164

R

RABENHORST, CHRISTIAN, 175, 176
Rabenhorst, Christian, 81, 82, 175
RADDICK, JOHN, 176
Raddick, John, 140, 176
RADDICK, MICHAEL, 105
Raddick, Michael, 105
RAE AND BARKSDALE, 19
RAE, JOHN, 19, 20
Rae, John, 20, 204
RAHN, CASPER, 176
Rahn, Casper, 176
RAHN, CUNRAD, 54, 176
Rahn, Cunrad, 53, 54
Rantowle, Alexander, 101
RASBERRY, THOMAS, 98
Rasberry, Thomas, 86, 98
Rau, John Georg, 47, 48
Rauner ---, 48

R

Rawcliff, 177
RAYMOND, JOSEPH, 176
Raymond, Joseph, 140, 177
Raynour, Laurence, 33
Rea and Barksdale, 144
READ, JAMES, 205
Reatter, Simon, 62
Red Bird Neck, 127
Red Bud Marshes, 128
RED, THOMAS, 177, 201
Red, Thomas, 90, 177, 201
Redford, Robert, 135
REIDELSPERGER, CHRISTIAN, 82, 83
Reidelsperger, Christian, 57, 67, 82, 159
Reinstettler, Adam, 116
REINSTETTLER, MATTHIAS, 119
Reinstettler, Matthias, 119
Reiser, Bath., 205
Reiser, George, 78, 84
Reiser, Michael, 83
Reiser, Michael, Sr., 78, 79
Reitnaurer, Laurence, 115
Relch, Andrew, 72
REMSHARDT, DANIEL, 73
Remshardt, Daniel, 74, 82
RENTZ, JOHN, 62
Rentz, John, 40, 42
Resch, Andrew, 61
Resch, Widow, 70
REUTTER, JOHN, 84
Reutter, John, 77, 79
Reutter, Peter, 67
REUTTER, SIMON, 73
Reutter, Simon, 52, 55, 73, 83
Reynolds Ward, 1, 2, 6, 9, 13, 28, 29, 36, 90, 129, 130, 135, 158, 160, 191, 192, 204
RHEINLANDER, JOHN MARTYN, 48
Rheinlander, John Martyn, 47, 48, 76, 80, 176
Rheinlander, Widow, 176
RIESER, BALTHAZER, 42, 43, 44
Rieser, Bartholomew, 56, 66
Rieser, George, 51, 62
RIESER, MICHAEL, 66, 67
Rieser, Michael, 51, 65, 66, 67
Rieser, Michael, Sr., 54, 60, 69

R

RIETER, CAUL (PAUL ?), 113
RIGBY, NICHOLAS, 176
RIGBY, SARAH, 176
Rihsh, George, 180
RING, CHRISTOPHER, 104
Ring, Christopher, 104
RISER, GEORGE, 178
Riser, George, 178
Roan, George, 163
ROBINSON, PICKERING, 177, 178
Robinson, Pickering, 92, 177
ROBINSON, THOMAS, 177
Robinson, Thomas, 177
ROCHE, MATTHEW, 178
Roche, Matthew, 178
Rockingham, 8
ROGERS, CHARLES, 88
Rogers, Charles, 88
Rogerson, John, 26
Ross, Alex, 17
ROSS, DONALD, 151
Ross, Donald, 151
ROSS, HUGH, 105, 106
Ross, Hugh, 105, 144
Ross, John, 142, 182
Ross, Thomas, 27, 32, 136
Rotten, 131
ROTTENBERGER, CHRISTOPHER, 52, 53
Rottenberger, Christopher, 52, 55, 68
Rotten Possum Island, 39
Rumney Marsh, 193
RUTHERFORD, JAMES, 175
Rutherford, Williamina, 175
RUSSELL, WILLIAM, 99, 100, 101
Russell, William, 99, 100, 133
Rutledge, John, 34

S

Saint Catherine River, 96
Saint Simons Island, 30
Salter, Thomas, 33, 34
Salters Creek, 85
Salters Island, 34
Sandford, Cornelius, 95

S

Sanfftleben, George, 55, 74, 75, 76, 80, 81, 144
Sapola River, 23, 34, 147, 148, 149, 150, 151, 153, 154, 155, 156, 157
Savannah, 1, 2, 4, 5, 9, 12, 13, 18, 20, 21, 22, 23, 24, 25, 26, 27, 28, 29, 31, 32, 33, 34, 36, 37, 38, 55, 85, 86, 87, 88, 89, 90, 91, 92, 93, 96, 97, 98, 102, 103, 105, 106, 107, 108, 109, 110, 125, 126, 127, 129, 130, 131, 135, 137, 138, 139, 143, 146, 157, 158, 159, 160, 161, 162, 163, 166, 168, 169, 170, 172, 173, 174, 176, 178, 179, 180, 181, 184, 185, 186, 191, 192, 193, 195, 196, 198, 203, 204, 205
Savannah River, 3, 7, 20, 24, 27, 28, 38, 44, 45, 47, 48, 50, 55, 58, 63, 65, 66, 67, 85, 93, 95, 102, 111, 120, 121, 123, 125, 126, 130, 131, 136, 139, 140, 142, 144, 145, 161, 164, 172, 177, 178, 191, 194, 197, 199, 200, 201, 202, 204
Savannah River Swamp, 130
Saw Mill, 75, 129
Saw and Grist Mill Plantation, 76
Schartner, Jacob, 76
SCHNEIDER, ANDREW, 183
Schneider, Andrew, 183
Schrempff, Rupert, 45, 81
SEALES, WILLIAM, 107
SECKINGER, ANDREW, 182
Seckinger, Andrew, 182
SECKINGER, MATTHEW, 184
Seckinger, Matthew, 184
Seckinger, Matthias, 142
Second Swamp, 150
Second Tything, 28, 138, 143, 157, 159, 178, 203
Second Ward, 204
Serjeant, Henry, 132
Seymour, Christopher, 164
SHAD, SALOMO, 182
SHAVE, JOHN, 183
Shave, John, 183
Sheffler, John, 41, 64, 82
Sheffter, John, 45
SHEFTAL, BENJAMIN, 108, 109
Sheftal, Benjamin, 37, 108
SHEFTAL, MORDECAI, 108
Sheiner, Rupert, 55
Sheinhulst, William, 112
Sherais, John, 182

S

SHERAUSE, GEORGE, 183
Sherause, George, 183
SHERAUSS, JOHN, 183
Sherauss, John, 149, 183
SHERIFF, JOHN, 180
Sheriff, John, 180
SHIELE, JOHN, 51
Shiele, John, 51, 52
Ship, Prince of Wales, 162
Shneider, Michael, 175
SHREMPFF, RUPERT, 45
Shrempff, Rupert, 45, 47, 60
Shubdrin, Daniel, 39, 59, 68
SHUBDRIN, DANIEL, JR., 40
Shubdrin, Daniel, Jr., 39, 40, 41
Shubdrin, John, 41
SHUBDRIN, JOHN PETER, 40
Shubdrin, John Peter, 40, 41, 42
SHUBDRIN, JOSEPH, 39
Shubdrin, Joseph, 39, 40, 41
SHUBDRIN, NICOLAUS, 41
Shubdrin, Nicolaus, 40, 41, 42
Silver Bluff, 102
Sinclair, Archibald, 207
Skidoway Island, 17, 29, 35, 37, 39, 86, 87, 91, 103, 111,
    112, 143, 146, 158, 163, 186, 192, 193, 197, 205
Skidoway River, 105
SLITERMAN, JERE:, 106, 107
Sliterman, Jere:, 107
Sliterman, Peter, 98
Sloan, John, 6
Sloper Tything, 4, 22, 35, 93, 96, 97, 98, 172, 175
SLYTERMAN, PETER, 180
Slyterman, Peter, 3, 132
Smith, Ann Skidoway, 163
SMITH, JOHN, 55, 56, 126, 127
Smith, John, 34, 55, 56, 58, 64, 66, 71, 133
SMITH, MARY, WIDOW, 181
Smith, Thomas, 20, 163
SMITH AND GORDON, 127
Smiths Island, 34
SNEIDER, JOHN GEORG, 81
Sneider, John Georg, 64, 73, 80, 81, 82, 84
SNEIDER, MICHAEL, 82
Sneider, Michael, 61, 68, 81

S

SNIDER, GASPER, 116
Snider, Gasper, 116
SNOOK, DAVID, 107, 108
Snook, David, 107, 108, 179
SNOOK, JOHN, 108
Snook, John, 108
Soap Creek, 202
Soldner, Martyn, 53
Solener, Martyn, 54
South Carolina, 3, 110, 193
South Swamp of Midway River, 130, 183
Spencer ---, 196
Spencer, John, 104
SPENCER, RICHARD, 182
Spencer, Richard, 182
SPENCER, WILLIAM, 106
Spencer, William, 106, 199
Spirit Creek, 6, 143
Spood, William, 3, 26
Springfield, 35
Spring Groves, 121
Stahle, John, 83
STALEY, GOTLIEB, 180
Staley, John, 145
STANLEY, ELIZABETH, 179
Stanley, Isabel, 179
STANLEY, JOSEPH, 179, 205
Stanley, 21, 137, 179
STEHELY, JOHN, 183
Stehely, John, 184
STEHELY, JOHN, JR., 183
Stehely, John, Jr., 183
STEINER, CHRISTIAN, 73, 74
Steiner, Rupert, 68, 72, 73, 74, 76
Steiner, Simon, 55, 64, 66, 69, 76, 78
Steinhaville, Anna, 117
Stephens, Col., 39
STEPHENS, NEWDIGATE, 181
Stephens, Newdigate, 95, 110, 157, 181, 186
Stephens, Thomas, 181
Stephens, William, 89, 181
Sterling, Messrs., 128
Sterling Swamp, 8, 102, 141
STEUART, ANN, 107

S

Stevens, Anna, 148
STEVENS, JOHN, 147, 182
Stevens, John, 147, 182
Steward, Donald, 104
STEWARD, JOHN, 104
STEWART, JAMES, 151
Stewart, James, 151
STROUB, ADAM, 70
Stroub, Adam, 69, 70, 71, 84
Stroubler, Jacob, 16, 114
Stuart, John, 151
Summerour, Joseph, 206
Summers, James, 179
SUMMERS, JOSEPH, 178, 179
Summers, Joseph, 26, 110, 179
SUMNER, EDWARD, 182
Sumner, Edward, 182
Sumner, Thomas, 148
SUTHERLAND, PATRICK, 147
Sutherland, Patrick, 147
SWEIGER, GEORG, 77
Sweiger, Georg, 61, 65, 76, 77
SWEIGHOFFER, THOMAS, 42
Sweighoffer, Thomas, 42, 53
SWINEA, JOHN, 191
Swinea, John 181
SWISER, MICHAEL, 180
Swiser, Michael, 180

T

Tailfer, Patrick, 125
Talbot Street, 148
TANNATT, EDMUND, 186
Tannatt, Edmund, 1, 186
TARIAN, STEPHEN, 109
Tarian, Stephen, 109
Taylor, James Stuart, 23
TAYLOR, NATHAN, 186
Taylor, Nathan, 165, 186
Taylor, William Watkins, 120
T'BEAR, DAVID, 16
T'Bear, David, 16
Teasdale, John, 158
Tebeau, Daniel, 186
TEBEAU, JAMES, 186

T

Tebeau, James, 8, 12, 93
Tertler, John, 113
Thebault, James, 37
THILO, CHRISTIAN ERNST, 57, 58
Thilo, Christian Ernst, 59, 62, 83
Third Tything, 1, 7, 13, 25, 30, 36, 88, 90, 97, 106, 130, 133, 158, 204
THIS, HANNAH DOROTHY, 122
THIS, JACOB, 122
This, Jacob, 122
THOMPSON, JOHN, 203
Thompson, John, 194, 203
Thunderbolt, 1, 86, 105, 174, 192
TINLEY, JOHN, 122, 123
Tinley, John, 8, 27, 31, 123
TISDALE, JOHN, 185
Tisdale, John, 130, 158, 185
TODD, JOHN, JR., 120
Todd, John, Jr., 120
TODD, JOHN, SR., 196
Todd, John, Sr., 196
TONDEE, PETER, 109
Tondee, Peter, 109
Tower Tything, 10, 109, 139, 169, 170
Traces Ward, 148
Tracy Ward, 33
TREUTTLIN, JOHN ADAM, 49
Treuttlin, John Adam, 47, 50
TRIBOUDET, JOHN FRANCIS, 185
Triedling, Frederic, 189
TRIPP, ISAAC, 184
TRIPP, THOMAS, 184
Tripp, Thomas, 184
TRUAN, DAVID, 110
Truan, David, 110
TRUAN, JACOB, 185
Truan, Jacob, 185
Trustees, 4, 6, 9, 11, 12, 13, 14, 20, 21, 22, 29, 32, 33, 37, 38, 86, 90, 91, 93, 96, 97, 98, 103, 107, 108, 109, 110, 113, 116, 117, 118, 119, 121, 123, 124, 125, 126, 129, 132, 133, 134, 135, 137, 138, 139, 141, 142, 143, 146, 157, 158, 159, 161, 162, 168, 169, 173, 176, 178, 179, 181, 184, 185, 187, 188, 191, 192, 193, 195, 197, 202, 203
Trustees Farm, 21

T

Trust Farm Lots, 98
Trust Lots, 91, 93, 107, 108, 110, 173, 184
TUCKWELL AND PYTT, 138
Turkey Camp Swamp, 150, 155
Turkey Cock Hill, 140, 177
Turner, James, 205
TURNER, RICHARD, 108
Turner, Richard, 108
Two Sisters, 145
Tybee Island, 12, 22, 121
Tyrconnel Tything, 13, 22, 33, 92, 100, 103, 146, 172, 178, 186

U

Uchee Island, 19, 206
Uland, Elizabeth Barbara, 118
ULAND, GEORGE, 114, 115, 118
Uland, George, 115, 133
Unseldt, David, 82
Upper Landing at Savannah, 18
Upper New Tything, 198
Upper New Ward, 7, 25, 30, 86, 88, 91, 94, 97, 104, 106, 133, 143, 157, 159, 192, 193
UPTON, THOMAS, 110

V

VALATON, JEREMIAH, 110
Valaton, Jeremiah, 110
Vale, Isaac D., 87
VAN BEVERHOUDT, ADRIAN, 17, 18, 104
Van Beverhoudt, Adrian, 18, 104
Van Beverhoudt, Johann, 104
VAN BEVERHOUDT, JOHN, 18
Van Beverhoudt, John, 18
VAN BEVERHOUDT, JON, 104
Van Beverhoudt, Jon, 104
Van Brahm, Mr., 85
Vaughn, Robert, 168
VENING, SAMUEL, 202
Vening, Samuel, 121
VENNING, SAMUEL, 194
Vernon River, 139, 142, 157, 181
Vernon Tything, 38, 90, 103, 109, 110, 160, 161, 179, 184

V

Vernonburgh, 16, 25, 86, 108, 114, 115, 116, 117, 119, 122, 129, 133, 147
Visley, Mister, 123

W

WACHTER, JOHN, 190
Wachter, Joseph, 190
Waggener ---, 123
Waldbourger, Jacob, 111
WALKER, ANDREW, 203
WALL, JAMES, 127
Wall, James, 127
WALLISER, MICHAEL, 63
Walliser, Michael, 63
Walnut Point, 6
WALSET, ANDREW, 207
Walthour, George, 87
Walthour, Jacob, 95
WALTHOUR, JACOB CASPER, 187
Walthour, Jacob Casper, 39, 187
WARNOCK, JOHN, 147
Warren, Richard, 5, 86
Warsaw River, 111
Waterman ---, 172
Water Mellon Bluff, 168, 203
Watkins, William, 120, 203
Watson, Ann, 192
WATSON, CHARLES, 109
Watson, Charles, 2, 3, 4, 5, 6, 8, 9, 12, 13, 14, 17, 18, 19, 22, 28, 29, 36, 37, 90, 91, 92, 93, 94, 103, 106, 107, 108, 109, 110, 112, 113, 114, 115, 116, 117, 118, 119, 120, 121, 123, 124, 126, 129, 130, 131, 132, 135, 140, 141, 143, 145, 146, 157, 158, 159, 160, 161, 162, 163, 168, 169, 171, 172, 173, 174, 175, 176, 178, 179, 180, 181, 184, 185, 186, 188, 189, 191, 192, 195, 196, 207
WATSON, JOSEPH, 187, 188
Watson, Joseph, 111, 132, 187, 188
Watson, Nathaniel, 85
Watts, Francis, 89
WAY, EDWARD, 190
Way, Edward, 190
WAY, MOSES, 190
WAY, NATHANIEL, 190

W

Way, Nathaniel, 190
WAY, PARMENUS, 189
Way, Parmenus, 189
WAY, SAMUEL, 190
Way, Samuel, 190
WAY, THOMAS, 189
Way, Thomas, 189
Webb, Thomas, 27, 123
WEBER, JOHN MICHAEL, 84
Weber, John Michael, 83, 84
Weddell, Austin, 97
Weddell, Benjamin, 97
WEIDMAN, LUDWIG, 41
Weidman, Ludwig, 41, 42
Weinjauff, Michael, 44
WEINKAUFF, MICHAEL, 43
Weinkauff, Michael, 43
Weisenbach, Jacob, 187
WERTSCH, JOHN CASPER, 49
Wertsch, John Casper, 47, 49
Wertsok, John Casper, 45
WEST, CHARLES, 102
West, Charles, 102
West, John, 100
WEST MATTHIAS, 189
West, Matthias, 145
WEST, WILLOUGHBE, 191
West, Willoughbe, 191
WHITE, JAMES, 108
White, James, 108
White, Richard, 172
Whitmarsh Island, 6, 29, 174
WILLIAMS, GRIFFITH, 127
Williams, Griffith, 127
Williams, James, 125, 197
Williams, John, 125
Williams, Robert, 95, 126
WILLIAMS, ROBERT, JR., 125
WILLIAMS, ROBERT, SR., 125
Williams, Robert, Sr., 125
Williams, Samuel, 32
Williams, Stephen, 141
Williams, Thomas, 202
WILLIAMSON, SOPHIA, 204
Willson, John, 167, 196

W

Wilmington Island, 9, 22, 204
Wilmington Tything, 5, 13, 86, 89, 91, 100, 133, 135, 158, 185, 193
WILSON, BENJAMIN, 188, 206
Wilson, Benjamin, 110, 188, 206
Wilson, James, 103
WILSON, JOHN, 188
Wilson, John, 188
WILSON, THOMAS, 110, 206
Wilson, Thomas, 110, 206
WILSON, WILLIAM, 189
Wilson, William, 26, 186, 189
WINKLER, GEORGE, 191
Winkler, George, 191
Wisely, George John, 121
Wisenbacker, Christopher, 180
Withrington Bluff, 126
WOOD, JOSEPH, 190
Wood, Joseph, 191
WOODROFFE, WILLIAM, 138
Woodroffe, William, 138
Wright, John, 132
Wright, John Norton, 99, 133
Wright, Samuel, 120
WYLLY, ALEXANDER, 105
Wylly, Alexander, 102, 105

Y

Yamacraw, 188
Yoakley, John, 174
YONGE, FRANCIS, 111
Yonge, Francis, 112
YONGE, HENRY, 111, 112, 193, 206
Yonge, Henry, 111, 197, 198
Youchee Island, 202
Young, Elizabeth, 192
YOUNG, ISAAC, 191, 192, 193
Young, Isaac, 191
Young, Jerry, 119
Young, John, 192
YOUNG, MARY, 193
YOUNG, PETER, 119
Young, Thomas, 192, 193
Young, William, 193

Z

Zantt, Bartholomew, 61
ZANTT, SALOMO, 61
Zantt, Salomo, 60, 61, 72, 80
ZEIGLER, JOHN GEORGE, 205
Zeigler, John George, 205
ZETTLER, MATTHEW, 52
Zettler, Matthew, 45, 52, 53, 55, 73
Ziegler, John Georg, 43
ZIMMEREBEN, RUPERT, 74
ZIMMEREBNER, RUPERT, 75
Zimmerebner, Rupert, 68, 70, 72, 73, 75, 76
Zittrauer, Paul, 40
ZITTRAUER, PAULUS, 68
Zittrauer, Paulus, 58, 60, 67, 68, 70, 81
Zittrauer, Rupert, 69, 71
ZOUBERBUHLER, BARTHOLOMEW, 111
Zouberbuhler, Bartholomew, 111

***

www.ingramcontent.com/pod-product-compliance
Lightning Source LLC
Chambersburg PA
CBHW030546080526
44585CB00012B/279

After dropping the Centennial League title in 2009, the girls set out to recapture that championship. They did just that. They swept the singles and doubles championships and added a fifth-place finish by Stoica. Combine that with a second-place finish in doubles by the team of Hirsch and Peterson, and that left little doubt about the team champion. Rural scored a 92-73 win over Manhattan.

"It was a great day for the kids," Hedberg said. "The doubles teams performed really well, and we got a great performance out of Smith and Stoica in singles, so it was everything we hoped for." Hedberg said that last year's team loss to Topeka West motivated his players to improve and get better in the off-season.

So it was on to regionals where Rural would try and run their string of regional titles to ten in a row despite some misfortune.

The doubles teams placed first and third, respectfully. Shepler and Mackenzie Hill won the doubles event, while teammates Peterson and Hirsch took third place. Smith continued her string of wins as the singles champion. The downside was Stoica having to withdraw from singles competition due to a knee injury that she had been battling all season. In fact, it was Hedberg's decision to have her withdraw. He said it was one of his most difficult decisions. So the team of five advanced to the weekend state tournament.

Hedberg entered the state weekend hoping for a top six team finish. He got that and then some as the Junior Blues propelled themselves to third place and a trophy. Hedberg said this team was made-up of overachievers and clutch performers. The third-place finish in singles and the fourth-place finish by the doubles team of Shepler and Mackenzie Hill gave the Junior Blues third place with 27 points, finishing behind Blue Valley North and Shawnee Mission East. "The doubles team showed up and played really well today, and Taylor Smith getting third (in singles) is fantastic. I'm thrilled with the team finish."

2011—KING OF THE HILL: FRESHMAN NEWCOMER HILL SHINES

The Capital-Journal's preseason look at the city tennis teams didn't reveal too much of Coach Hedberg's enthusiasm. Rural had finished third at the state tournament as a team and returned a doubles team that placed fourth in 6A. He also mentioned that Maria Stoica was once again healthy. He didn't mention that he undoubtedly had one of the best freshmen entering the program, and not just one of the best in the city. Perhaps one of the best in the state. He low-keyed it saying, "We look forward to a good season." Sometimes coaches don't tip their hands. They wait and let it play out on the courts.

When newcomer freshman Madeline Hill went 3-0 in her first quadrangular, Hedberg revealed, "Madeline's a very talented young lady, and she's got a lot of tennis, a lot of game. I've kind of known what I had as far as the ability and talent level, but it was really great to watch her battle and not give up." In her second match of the day, she fell behind 7-3, but came back to win the match.

At the city tournament, Rural left no doubt about their skills. They swept all four events and secured a 31-22 team victory over second-place Hayden. In addition to Hill's number one singles championship, sophomore Irene Nicolae also won the number two singles event. The number one doubles team of senior Gwen Shepler and junior Mackenzie Hill took care of business winning their event, and their junior teammates Maria Stoica and Alix Welch captured the number two doubles event. Four events, four victories for the talented Junior Blues. Hedberg commented, "It's nice to have all the girls have success like that. We had some difficult matches in the finals, and it was good to see all the girls in town. We had a really nice day." Perhaps a bit of an understatement, but it was early in the season.

Again, at the Centennial League meet, Rural took the top two spots in doubles and Hill won her first league singles title. Washburn Rural outdistanced Manhattan 91-73 to take the Centennial League title. Coach Hedberg was hopeful that the Junior Blues could successfully defend last year's league championship and start another streak. But he also wanted to come out of the meet healthy. Injuries had plagued this bunch the last couple of years. This was simply a tune-up for the regionals to be played on Saturday.

Hedberg mentioned, "I thought this morning we were in some degree of difficulty, and the girls came through nicely. It's a long day and a grueling event."

For the singles event, the freshman Hill had to play six matches. She not only won them all, she claimed every game. When interviewed by Capital-Journal sportswriter Rick Peterson, Hill reflected, "I think I've improved a lot during the season, so I'm really happy about that." It's hard to think she could be much better against city and league competition. Her real test would be at regionals.

Washburn Rural proved worthy, taking first place at their regional meet. So Madeline Hill, who captured first place in singles at regionals, took a 27-2 record into the 6A state event. The doubles team of Shepler and Madeline Hill also took first place in the doubles event, running their record to 26-3. Nicolae placed fifth in singles at regionals, running her record to 21-9, and the doubles team of Stoica and Welch also qualified for state and had a record of 17-6 going into the weekend state tournament. All six girls qualified for state. Hedberg mentioned a couple of powers from Kansas City—Shawnee Mission East with two great singles players and Blue Valley North who won the state title in 2010.

At the state tournament Hill made it to the semifinals, finishing fourth place in her first high school season. The doubles team of Stoica and Welch finished tenth while Nicolae was twelfth in singles. Those three placings earned Rural a trophy, finishing third at state.

It is interesting to note that Stoica continued her formal education both at MIT and Harvard. Nicolae continued hers at Harvard. As good as they were at tennis, they were even better students.

2012 – A HISTORICAL FIRST FOR HEDBERG AND HILL IN GIRLS' SINGLES

The Capital-Journal's preseason capsule of city tennis mentioned that Rural was city, league and regional champions and finished third as a team at the 6A state tournament. Hedberg also listed twelve returners from the previous season in addition to three good newcomers joining the program. Hedberg told the Capital-Journal, "We have a very deep team and we return five starters from 2011." Sophomore Madeline Hill and senior Mackenzie Hill were expected to be the singles players.

At the city meet, Madeline Hill won her second consecutive singles championship, and Mackenzie Hill captured the number two singles event. On Tuesday, Madeline Hill became the first Topekan to win the singles event at the prestigious St. Thomas Aquinas invitational. And on Thursday, she helped lead the Junior Blues to their eighth straight city championship. Newcomer freshman Laura Nicolae (who went on to attend Harvard) and her doubles partner, junior Melaina Piyassaphan, won the number two doubles event, propelling Rural to a 28-22 team victory over runner up Topeka West.

The road to the Centennial League team title saw Rural topping Hayden 90-74, but also saw Madeline Hill's ability to dig deep and recover when behind. Hill overcame a 3-2 deficit at the hands of an Emporia singles player, but she came back to capture the league title 8-3. She ran her season record to 22-0. Mackenzie Hill took fourth in the singles event. Rural seniors Maria Stoica and Alix Welch captured the doubles event while their teammates Nicolae and Piyassaphan took fifth place to round out the deep Rural point getters.

The doubles team of Stoica and Welch avenged their city losses. Stoica said, "We were just hitting really well today. We were able to beat West in pool play, and then we went on to beat Hayden who also beat us at city. It was a good day."

Washburn Rural geared up for the regionals and captured that championship too, finishing first and second in both singles and doubles. They qualified their whole team for the 6A state tournament. There was a lot of pressure on undefeated singles player Madeline Hill. Hill would join four really good tennis players from the Kansas City schools, and she had a good strategy going into the state event. "Fourth place last year I guess—like I said last year—I'll try to go for third. If better happens, that's awesome, but I'm not going to put too much pressure on myself," Hill told Capital-Journal sportswriter Rick Peterson. Teammate Mackenzie Hill took a 21-9 record to state. The doubles team of Nicolae and Piyassaphan took a 28-5 record to the state event, and their doubles teammates Stoica and Welch boasted a 21-7 record.

At the state event, Madeline Hill worked her way into the semifinals, winning her first two matches to hold an unblemished record at 28-0. The doubles teams of Stoica and Welch and Nicolae and Piyassaphan also advanced to Saturday.

On Saturday, Nicolae and Piyassaphan finished eighth while the other doubles team of Stoica and Welch placed eleventh.

But the big news of the day, really the season, was Madeline Hill remaining undefeated and winning the 6A state singles. Just a sophomore, she fought exhaustion in both her semifinal victory and in the final. "I really felt empty that whole last set honestly," said Hill. "I just tried to stay in it and keep my mind there, because my body wasn't. It was extremely exhausting. I would say I was more worried than confident. I didn't know if I would make it through that last set because I'm not in shape. I was more on the worried side."

For Hedberg, Hill became his first girls' state singles champion after having some very successful individuals at Rural in his first 22 years coaching the Junior Blues. And he sensed that Hill was wearing out. "I know she's a terrific fighter so I never gave up on her, but in the first set when she had a lead and kind of let it get away, I was kind of concerned about having to go back to back, three set matches. But she stepped up, and the way she played I think she wore her opponent down a lot in the second set, and she got stronger as the third set went along."

As a team, Washburn Rural was in the hardware with a third-place team finish.

In a follow-up article about Hill's state singles championship, Hill told Capital-Journal sportswriter Rick Peterson, "I wanted to win state for Hedberg, I was not playing for myself."

Hill went on to express how many Rural tennis players feel about their coach saying, "Hedberg is such a great coach. He has helped me through everything. Without him, I wouldn't have won." Hill became only the fifth Topeka girls tennis player to win a state singles championship as of 2022.

2013—WHAT DOES THE JUNIOR HILL DO AFTER THE PREVIOUS YEAR'S WIN?

This would be an unusual and unprecedented start to any season Kevin Hedberg had kicked off in his high school coaching career. The 6A singles champion, now junior Madeline Hill, was not practicing yet, albeit there were ten players returning from the previous season and three young newcomers with promise according to Hedberg's preseason tennis capsule he gave to the Capital-Journal. "We should have a good season and are looking forward to our young players getting experience," Hedberg said.

By the time the city event rolled around, Madeline had rejoined her Junior Blue tennis team. It was her first meet of the year, and she knocked off whatever rust there might have been and won her third straight singles championship, although it would take some time to return to the form from last season when she capped an undefeated high school season with a state singles championship. Hill received a first-round bye and dropped just two games all day and defeated Shawnee Heights number one singles player 8-1.

Hill told Capital-Journal sportswriter Rick Peterson, "I've never completely loved tennis, and I lost a lot of love for it this summer. I kind of went through a rough time and kind of got out of it a little bit. I just figured that if I stepped back, my goal was to try to gain that (love for tennis) back. The reason I'm out here today is because I love my coach (Kevin Hedberg) so much and my teammates. I've been taking a step back to try and figure out what God wanted me to do with (tennis), and I just thought I would go out and just try to play for the team and help them out the best I can." Other than acknowledging that she felt a bit rusty mentally and with her game, she said she hoped she'd get her spirit back.

Seniors Irene Nicolae and Melaina Piyassaphan captured the city title in number one doubles with an 8-4 win over a Topeka High duo. The previous year, as juniors, Nicolae and Piyassaphan captured the number two doubles at city. They won their title with aggression at the net and by staying positive during the volleys. Sophomore Darby Hirsch and junior Mikaela Steinagle won the number two doubles event over a Hayden pair. Freshman Avery Munns made it all the way to the number two singles championship, dropping and 8-2 match to a Shawnee Heights singles player.

It was much the same and business as usual at the Centennial League meet. Hill once again dominated singles. Hill lost just two games in six matches all day, capturing her third straight league singles title. She told Capital-Journal's Peterson, "I was actually able to get my mind out of the way today, and I'm happy." Hill confided, "I was able to go for my shots, and I played free."

Hirsch and Steinagle continued their dominance by capturing the doubles event, and this helped carry Rural to an 88-79 team margin over Emporia. Nicolae and Piyassaphan, who captured the number one city doubles last week, took fourth in league. Hedberg commented on the parity in doubles. "The four schools that were in the semifinals were all so close. All those doubles teams could beat each other on any given day, but today was Mikaela and Darby's day, and they played great."

Despite her successes, Hill mentioned that the original plan was to compete only in city and league, and bypass regionals and possibly state. Now she'd reached that point in the season where she said she would like to sit down and re-evaluate that original plan.

Veteran coach Hedberg said he was a hundred percent behind Hill's decision either way. "She's such a talented kid, and she's just got to sort through things and see how all this is going to play out for her," Hedberg told sportswriter Peterson,

"We want her to do what's best for her. We'll be glad to have her, if we have her and, if we don't have her, we'll play as hard as we can without her." Would all coaches show this much patience? If they care about their players as people, yes they would.

After some long and careful thought, and likely some chats with folks close to her, Hill decided her game was pretty decent, so she rolled to 15-0 after capturing her third straight regional singles title. Hill's championship, combined with Steinagle and Hirsch second place finish in doubles and their teammates Nicolae and Piyassaphan's third place finish, rolled Rural to a 20-13 team scoring margin over Derby. The icing on the cake was freshman Munns qualifying for state also with a sixth-place finish in singles. Once again, Rural would send all six tennis players to the 6A state event.

"It was a great day for us," Rural's Coach Hedberg told the Capital-Journal's Peterson, "I was pleased my freshman girl got in and my doubles teams played well. Madeline's Madeline and I knew what I'd get out of Madeline."

At the 6A state tournament, the previous year's state singles champion finished fourth, and she was relatively upbeat about it. After a weather delay, Hill dropped her Sunday semifinal match to nationally-ranked Shawnee Mission East's Olivia Sneed. Hill said, "I'm glad I did it." Now 76-6 in three high school campaigns, she said, "I would say I learned to just push through things even if you don't feel like you can make it, and sometimes you're surprised. It wasn't in the cards today. I'll come out and try and be stronger next year. I'm excited."

Hedberg said, "I told her before her third-place match that I was as proud of her for playing as I was for her winning it last year because I know she had struggled with it. She belongs on a tennis court." And Hedberg belongs on the sidelines coaching kids like Madeline Hill.

With Hill and Hedberg and the rest of the cast of excellent tennis players, Rural managed to finish third place as a team which meant they received a trophy. Melaina Piyassaphan and Irene Nicolae were equally important in helping Rural to their third-place team finish as they medaled and scored valuable points, placing ninth in doubles.

2014—HILL EXCITED FOR FINAL SEASON AS RURAL WINS FOURTEENTH STRAIGHT REGIONAL

For a three-time city singles champion, three-time singles league champion and a three-time regional champion to question her desire to continue to play tennis, there had to be some issues. There were and, according to Madeline Hill, she worked through them and was not only anxious to play tennis again, she planned to continue playing in college—at the Division One level, if the opportunity presents itself, and it likely would. Southern Illinois in Edwardsville wanted her to attend and play.

It should be a lesson to all of us; just because an athlete can perform at a high level, doesn't mean everything is all right. We've learned that in recent years with the Olympic gymnast Simone Biles. Not insinuating their two situations were the same, nor even comparable, but there is the public side for athletes and there is the private side. We should respect both. Many things can affect an athlete and their ability or desire to compete, and just because we can't see it, the mental disposition is just as important as the physical abilities.

Hill told the Capital-Journal sportswriter Rick Peterson, "I'm super excited for this year. I'm going to get all emotional talking about it, but Hedberg, I can't wait to play for him one more year. I love him to death, and I'm hoping I can give him something good before I leave." That, coming from a player who had already won a state singles championship her sophomore year and finished in the top four places the other two years. She already had given plenty.

Hedberg hoped his team could at least finish in the top three team places at the 2014 6A event. He had a solid core of upperclassmen, and his younger players showed a lot of promise too.

In the city meet, Hill was her usual self—albeit some butterflies. She became one of a handful of girls or boys to capture four city singles titles, and Rural won their tenth straight city championship. The number two doubles team of Anna Fritz and Annie Tessendorf also captured a city championship. Laura Nicolae chipped in a third-place finish in number two singles. Mikaela Steinagle and Avery Munns rounded out the placings with a fourth-place finish in number one doubles. Washburn Rural outdistanced their nearest competitor, Hayden, by a score of 25-20.

Hill remained undefeated despite a nagging tennis-elbow injury, winning a very competitive field at the Topeka West Invitational. With two and a-half weeks left in her senior season, there was no injury stopping her now. Sydney Pretsch finished fourth in number two singles. The doubles teams finished second and fourth place respectfully. The championship was won by the number two doubles team of Fritz and Tessendorf. The number one doubles team of Hirsch and Steinagel took second place to round out the scoring as Rural topped all teams.

Rural won their fifth straight Centennial League championship, barely holding off challenger Emporia 78-76. Hill won her fourth straight singles league title and remained undefeated. Hirsch and Steinagle finished third in doubles, while Rural got a seventh-place finish in singles from Nicolae. The doubles team of Fritz and Tessendorf finished ninth.

"This tournament's a grind and a battle, and it was certainly that today," Hedberg said. "Hayden has a great young team, Emporia played great, and we feel real fortunate to have won. We had some ups and downs, but we got some great performances in the last round and that's really gratifying."

Rural came into regionals with fourteen straight titles and, after this one, they had fifteen in a row. Hill captured her fourth regional title in singles, and the doubles team of Hirsch and Steinagle won the doubles championship in a close 7-6, 7-6 matches taking both tiebreakers for first place. Tessendorf and Fritz finished fourth in doubles, and Nicolae captured fifth in singles to round out the scoring and give Rural the regional championship, qualifying all six players for the state tournament.

Heading into the tournament, what does a player who is currently undefeated this season and already had the successes do? What does her coach expect? More importantly, what does her dad expect? Hill told Capital-Journal sportswriter, "My dad always tells me the two things I can control are attitude and effort. A lot of times I don't stick with that, but I really need to focus on that."

The field for singles in 6A was really loaded, so it came down to who each player drew. The eventual finish depended a lot on who got hot and, of those players, who would be going to leave it all out there on the courts the day of the tournament. Hill said, prior to the tournament, "My biggest thing is I don't care if I lose as long as I play well, although it's still heartbreaking when you lose. Last year for third and fourth (place), I regret that match a lot because I didn't leave it all out there. The biggest thing for me is going to be leaving it all out there and enjoy it." Really, when you put it in perspective, can you really approach something with any more maturity or with a better perspective than that?

Hedberg concurred. "If she competes and fights and fights and fights, I'll be happy with whatever we get. Sure I want her to win, she is one of my favorites of all time, but by the same token, I realize how hard the road is and she's going to have to just bring it and bring it and bring it. That's what I want." Hedberg sounded like a coach who knows what competition is really all about.

At the state tournament held in Topeka, Hill met Shawnee Mission East's Elizabeth Barnickel for the third straight year. Hill had beaten Barnickel in the 2012 semifinals and Barnickel had beaten her in 2013, so this was the rubber match. Not taking anything away from Barnickel, but this year, Hill played a marathon of a semifinal and came into the championship with very little gas in the tank. Hill's semifinal was a two-hour and fifty-minute marathon. Barnickel, on the other hand and to her credit, made quick work of her semifinal match. It only lasted an hour. Barnickel recognized this, but didn't take anything for granted. Champions seldom do. She ended up winning over Hill 6-0, 6-2. Hill told Capital-Journal sportswriter Rick Peterson, "I just had absolutely nothing, which sucks," as she fought back tears. "I was trying to get myself just a little bit of energy, but I just couldn't create it. I just couldn't do it today."

As a team, Rural also got a ninth-place doubles finish from Steinagle and Hirsch to take home the third place trophy.

Hedberg said it best. "It's a really good day for us, and I'm proud of all of them." Tennis is such an individual sport, but the scoring system also makes it a great team sport, and Rural could be proud of a third-place team finish.

Capital-Journal sportswriter Rick Peterson said it best in the article about the All-City tennis team. "Washburn Rural senior Madeline Hill, who closed out one of the most successful careers in city history with a second-place singles finish in the class 6A state tournament, headlines the 2014 All-City girls tennis team."

STATE CHAMPION MADELINE HILL'S REFLECTION

"I grew up playing tennis from a young age. Therefore, I played under the direction and instruction of many skilled coaches, and I spent countless hours on the court...but there are only two tennis coaches throughout my entire lifetime that left a permanent mark on me—Hedberg being one of those two.

"I remember entering high school as a freshman. I was the new kid on the block, and I felt a lot of pressure from all different directions to perform the way everyone knew I 'could' for our high school tennis team. My sophomore year of high school, I almost didn't play on the tennis team because of the pressure I put on myself, and the pressure I felt from others had mounted up into overwhelming negative emotions within me.

"To give a little back story, throughout my entire life up until that point, I had quite the love/hate relationship with tennis. Most kids playing competitively at my age were out practicing upward of three hours a day...but for me, it was a struggle to get myself excited enough to even want to be on the tennis court more than three hours a week. To depict this, my dad would always tell me a story of when I was younger. We were at a tennis tournament, and I looked at him and said, 'Dad... you would think, if God truly wanted me to play tennis, He would've given me a lot more desire for the game...and He would've given you a lot more money.' We laughed out loud.

"I don't know how old I was when I made this comment to my dad, but my comment always seemed to make a little bit of sense to me whenever my dad reminded me of this story.

"However, despite my lack of desire for the game of tennis at times, God did gift me with a natural ability for it. The only thing was, I had a really hard time in being motivated playing for 'myself.' I didn't care so much about my personal accolades. I didn't care about being in the newspapers or being 'regarded' as a great tennis player—no, what I cared about was playing for a team, for other people, and playing for a purpose bigger than myself. And Hedberg became one of those purposes. In fact, he was one of the biggest purposes I ever played for throughout my years of tennis. And he was the sole reason I decided to pick up my racket my sophomore year of high school and play that season.

"I'll never forget that season. One of my fondest memories, that I remember so vividly, was being in the finals of the state tournament that year. Hedberg had coached countless numbers of incredible tennis athletes throughout his career who had accomplished amazing feats, but the one thing that hadn't happened at that point yet was a female winning the state singles championship, and I wanted so badly to be able to win that for him. I was up against a rival opponent from that year from one of the top high school programs in Kansas City, and it was an absolute battle, mentally and physically. Things weren't looking that great for me during several moments throughout that match. We were tied up in a third and final set. But somehow I scrapped away and finally earned myself a few match points.

"I remember looking over and seeing Hedberg talking to someone on the phone with one hand and his other pressed up against the fence watching the match closely. (It turned-out that he was updating his wife, Sherri, who was interested in how Madeline was doing). He knew it was a match point and, despite my exhaustion, I knew this was my chance to close this match out and win the championship. My opponent and I played the match point intensely and, at the end of that point, I came out on top and won. Game. Set. Match. I looked over at Hedberg, and I'll never forget what I saw. He walked away from the court with a huge, beaming smile on his face and threw his fist high up in the air. It's been years since this moment, but I can still picture it perfectly to this day. It was one of those memories that stays burned into your brain forever.

"My junior and senior year, playing under Hedberg, was incredible as well. So many memories were made with the team and him. And when my final senior season ended, I was saddened knowing I would never have the chance to play under Hedberg again—one of the most amazing coaches and people I had ever known.

"Hedberg, if you're reading this, know that I will forever cherish many of the memories we had the chance to create during the four years I played for you in high school. Even though tennis wasn't a strong 'love' of mine, you made playing those four years so enjoyable and worth it for me. Although life has pulled us both in different directions and we both reside in different states now, I will always consider you like a father to me. There are few people throughout life who truly leave lasting marks on us and you, my friend, are one of those people to me."

With love, Madeline

2015—CAPTURE A FIFTH PLACE 6A STATE FINISH

The 2015 tennis team was composed of twelve returning, experienced players and three newcomers. One of the biggest losses for this team was Maddie Hill who owned a state singles title and a runner up as well. Hill qualified for the state tournament all four years before moving on to NCAA Division 1 competition at Southern Illinois in the fall of 2015.

Hedberg told the Capital-Journal that, "Life without Madeline will be an adjustment, but we still have a solid team. Outside of my three varsity returners, we are still playing matches to determine our lineup."

In the first match of the season, a quadrangular, Rural took first in all four divisions of singles and doubles. Senior Laura Nicolae won number one singles, senior Olivia Taylor took the number two singles title. Rural senior Darby Hirsch teamed with junior Avery Munns for the number one doubles title. The number two doubles team of senior Hayley McDonald and sophomore Maddie Aarnes won the number two doubles competition.

After ten consecutive city team titles, the Junior Blues finished in an unfamiliar third place this year by the thinnest of margins. Champion Seaman had 25 points, Shawnee Heights 24 and Rural 23. Nicolae finished third in number one singles, and Aarnes took second in number two singles. Based on practice matches, Hedberg did some shuffling of his lineup in both singles and doubles. The doubles team of seniors Lindsey Wagaman and Taylor took second in the number two doubles event.

Hirsch and Munns also took second in the number one singles event.

Washburn Rural fared better in the larger Centennial League meet (ten teams) as they outdistanced second place Shawnee Heights 80-75 for the team title. With the addition of Emporia, Junction City and Manhattan, the format favored the deeper Rural. Rural put both its doubles teams in the top three places as both their singles finished in the top seven.

Answering the inevitable question after dropping the city event, Coach Hedberg told the Capital-Journal sportswriter Rick Peterson, "Hats off to the Seaman girls (Hedberg coached at Seaman his first eleven years in the business)." He added, "They (Seaman) took it, and I think it did remind our girls that this is competitive and people do want to beat you and you should respect them for wanting to beat you because we're all trying to do the same thing."

Kevin Hedberg and I had a chat about this competitive coaching dynamic. He said he thinks that the really good coaches have this perspective: "We all are trying to do the same thing, have our teams and our individual players play up to their potential, and we should all support each other's efforts." Hedberg told me that, for him, it's never been about HIM against some other COACH. Everybody who's in it for the right reasons appreciates their counterparts' efforts and also their trials and tribulations. Each coach faces different variables—factors within their school and within their team—and you work with the talent you inherit, and you try your very best to make your players better each day.

At the league meet, Hirsch and Munns led the team with a second-place finish in doubles while their teammates Taylor and Wagaman finished third. The singles players Nicolae and Aarnes finished sixth and seventh, respectively. The overall performances allowed the Junior Blues to win their sixth straight Centennial League title. Hedberg had this to say about his team's efforts, "We just came back with a little more determination, and we had a really good week. We won the Emporia tournament and then turned around and won the Topeka West Invitational—both I felt were really good tournaments—and then we came in and won today."

In the following weekend, Rural took second place at the regional event led by the doubles championship won by Hirsch and Munns. Interestingly, both girls are soccer players as well, and they spent part of their weekend competing in club soccer and still had enough gas in the tank to win their high school tennis regional. Hirsch and Munns pushed their record this season to 27-5 and defeated a solid Derby duo. Derby won the regional team title, so it was a good win for Hirsch and Munns, 6-3, 6-1.

The Capital-Journal sportswriter Rick Peterson asked Hedberg about his good doubles team doubling up with tennis and soccer. Hedberg said he had no problem with it, but hoped they could avoid injuries as a result of playing competitive soccer and tennis during the same season. Last season both were injured, and it affected their tennis season. Hedberg was still willing to let them compete in soccer during the tennis season because that's what they loved.

Rural finished second to Derby. "Derby is a little bit deeper team than we are, but I'm happy to get five of them in (to the state tournament the following weekend). No complaints," Hedberg said matter of factly. Nicolae took third in singles with a 6-1, 6-1 win over Manhattan. Taylor and Wagaman made it to the fifth-place match, but lost a 6-1, 6-2 decision to Wichita East for a sixth-place finish and qualifying for the 6A state tournament.

At the state tournament, the doubles team of Hirsh and Munns finished seventh. Nicolae placed eleventh in singles, and Washburn Rural finished fifth as a team.

2016—DOUBLES DOMINANCE AND MUNNS PLACES AT 6A STATE; TEAM 7TH

A good way to ensure it's going to be a good tennis season at Rural is to begin with a win of the city title—or the Town Title as it was referred to in the Capital-Journal coverage. Since that had escaped them last season, they might as well start a new streak. With Hayden sophomore Brooklyn Hunter winning her second city singles title, there were points that needed to be won to secure a team title for Washburn Rural.

So Washburn Rural finished third and second in singles. Senior Avery Munns finished third in number one singles, and freshman Lauren Pryor finished second in number two singles. No champion, but good depth. What sealed the deal was a sweep in doubles for the Junior Blues. The doubles team of juniors Maddie Aarnes and Hallie Beard dominated the Hayden duo 8-1 in number one doubles. Their teammates, senior Lauren Ailslieger and junior Cortlyn Wolfe, took the number two doubles 8-2. The team title went to Rural, 27 over Hayden's 23.

"We've grown a lot in the last two weeks, and I'm real happy with the way they played," Coach Hedberg told Capital-Journal sports reporter Rick Peterson. "We had some good fortune. The Seaman number one doubles team is a very good team, and they had us (in the semifinal match), and we made a comeback and got them.

That was a huge win for my girls (Aarnes and Beard). According to Beard, "We knew there were some really good teams out here, and we knew we'd have to play our hardest. We needed to start off better, and that's what we did." Beard and Aarnes came back from 5-2, 6-3 deficits in the semifinals against Seaman.

According to Capital-Journal sportswriter Rick Peterson in his Centennial League article, he said, "Washburn Rural may have played its best tennis of the year en route to a 90-74 win over runner-up Seaman." Manhattan was a distant third in team points with 58.

The Junior Blues once again rode their strong doubles teams. Beard and Aarnes won the doubles title, while their teammates Ailslieger and Wolfe finished third. Singles held their own with teammates Munns and Pryor meeting in the third-place match. Munns won the friendly competition 8-2 over Pryor who took fourth.

Hedberg said, "It's been a great day, we've really played well. There was no falter in any of the girls. They really came ready to play, and I'm very pleased with them." Hedberg said the key to Rural's team title was the way the Junior Blues played in their four pool matches, with all six players rolling to semifinal berths. Depth.

Washburn Rural continued to roll as a team at regionals and qualified all six tennis players for state. Munns took the regional singles title while the doubles team of Aarnes and Beard won the doubles competition. Pryor took third in singles, and Ailslieger and Woolfe took fifth in doubles. Rural once again claimed the regional team title after not winning it in 2015.

At the 6A state event, Munns placed eighth in singles—the only Junior Blue to place—propelling the Junior Blues to a seventh-place team finish.

2017—SUCCESS AT CITY, LEAGUE AND REGIONALS AND LAND 4TH AT STATE

Washburn Rural coach Kevin Hedberg liked the experience that was coming back from the previous year. His doubles teams, in particular, was set. The other two spots boiled down to who would win the singles battle. Freshman Rachel Osborn looked like a favorite to play number one singles. Hedberg told the Capital-Journal reporter covering preseason outlooks, "We are optimistic. We have experience returning in doubles and have our combinations set. We still have competition in singles."

The experience was enough to carry the Junior Blues to the city title—their second straight.

With the league additions of Emporia, Junction City and Manhattan, would Rural also have enough to win the Centennial League event? Rural had won that league championship each year since 2010—seven straight. Going for number eight was made that much more difficult with Hunter from Hayden entering the singles field again, the clear favorite. But Rural had an answer for that when freshman Rachel Osborn played well enough to take second place, losing to Hunter 8-1 but defeating all of her other opponents on the way to second place.

Rural's doubles teams were stronger than the rest of the field too. The duo of

Cortlyn Wolfe and Lauren Pryor followed up their city championship by winning the league doubles competition for Rural, and they played their teammates in the championship as Maddie Aarnes and Hallie Beard took second place. Junior Haley Kucera played well enough to take fourth in singles to round out the scoring. Two first places, a second and a fourth propelled Rural to 92 points. Next closest team score was 76 for Manhattan.

Hedberg recognized his team's efforts on an extremely windy day saying, "The girls have had a really good season, and they played well today in the conditions because this is a tough day." Commenting about the upcoming regional Rural hosts, Hedberg said, "I know we're playing better as doubles teams right now than we did at the start of the season, and my number two singles player (Kucera) has just gotten better and better and better, and she kind of set us up. And Rachel Osborn is growing every time she plays a match, so it's all good."

It was all good for Osborn at regionals where she picked her first tournament to win a singles championship which helped boost Rural to a team title. Back-to-back regional titles. Osborn capped a 4-0 match day by defeating teammate Kucera in the championship match 6-0, 6-1. A one-two finish in singles was great. Osborn would take a 26-6 record to the 6A state event. Doubles did almost as well with a first and a third place finish. Wolfe and Pryor were regional champions. Aarnes and Beard finished third and helped lead the Junior Blues to a 25-12 title with the closest competitor league foe Manhattan.

Hedberg told Capital-Journal sports reporter Rick Peterson that, "It's been a wonderful day for us. It's a good field, and there's several good teams. Manhattan has some very good entries, and we're just happy to be moving on and getting everybody to be able to travel to Wichita for state." He added, "It's about surviving to the second day. It's a really tough field, and you've just got to get as ready as you can."

Hopes of playing for a state title dwindled on Friday when both Wolfe and Pryor and Osborn slipped into the consolation bracket. But Wolfe and Pryor played well enough to medal at state with a seventh-place finish. Osborn, too, would medal as a freshman by finishing eighth place. It would have likely taken a fifth-place finish by all three to stand a chance at the title. Rural finished fourth place behind Blue Valley

North, Shawnee Mission East and Blue Valley Northwest. Sound like a Kansas City-metro dominated field? The Junior Blues were just six points off the trophy hunt.

2018—LOSS OF OSBORN A BIG BLOW FOR RURAL BUT QUALIFY FIVE FOR STATE

Before Rural stepped on the court in 2018, they suffered a big loss as last year's seventh-place state singles winner, Rachel Osborn, a sophomore, transferred to Las Vegas. But they did return two other standouts from last season. Lauren Pryor was a placer at state, and Haley Kucera qualified for the state tournament.

The previous year, Rural captured the city, league and regional championships and finished fourth at the state meet.

Nobody in Topeka city schools or their league competitors would feel sorry for Hedberg losing a key player. He would spend no time dwelling on the loss of a good player either. Instead, he chose to convey optimism about players who WERE members of the Junior Blue tennis team this upcoming season. "I like my team, and I've got some senior girls who've worked real hard in the off season," Hedberg told Capital-Journal sportswriter Rick Peterson. "Haley Kucera has worked hard and is going to be good and have a good year, Harper Zimlich has worked hard as well, and we've got some good young girls coming in, so it's an exciting time for us. I'm pretty optimistic."

Rural showed its resiliency early in the season. After suffering through a tough day in a loaded St. Thomas Aquinas invitational, the Junior Blues bounced back to claim their third straight city tennis team title, beating Hayden by a mere one point, 26-25. Rural swept the doubles events and took two third places in the two singles events.

"We had a miserable day Tuesday (at Aquinas) and, honestly, we didn't play badly," Hedberg said. "The level of competition was just so high that we got kind of eaten up and beaten up, but it does help. You're just a little bit more ready when you come in here (city schools), and maybe a little bit more hungry, and I thought we played that way."

Rural got third-place finishes from senior Kucera in number one singles and a third from senior Pauline Kosch in number two singles. Pryor teamed with Wichman to win the number one doubles event. Bradbury and Robinett also won the number two doubles event.

Washburn Rural would finish third (65 points) at the Centennial League meet behind Manhattan (75) and Hayden (71). Kucera placed third in singles. Pryor and Wichman took second in doubles.

Five girls qualified for the state event as a result of their regional finishes. At 17-11, Kucera finished third place in singles. The doubles teams both qualified. Wichman and Pryor placed third and took a 24-6 record to state. Bradbury and Robinett (21-9) finished fifth place.

Pryor and Wichman placed eleventh at the 6A state tournament.

2019—RURAL GAINS VALUABLE EXPERIENCE WHILE WINNING CITY EVENT

Coach Hedberg had six returning players from 2018 and five newcomers. State placer Sheridan Wichman was tabbed by the Capital-Journal as a city player to watch in the upcoming season.

Hedberg knew his team's makeup and told the Capital-Journal, "We are young and will be improving each year with the freshmen and the sophomore classes. This year will be a challenge to get experience and still perform at a high level." Sounds like a rebuild.

The Capital-Journal said that Seaman was the "prohibitive favorite" to win the city team title this year which would have ended Rural's three-year reign as champions of Topeka schools. The Seaman team held the top seed in three of the four events and looked to be in a position to win the city title, which would be their first since 2015.

Brent Maycock, Capital-Journal sportswriter, covered the city tournament and wrote, "Funny thing about streaks, though. The team owning one tends to rise to the occasion, and Rural did just that on Monday at Kossover Tennis Center."

In fact, it was the Junior Blues that walked away with three of the four events' champions. Rural won the number two doubles, and number one and two singles.

The number one singles title victory was thanks to sophomore Wichman. Gone was Hayden's Brooklyn Hunter (2015-2018), so it cleared the way for a new singles champion. Wichman was glad to oblige and took the opportunity. Wichman topped Marisol Blair from Hayden 8-4 in the semifinals and defeated top-seeded Seaman singles player Elise Schreiner by a score of 8-5.

Wichman said, "I knew I'd have to just stay consistent with Elise because she's a really great player and puts good spin and hits good shots."

Rural freshman Meredith Kucera captured the number two singles event by upsetting Hayden's Rhen Calhoon 6-3.

Another pair of freshmen, Hailey Beck and Kate Fritz, also pulled an upset in the number two doubles event, downing a good Seaman duo, 8-4. The number one doubles team of senior Halley Robinett and senior Grace Bradbury added a third-place finish in number one doubles.

"I hope this will be a springboard for all my young kids to keep working because in tennis right now, if you work hard you can really cover some ground," Hedberg said, "I'm happy for the girls. I hope they feel like they accomplished something, because they did. The Seaman team is very good and, if we play them again tomorrow, it might be very different." But it was the same story this year with Rural outdistancing the Vikings 29-25.

The Centennial League event was all Manhattan—again. They captured championships in singles and doubles, outdistancing second-place Rural 83-72. Wichman took third in singles, and her teammate Kucera took sixth place. The doubles team of Bradbury and Robinett finished fourth in doubles, while their teammates Beck and Fritz took fifth place.

Hedberg told Capital-Journal sportswriter Rick Peterson, "I've been real pleased all season with them. We've played well. Manhattan's a very good team, real solid at all their spots, and we've been chasing them, but we can't catch them. But I'm real pleased with where we sit, and now we've just got to play a really good regional this coming Saturday."

Once again at regionals, Rural fell runner-up to Manhattan but managed to play well and qualified their entire team for the state tournament. Wichman finished third in singles and Kucera was fourth. The best finish of the day came in doubles with Bradbury and Robinett capturing second place. Beck and Fritz finished fourth at regionals. It was a year that saw Topeka schools send twenty individuals to their respective state tournaments.

There would be no places won by Rural at the 6A state tournament, but the valuable experience some underclassmen got would pay dividends for the Rural team in the future.

2020—JUNIOR SHERIDAN WICHMAN CALLED "A CITY PLAYER TO WATCH"

According to the Topeka Capital-Journal, Washburn Rural returned one of the city's top six individual players in junior Sheridan Wichman. Just a season before, Wichman was the reigning city singles champion. She placed third in the Centennial League singles as well as third in the regionals. Wichman was also a state qualifier for the second straight year. As a freshman, she had earned a state doubles medal.

In an early season invitational tournament hosted by Topeka West, Rural finished third in the ten-team tournament. Rural was led by a first-place finish in the doubles competition from the duo of Kate Fritz and Meredith Kucera, who upset the undefeated Seaman doubles team. Wichman finished third in a very good field of entries.

Wichman also captured her second straight city singles championship, defeating Hayden's Rhen Calhoon 8-2.

At the Centennial League meet, Rural finished fourth as a team. Wichman advanced to the singles championship by defeating one Manhattan singles player, but finished second to Manhattan's Harkin by a score of 8-2.

Fritz and Kucera finished third in the league doubles championship. Manhattan captured the league team title.

On the following Friday, Washburn Rural competed in the 6A regionals. Due to the Coronavirus, the activities association made the determination to lessen the number of qualifiers by only allowing the top four placers to qualify for the state event. This would mean fewer participants, fewer spectators.

Rick Peterson interviewed Rural's Wichman about the upcoming regional event. "I feel like there is still a lot of room for improvement for me," said Wichman. "My goal is to make it to state and place this year, but I feel like I just need to keep training and keep going and not fall back. I have a lot of opponents coming up that are going to give me a real run for my money."

At the 6A regionals, Washburn Rural once again had multiple qualifiers for the state tournament. Sophomore doubles team Kucera and Fritz won the regional doubles event with a 6-2, 6-3 win over the Manhattan team of Loub and Wiens.

Hedberg had this to say about his very good pair of sophomore champions, "We threw this team together, and I've got to tell you, I was a pretty big skeptic when I did it, but they've played really well together. They have a really good chemistry together."

Wichman also met her goal of qualifying for state by finishing third in the singles competition. She defeated Topeka High sophomore Lorraine De La Isla 6-0, 6-1. Hedberg said, "I'm real happy for Sheridan." As a team, Rural finished second, just six points behind Manhattan.

There was to be no placing at the state tournament, but Wichman completed a 21-8 singles record for the year, won her second straight city singles championship, finished third at league and in regionals. Fritz and Kucera finished their doubles season with a 25-6 record, including a first-place regional finish, a second-place city finish and a third-place league finish. All three would return next season.

2021—WOULD BE THE LAST FALL SEASON FOR COACH HEDBERG

In what would be Kevin Hedberg's last fall of high school tennis, the Washburn Rural girls had an amazing season to close out his thirty-year career as coach of the girls tennis team. He was named the Centennial League Coach of the Year.

The culmination of the season saw the girls finish eighth as a team at the 6A state tournament. Individually, Sheridan Wichman placed ninth in singles. Katherine Fritz and Meredith Kucera took ninth in doubles.

During the season, the team placed first in the WRHS Quad, Lawrence Quad and also the Manhattan Quad.

In the big Washburn Rural Invitational, they tied Manhattan for the championship of that event.

In the city meet they once again captured first place as a team. Sheridan Wichman, Mena DiMarzio, Kate Fritz, Meredith Kucera, Hailey Beck, and Shelby Schmutzler were named to the All-City team.

For the first time ever, the team took first place at the Topeka West Invitational. They also captured second place at the Centennial League tournament, dropping the championship by a mere one point. Wichman, Fritz, Kucera, Beck and Schmutzler garnered all-league honors.

At regionals, seniors Fritz and Kucera led the Junior Blues, capturing the doubles title. Their teammates Hailey Beck and Claire Ireland posted a third-place finish in doubles. The Junior Blues were also strong in singles with Di Marzio and Kayla Peter placing third and fourth-place respectfully.

HEDBERG REFLECTS ON HIS TIME AS GIRL'S TENNIS COACH

Through the 90's, the girls also had their share of players who went on to attend college and play tennis, and it was not a small number of girls.

In one reflection—not really a comparison—Hedberg mentioned that, overall, the boys teams were committed to the team finishing first, and they were tight groups when it came to teammates and chemistry. But he felt that the bond the girls established may have seemed tighter, and they truly became friends on and off the court. He says, "There were few exceptions, but their closeness was palpable. You could feel it."

He also coached so many girls teams and individuals that it was hard to single them out. He mentioned that Madeline Hill was a more recent graduate and was amazing in so many ways. Hedberg said, "For her size, she was really something."

"Danielle Knipp was spirited and gutsy and had the same match toughness as Madeline even though they were separated by twenty-five years." He also said, "To be a really good girls player requires you to be able to conjure a little bitchiness in yourself. And I mean that as a compliment. You have to stand up for yourself, deal with a lot of on court nonsense. Not only did Madeline and Danielle have that, so did Sherri Olivier. They had that wonderful toughness it takes to be really good.

Taylor Smith had it as well, but she had a quieter version of it."

Those were some of the standouts he mentioned, but he also recognized that so many of his players stood out as exceptional young women (and men).

In reference to both, Hedberg said, "I now realize just how lucky I was to have had all of them enter my life. What an experience to have all these exceptional young women and young men coming together to seek a common goal playing a game that you, as a coach, truly love. I was truly blessed and will be forever thankful I spent my time with them in the classroom and on the court."

Another plus was doing nine to ten weeks of morning tennis lessons and practices in the summers. "I got to watch many of them grow up from the third grade on. So fun," he reflected.

Additionally, a good head coach knows the value of their assistant coaches. "I had great assistant coaches at all times," Hedberg said. He mentioned Susan Sittenauer, his first assistant at Seaman High School. She knew little about tennis, but had faith because Hedberg had faith in her. He also mentioned Jim Dinkel, who was his first assistant coach at Washburn Rural, along with long-time assistant Kyle Fowler. As of this writing, Fowler is still teaching at Washburn Rural, and when I asked him what made Hedberg so successful, he said, "That's easy. He's a relationship guy. Coach Hedberg always had the ability to build rapport with all types of people, and this is what made him so special on and off the court, as well as in the classroom."

I think we all appreciate how fortunate we were to work directly with Kevin. As his athletic director, I considered him one of the safest coaches. What I mean is, you could always count on Hedberg to act sensibly and reasonably. And he taught me a lot about the ins and outs of high school tennis. It was also fun, according to Hedberg, in the later years, to bring along new assistants Hannah Armand and Diann Faflick. According to Hedberg, they were fast learners and all invaluable to his program and the program's successes.

HEDBERG'S RETIREMENT

As the old adage goes, "All good things must come to an end." But it's a whole lot more palatable when an individual can make their own decision about when enough is enough. Kevin Hedberg's success and his continued relevance, both in the classroom, and on the high school tennis courts, definitely gave him the right to decide when and how to hang em up. Being a reflective individual and a calculated person, you can bet Hedberg had given careful consideration to announce his retirement in the early spring right before his final tennis season with the 2022 Washburn Rural boys team.

In an online article written by Rick Peterson of Top Sports News, Hedberg made his public announcement after a forty-three-year teaching and coaching career. The 2021-2022 school year would be his last. He told Peterson, "The classroom was fine, the kids were absolutely fantastic and treated me with a lot of respect and did what I asked—teaching and tennis—but it just seemed like time." Hedberg said, "For whatever reason, it just felt like time."

In February of 2022, Hedberg had his 70th birthday. That benchmark caused him to have some thoughts about retiring. In Peterson's article, Hedberg said, "When I turned 70, it was kind of a weird thing. You start thinking, 'Wow, when I was a kid, 70 was ancient,' and I'm there."

At this point Hedberg had established himself as one of the most successful and best known tennis figures in the state of Kansas. Prior to the last boys season of 2022 at Rural, Hedberg had coached five state-championship teams (four boys and one girls) as well as numerous individual singles and doubles champions. Along with that came forty-one Centennial League titles (twenty girls and twenty-one boys). As far as Topeka city dominance, the Rural teams captured forty-seven city championships (twenty girls and twenty-seven boys). Washburn Rural won forty regional championships (twenty girls and twenty boys). At the state tournament, Rural finished in the top three team placers twenty-six times (twelve girls and fourteen boys). That kind of consistent dominance over a period of thirty-two years at Washburn Rural definitively puts Hedberg and the program in the elite category. If there's a better program over that same period of time, it would be fun to compare them.

Hedberg would tell you that, while he enjoys the successes, it is far more rewarding to see his players excel year in and year out. His ultimate reward is for players from the last forty years to come back and see him, let him know how they are doing. He remains the same humble individual regardless of the numerous great years of tennis. Hedberg reflected upon the important aspect he will miss and told Peterson, "There's always going to be things at every job you don't like, but the hardest thing about it (retiring) for me will be walking away from the kids, because I honestly think the kids have kept me young. Ending that association with them is going to be hard, but I've got to fill that void, and I will. I'll figure something out to keep my spirits up that way."

So, with that kind of success in a city with multiple high schools competing in tennis, you might expect that there would be some resentment toward the Junior Blues, toward Coach Hedberg. It's human nature for people not to root for the favorites, the consistent winners. It's a funny society. We place a high priority and emphasis on success and winning, but we don't want someone or some team to dominate. Maybe not the case here.

Veteran Topeka West coach Kurt David told Rick Peterson of Top Sports News that he has a great deal of respect for Hedberg and said he will definitely be missed. David went on to say, "When I came here (West) in 1993, it was easy to hold a grudge against Washburn Rural because of their success, but as time went on and I got to know not just Kevin but the rest of the coaches in town and in the league, you realize that everybody cares for each other, and everybody wants everybody to be successful against everybody but themselves."

David also commented that, "Kevin was always a good example of that—good advice, understood what we (coaches) had to do and understood how we were trying to do things."

He went on to say, "I consider him (Hedberg) a very dear friend now, more so than a mortal enemy. He wants to be successful, we want them to be successful, up until the time they play us."

Isn't it interesting that, in Hedberg's chosen sport of competition for himself, tennis, it is basically a competition between two individuals to see who can better the other. Who can score more points and win the match. But as a coach, he and his colleagues had a tendency to wish each other successes with their high school athletes and with their teams—except when their two teams meet. Hedberg's own lessons in sportsmanship that he was forced to learn at an early age helped shape his solid sportsmanship attitudes for so many years, but never dispute the fact that it's much more fun when your kids are successful. There may be very few coaches in the state of Kansas with the consistent type of success that Washburn Rural's Kevin Hedberg has had the chance to experience and be a part of year in and year out.

When both Hedberg and I would talk in the school's hallway pre-2015, the topic of retirement would inevitably come up. Neither of us felt like we had lost the fire for working with teenage students, but we both had seen and experienced a few teachers hanging on too long and becoming bitter about their job, their career. Hedberg and I made a pact with each other that, if either of us recognized that we were becoming "that guy" (burned out and cranky), we would let the other know. I retired at an age that would be twelve years younger than Kevin's retirement age. I felt blessed that he never told me I was becoming "that guy." I kept my eye on him, even after I had hung it up, and I can honestly say I don't believe Hedberg would ever become that guy. His fire for teaching, for tennis and for kids stayed lit during his entire forty-three-year career. He could have gone longer. I'm glad for the time he gave all of us.

THE FINAL CHAPTER FOR KEVIN HEDBERG

How do you summarize a teaching and coaching career that does justice to an individual so impactful as Kevin Hedberg? There is really no way to do it justice. The body of work portrayed in this book should do the loudest talking. The early days of coaching at Seaman in which he began the solid building blocks by establishing a quality summer youth program— putting more kids from the Seaman district on the courts—paid dividends for the high school program, but it also provided opportunities for individuals to learn a lifelong sport. It was something they could enjoy whether they played competitively or just for the sheer enjoyment of the game.

Then there is the lengthy span of excellence established at Topeka-Washburn Rural High School—a school that competed in 5A and also competed in the largest classification of schools, the state's thirty-two largest by enrollment. The success of Rural at the local level is unprecedented. The consistent, year-to year dominance among the city's seven local high school's is nothing short of miraculous. The consistent successes in the Centennial League and the regional competitions set a standard that will be hard, if not impossible, to match. The quality of players matched the quality of coaching they received.

Of course, there was success at the state level—both by individual players and by teams. Over the span of thirty years, the players attended, played and graduated, but the coach was the consistent factor. The coach played a significant factor in molding and guiding his players on the path of unselfish, team-oriented groups of young people who took pride in their abilities and in their displays of character. Coach Kevin Hedberg would downplay his role in these successes, but those of us who know youth—know coaching and all of the nuances that each of those entities contain—can appreciate the accomplishments of one Kevin Hedberg. Kevin Hedbergs don't come along every day. They are a special breed.

But tennis was but a small contingency of the youth that Hedberg affected. For forty years he taught six to seven periods per day with classes that numbered twenty-five to thirty kids each period, so his impact from the classroom shined brightly as each semester he taught over one hundred kids the important factors associated with government. The very basis of a democratic government was instilled in so many young people, and he taught them how to learn, how to fact find, how to think. When it is all said and done, what could be more important or rewarding than the thought of all those young people carrying those principles and those ethical ideals into society.

Kevin Hedberg was an individual who played the game of tennis with passion and a competitive nature that served him well. He not only played tennis, he was an ambassador for the sport. The sport was important to him, but the lessons learned from preparing and from competing that he passed onto his players served them well as they made their way into the world. He and tennis provided them life lessons.

There are great coaches. There are great teachers. There are great people. When all three of those get rolled into one individual, you see an ordinary person do some extraordinary things. That sums up Kevin Hedberg. There may be folks who do it as well, but none better.

(Photo credit: *Topeka Capital-Journal*)

ALL-STATE TENNIS PLAYERS FOR WASHBURN RURAL HIGH SCHOOL

*All recognition until 1990 Classification 5A
Post 1990 recognition Classification of 6A

5A Classification		1st-3rd State Team Finish
1980-81	John Hughes 3rd in Doubles	
	Sean Roberts 3rd in Doubles	
1981-82	Jennifer Pasley 3rd in Doubles	
	Erica Anderson 3rd in Doubles	
	John Hughes 2nd in Doubles	
	Huston Pulford 2nd in Doubles	
1982-83	Sean Roberts 1st in Doubles	
	Huston Pulford 1st in Doubles	
	Sarah Craig 4th in Doubles	
	Reina Roberts 4th in Doubles	
1983-84	Jeff Watson 3rd in Doubles	
	Mark Dillon 3rd in Doubles	
1985-86	Powell Crosley 1st in Singles	
	Lisa Schmoller 5th in Singles	
1986-87	Michelle Knipp 2nd in Singles	2nd Girls Team
	Lisa Schmoller 3rd in Doubles	
	Paige Evans 3rd in Doubles	
1987-88	Powell Crosley 1st in Singles	1st Boys Team
	Michelle Knipp 2nd in Singles	
6A Classification		**1st-3rd State Team Finish**
1990-91	Danielle Knipp 3rd in Singles	1st Girls Team
	Heather Dobbs 3rd in Doubles	

1991-92	Marie Gruffy 3rd in Doubles Danielle Knipp 2nd in Singles Anne Wiksten 4th in Doubles	2nd Girls Team
1992-93	Megan McBride 4th in Doubles Danielle Knipp 2nd in Singles Megan McBride 4th in Doubles Jenny VanVlack 4th in Doubles Colleen Pendley 5th in Doubles Kelly Roberts 5th in Doubles Phillip Pepperdine 3rd in Doubles Ryan Kuhn 3rd in Doubles	2nd Girls Team
1993-94	Danielle Knipp 2nd in Singles Megan McBride 2nd in Doubles Jenny VanVlack 2nd in Doubles Kelly Roberts 4th in Doubles Colleen Pendley 4th in Doubles Brian Hejtmanek 4th in Singles	1st Girls Team
1994-95	Megan McBride 1st in Doubles Jenny VanVlack 1st in Doubles	3rd Girls Team
1995-96	Danny Williams 5th in Singles Brian Hejtmanek 6th in Singles	3rd Boys Team
1997-98	Cheryl Catron 4th in Doubles Michelle Hollins 4th in Doubles	
1998-99	David Stauffer 4th in Singles Justin Keller 5th in Singles Blake Asbury 5th in Doubles Jared Keller 5th in Doubles	

1999-2000	David Stauffer 3rd in Singles	3rd Boys Team
2000-2001	Blake Asbury 1st in Doubles	2nd Boys Team
	Jared Keller 1st in Doubles	
2001-2002	Sumeet Patel 2nd in Doubles	3rd Boys Team
	Drew Hanson 2nd in Doubles	
	Matt Koupal 5th in Doubles	
	Jeff MIllberger 5th in Doubles	
2002-2003	Jeff Millberger 2nd in Doubles	3rd Girls Team
	Sumeet Patel 2nd in Doubles	1st Boys Team
	Whitney Hamilton 3rd in Doubles	
	Kassie Baxter 3rd in Doubles	
2003-2004	Matt Hansen 4th in Singles	3rd Girls Team
	Sumeet Patel 3rd in Doubles	1st Boys Team
	Trevor Hedberg 3rd in Doubles	
2004-2005	Drew Hanson 1st in Singles	1st Boys Team
	Sumeet Patel 1st in Doubles	
	Trevor Hedberg 1st in Doubles	
2005-2006	Ben Newell 1st in Doubles	3rd Boys Team
	Zach Newell 1st in Doubles	
	Sherri Olivier 4th in Singles	
2006-2007	Sherri Olivier 2nd in Singles	2nd Girls Team
	Ben Newell 3rd in Doubles	1st Boys Team
	Zach Newell 3rd in Doubles	
	Jason Lepse 4th in Doubles	
	Bronson Brassel 4th in Doubles	
2007-2008		3rd Boys Team
2008-2009	Bronson Brassel 5th in Doubles	3rd Girls Team
	Conner Edwards 5th in Doubles	
2009-2010	Conner Edwards 4th in Singles	3rd Boys Team
	Daniel de Zamacona 5th in Singles	
	Bobby Florence 3rd in Doubles	

Coaching Legacy of Champions

2010-2011	Max Cooper 3rd in Doubles Taylor Smith 3rd in Singles	3rd Girls Team
2011-2012	Gwen Shepler 4th in Doubles Mackenzie Hill 4th in Doubles Conner Edwards 3rd in Singles Daniel de Zamacona 5th in Singles Madeline Hill 4th in Singles Scott Ziegler 5th in Doubles Griff Koupal 5th in Doubles	3rd Boys Team 3rd Girls Team
2012-2013	Madeline Hill 4th in Singles	3rd Girls Team
2013-2014	Madeline Hill 1st in Singles	3rd Girls Team
2014-2015	Madeline Hill 2nd in Singles	
2015-2016		3rd Boys Team

www.ingramcontent.com/pod-product-compliance
Lightning Source LLC
Chambersburg PA
CBHW052133070526
44585CB00017B/1811